COMPETING VISIONS

COMPETING VISIONS

The Political Conflict
over
America's Economic Future

Richard B. McKenzie

Library of Congress Cataloging in Publication Data

McKenzie, Richard B.
  Competing visions.

    Includes index.
    1. United States—Economic policy—1981–
2. Economic forecasting—United States.   3. Industry
and state—United States.   4. Plant shutdowns—United States.
I. Title.
HC106.8.M36   1985   338.973   85-11305
ISBN 0-932790-51-8
ISBN 0-932790-52-6 (pbk.)

Printed in the United States of America.

CATO INSTITUTE
224 Second Street SE
Washington, D.C. 20003

Dedicated to My Son
David Loar McKenzie

Contents

Foreword

The economic doldrums of the 1970s—declining U.S. productivity, rising inflation, rising unemployment, and general malaise—not only ushered in a new president in 1980 promising deregulation, but gave new vigor to the debate over the legitimate role of government in a free society.

Indeed, the proper role of government is a critical issue that must be addressed if we are to prosper as a rich country with maximum personal freedom. Given widespread sentiment that government growth is necessary, and political pressures for even more of it, we have to return to some basic questions: How was it possible for Americans to advance smoothly from wood to coal, coal to oil, and oil to nuclear power *without* the U.S. Department of Energy? How was it possible for such huge monuments to ingenuity as New York, Philadelphia, and Chicago to be built without the services of the U.S. Department of Housing and Urban Development? How have U.S. scientists managed to win an increasingly disproportionate share of Nobel Prizes—through the efforts of the U.S. Department of Education?

The answers to these questions are obvious, and they challenge the assertion that government management and control are *necessary* conditions for economic growth, prosperity, and progress. In his superb book economist Richard B. McKenzie likewise challenges this argument, showing that government intervention in economic affairs almost always produces results that are inferior to those obtainable in an unfettered market environment.

Competing Visions would have performed an exemplary public service if it had stopped at the first chapter, in which the cabal of national industrial policies and the extent to which they would be expected to achieve their stated objectives are outlined. McKenzie examines the industrial plans of a broad range of NIP proponents, from 1984 presidential contenders Hart and Hollings to academics Robert Reich and Lester Thurow. The advocates of industrial economic planning propose a mix of price controls, the elimination of "wasteful" mergers and acquisitions, the re-formation of a Reconstruction Finance Corporation, plant closing restrictions, and a host of other government restrictions and mandates.

A cursory reading of their proposals is enough to inform the reader that economic planning is one thing, and one thing only: the forcible supression of other people's economic plans by a powerful elite. As such, the attitude underlying modern proposals for industrial planning differs little from the age-old notion that wisdom is the special domain of the elite, whose ordained mission it is to forcibly impose that wisdom on the rest of us. In other words, it is a matter of who makes the decisions. In the marketplace, outcomes are determined by millions of independent decisions, as was the case when millions of Americans decided to purchase Hondas instead of Chryslers in the late 1970s. Proponents of economic planning simply disagree with the decisions made by the majority of consumers and would like to preempt them with "superior" decisions. The mechanisms the planners would use to do this are tariffs, quotas, and domestic-content laws.

Critics of market resource allocation contend that industrial planning can replace "greed" with "cooperation," "social consciousness," and "social justice." They fail to explain the character transformation that makes politicians, bureaucrats, consultants, and civil servants non-self-interested. Proponents of industrial planning assume that good results can spring only from the well of good intentions.

But the facts of the matter belie such a contention. Texas cattle ranchers ensure that New Yorkers have beef, pharmaceutical houses provide drugs, and airlines transport people from one place to another. It requires unyielding, resolute ignorance to think that all this good is motivated by the intent to do good. To the contrary, as Adam Smith put it, "It is not from the benevolence of the butcher, the brewer, or the baker that we expect our dinner, but from their regard to their own interest."

Industrial planners everywhere face an information problem. From the standpoint of consumer and producer satisfaction, how can a planning board *know* which industries should be "born" and which should "die," which should be subsidized and which should be self-sufficient, which should receive tax credits and which should not? A computer the size of the United States could not manage the innumerable interdependent decisions made every day in our economy. Is it reasonable to expect an army of bureaucrats to do better?

In considerable measure, support for industrial planning derives from widespread perceptions of recent slow productivity growth, plant closures, regional disparities in economic growth, and other maladies. No doubt there is a bit of truth to the observations. But as said of the witches' predictions in Shakespeare's *Macbeth*, "And oftimes to win us to our harm, the instruments of darkness tell us truths, win us with honest trifles, to betray us in deepest consequence." McKenzie argues that, indeed, there is *some* truth to the planners' observations—and then proceeds to demonstrate how government tax policies, business regulations, and labor laws have brought the problems about.

The inescapable conclusion is that the advocates of industrial planning want to give us more of what weakened our economy in the first place: more federal restrictions on domestic and international trade, more taxes and government expenditures, more centralized decision making in Washington. As McKenzie says, "These industrial policy advocates offer the problem as the solution. They tell us that all they seek is more 'rational federal policies,' but suggest more of the same policies that have been tried repeatedly with results industrial policy advocates now seek to remedy."

In a free society there is no justification for the centralized planning and control advocated by national industrial policy proponents. In *Competing Visions*, Richard McKenzie has offered an alternative that cannot be ignored.

WALTER E. WILLIAMS
John M. Olin Distinguished
Professor of Economics
George Mason University
Fairfax, Virginia

Preface

This book is concerned with national industrial policies—particular legislative proposals and the extent to which they can or cannot be expected to achieve their professed objectives. Perusal of the table of contents suggests that my interest in the industrial policy debate ranges broadly.

However, the book is more fundamentally concerned with competing visions of America's economic future. One view of this country's future is founded largely on the proposition that America is "deindustrializing," mainly because we have for too long relied on the market system, which is necessarily animated by "greed and fear" and which is faltering because businesses in the country have lost their ability to adapt to current economic challenges. The proponents of national industrial policies who share this vision recommend that government be given greater authority to plan and control the future through expanded use of government's power to tax, subsidize, regulate, and protect businesses—most importantly, firms in "basic" industries.

These policy proponents have an abiding faith in the ability of Washington planners and regulators to rise above politics to "pick winners" and to "ease the pain of losers" solely with an eye toward enhancing societal welfare, as opposed to the welfare of particular political and economic interest groups. They truly believe that the "next American frontier" hinges on our willingness to rely to a greater extent on collective decisions. These national industrial policy enthusiasts often acknowledge that many of our economic difficulties can be attributed to faulty government policies of the past, but they remain convinced that policy outcomes can be improved through greater reliance on centralized democratic and bureaucratic decision-making processes.

The other vision of America's economic future emerges in these pages from an examination of a number of national industrial policy proposals. The proponents of this view also fully acknowledge the country's past economic difficulties but conclude, contrary to the claims of industrial policy proponents, that America is not deindustrializing. Even if it were, it does not follow that "more government" would be the solution; indeed, expanded government of the past is a major source of our economic difficulties. Entrepreneurialism still activates businesses, in spite of growing governmental efforts to control and distort economic decisions through higher taxes and subsidies, more regulation, and greater protection from foreign and domestic competition.

From this perspective the solution to our economic difficulties lies in policy changes that would reduce government intrusion in markets. Giving government greater power to pick winners and, in the process, also pick losers would serve only to divert scarce entrepreneurial talents from productive market activity to nonproductive and counterproductive political activitiy. If government decides to allocate the nation's real and financial resources according to firms' profitability, the government will do nothing other than what the market already does, but will do it more inefficiently. If the government channels resources to uncompetitive firms, it will simply waste the diverted resources and will encourage rent seeking, that is, the pursuit of profits through government transfer powers.

Added economic power in the hands of government would be power that could be expected to be used disproportionately by the current economic establishment—those industries that through their workers and stockholders and network of suppliers are sufficiently large to have the votes and funds to warp current political decisions to their favor. A policy shift toward an expanded "economic democracy," which is what many industrial policy proponents say they seek, could be expected to translate ultimately into greater protection of the status quo. This is because the emerging and the unknown future industries, which do not have the votes (because they do not now exist), will lack the necessary political muscle to hold their own in currently organized planning councils.

The vision of America's economic future developed in these pages is founded on the conviction, supported by extensive empirical and conceptual arguments, that America's economic future can only be dimmed by less reliance on market processes. It is a vision that recognizes that people in high government places are much like the rest of us, imbued with their own private interests and goals (which will distort and govern their view of what people want and what type of industrial structure should exist) and limited in the capacity to effectively manage any complex economy, much less one the

size of the United States. Greater reliance on government necessarily means that the complexity and vitality of the economy will
be restricted by the limitations of government managers to manage
and to understand the types of goods and services people really
want.

* * * * *

This book is the product of several years of work and brings
together a number of papers I have written on national industrial
policy topics, most of which have been published elsewhere. Chapter 1, which introduces the industrial policy debate by outlining
specific policy proposals, and chapter 4, which is concerned with
the proposed Reconstruction Finance Corporation, were distributed
as Backgrounders by the Heritage Foundation (respectively, "National
Industrial Policy: An Overview of the Debate," July 1983; and "A
New Reconstruction Finance Corporation: No Cure for U.S. Economic Ills," November 1983). Chapter 2, which lays out the myths
of deindustrialization, is drawn from the empirical section of a
pamphlet entitled "The Great National Industrial Policy Hoax,"
published in March 1984 through the sponsorship of the Manville
Lecture Series in the College of Business at the University of Notre
Dame. Chapter 3, which deals with the displaced worker problem,
was originally written for the National Center for Research in Vocational Education for publication in *Displaced Workers: Implications for
Educational and Training Institutions,* ed. Kevin Hollenbeck et al.
(Columbus: Ohio State University, 1984) but was also distributed
in revised form as a Backgrounder by the Heritage Foundation
("Displaced Workers: A Misadventure of Industrial Policy," December
1983).

Chapter 7, which views many industrial policies as a form of
capital taxation, was published in *The Political Economy of Capital
Formation: The Direct and Indirect Effects of Taxation,* ed. Dwight R.
Lee (San Francisco: Pacific Institute for Public Policy Research, 1985).
Chapter 9 discusses "rent seeking" in an industrial policy context
and is an expanded version of an article published in *Public Choice*
(Summer 1985). The final chapter, which develops an alternative
pro-market policy course, is a combination of the introduction to *A
Blueprint for Jobs and Industrial Growth,* which I edited and which
was published by the Heritage Foundation (Washington, February
1984) and a short article published in the *Cato Journal* (Fall 1984).

Over the past several years I have written extensively on industrial policies for newspaper audiences, and these columns have been collected in a volume entitled *National Industrial Policies: Commentaries in Dissent*, published by the Fisher Institute (Dallas, 1984); several of those columns have been revised and incorporated into chapters in this book. Almost all of the chapters have been extensively revised, expanded, and updated for inclusion.

I am, of course, greatly indebted to others for help in my writings. I owe the largest debt to the Heritage Foundation, which gave me the opportunity to direct its national industrial policy project during 1983 and 1984. I greatly appreciate the help several people at Heritage gave me in the form of substantive and editorial improvements to my own writings, especially Burton Pines, Herb Berkowitz, Stuart Butler, and Jean Savage. I am also pleased to say that Sue Jones and Debra Hoskin were indispensible in getting the manuscript organized and computerized for submission to the publisher. I am also indebted to Catherine England at the Cato Institute and Karen Albers at the Strom Thurmond Institute for reading over the entire manuscript for needed corrections in form and substance, and to Mark B. Foster of Cato for copy-editing the entire manuscript.

My colleagues in the Economics Department at Clemson University, particularly Hugh Macaulay, Clinton Whitehurst, Bruce Yandle, Rex Cottle, and John Warner, helped me work through a number of the arguments developed in the chapters that follow, and read over many of them. All along the way, they offered many valuable suggestions for improvement.

Lastly but most dearly, my son David was 10 at the time this book was completed. He, more than anyone else, understood that the period during which this book was written was an especially difficult one for me and that time with him was unusually important to me. Others can only envy me for having a son who is as thoughtful to his dad as David has been to me. For this and many other reasons, I am very proud and pleased to be able to dedicate this book to him.

I. Visions of America's Economic Future

America's economic future is, once again, being vigorously contested. The policy conflict, evident in proposed legislation in Congress, is largely over differing perceptions of the current state of the economy—especially the industrial sector—and over visions of America's future with and without greater government involvement in the economy.

Free industrial markets are under attack. Through the passage of a wide range of government initiatives grouped under the rubric of "national industrial policy," a growing coalition of American political, labor, religious, intellectual, and business leaders seek to change the future by realigning in a fundamental way public and private decision making in the economy. The proponents' objectives are laudable: to renew economic prosperity and growth in national wealth and to enhance social justice. However, the attendant rhetoric, founded on a particular vision of America's future, echoes appeals of bygone generations of social-economic reformers intent upon spurring social improvement through greater government control of the economy.

Sen. Gary Hart (D-Colo.), runner-up for the Democratic presidential nomination in 1984, has summarized a now familiar political theme within the movement: "Today, more than at any other time since the Depression, traditional policies are producing unintended consequences. They are increasingly irrelevant to the unique economic realities of this decade."[1]

What Hart and many other industrial policy champions argue is that a new holistic approach to public policy can be forged by "melding" the "Jeffersonian principle of free competitive economy" with the "Rooseveltian principle that economic success cannot be

---

[1]Gary Hart, "Restoring Economic Growth," policy statement presented to the Strategy Council, Democratic National Committee, February 6, 1982, p. 1. These views are recited by Robert Reich, professor of business policy at the Kennedy School of Government, Harvard University, in his book *The Next American Frontier* (New York: Times Books, 1983).

1

divorced from social conscience."[2] For instance, Sen. Ernest Hollings (D-S.C.), in his unsuccessful 1984 bid for the Democratic nomination, stressed that we need a "unity of purpose" to economic policy.[3] A founding father of industrial policy, Harvard University professor Robert Reich, contends in *The Next American Frontier* that "in the emerging era of productivity social justice is not incompatible with economic growth, but essential to it. A social organization premised on equity, security, and participation will generate greater productivity than one premised on greed and fear."[4] Mirroring Hart's vision of the industrial world (or, perhaps, having originally articulated that vision for Hart), Reich writes, "America has a choice: It can adapt itself to the new economic realities by altering its organization, or it can fail to adapt and thereby continue its present decline. . . . But failure to adapt will rend the social fabric irreparably. Adaptation is America's challenge. It is America's next frontier."[5]

The trouble with this new talk about industrial policy is that it is not new. It is at least as old as the eighteenth century's mercantilism and as familiar as this century's disastrous experiments with central planning, the corporate state, and five-year plans. While several specific policy proposals warrant examination by Congress, mainly because they attempt to correct problems with existing policies, much of what has been proposed as "national industrial policy" is a 1980s version of the social politics of the late 1960s and early 1970s. It calls for more federal money and more federal intervention in the activities of workers, businessmen, investors, and consumers. Strangely, the lessons painfully learned in the past decade seem to be willfully ignored.

From what industrial policy proponents have been saying so far, there is no reason to believe that their repackaged schemes would be any less catastrophic than the earlier models. To be sure, most industrial policy enthusiasts have noble concerns. But their arguments are replete with internal contradictions that draw into question the movement's intellectual foundation. What is most alarming is that backers of these policies fail to acknowledge, or choose to

[2]Ibid., p. 4.

[3]Ernest Hollings, "Statement of Candidacy," remarks presented at Midlands Technical College, Columbia, S.C., April 18, 1983.

[4]Reich, p. 20.

[5]Ibid., p. 21.

ignore, a critically important and central point in such debates: government control of capital ultimately translates into control of people, whether the control is instituted by democratic or by authoritarian means.

This study examines in considerable detail the factual foundation and conceptual consistency of the arguments recently articulated in favor of a new national industrial policy. It is written with a sense of urgency, not because the objectives sought by industrial policy advocates are uninspired and unshared by opponents, but mainly because the factual case is warped to the point that it has little tie with reality and because serious, if not damning, logical flaws abound in the theoretical arguments. These points will be substantiated in following chapters. The remaining pages of this opening chapter are devoted to a presentation of the types of policies advocated and to a brief overview of the case for a national industrial policy. The overriding objective of what is written below is to redirect policy discussions away from efforts to control markets to efforts to free market processes. The industrial policy debate is terribly important because the outcome of it (and similar debates that will likely be joined in the 1980s) will largely determine America's future.

Major Policy Proposals

As evidenced by the variety of policy proposals, national industrial policy (NIP) means different things to different people, a point that may go far in explaining the political appeal of calls to join the movement. Consider several of the major proposals, but certainly not all, of frequently cited industrial policy advocates.[6]

The Hart Proposals

Senator Hart offers a reasonably complete, broad-based policy menu:

- To encourage investment in physical and human capital, the tax code would be changed to a progressive expenditure tax, exempting savings from taxes and thus stimulating investment.

[6]For a sample of specific legislative proposals that were introduced in Congress in 1983 alone, see Gregory L. Klein, "Industrial Policy: A Summary of Bills before Congress," Heritage Foundation Issue Bulletin no. 96 (Washington, July 12, 1983).

- To encourage new investment and to reduce the tendency of the 1981 tax cut to favor existing firms over emerging firms that have limited capital bases and, therefore, have minimal depreciation allowance to deduct from taxable corporate profits, the tax code would allow capital expenditures to be treated as an expense. Further, a new form of common stock would be created. Called "new capacity stock," it would be used to finance new plant, equipment, and research and would be exempt from capital gains taxes.

- To encourage "new entrepreneurial frontiers," federally financed "Venture Development Centers" would be established to provide technical assistance and seed money to small businesses. The corporate income tax rate would be reduced for small businesses, and small business shareholders would be allowed to deduct company losses from their taxable personal income.

- To stimulate research and development, federal support of science and engineering schools would be increased, the patent laws would be strengthened, and government procurement policies would "pull technological progress forward."

- To expand global markets for American goods, the federal government would free international trade of tariff and nontariff barriers and eliminate export subsidies provided to other countries' industries.

- To reduce the crowding-out effect of government deficits, the 1983 tax cut was to have been postponed, while defense expenditures were to be trimmed by $20 billion. To reduce inflationary pressures, a "Tax-Based Incomes Policy" would impose a tax penalty on price and wage increases exceeding a "pre-established target" and would focus on the 2,000 largest firms in the country.

Hart would also revise antitrust laws to allow for more joint research and development projects among competing domestic companies and impose a "security fee" on imported oil that would reflect the now-hidden cost of our "energy vulnerability." He would expand federal aid to education, incorporating a "GI Bill in Reverse," meaning a program under which students would pay back their federally subsidized loans by work in areas of "national need."[7] Generally speaking, Hart's NIP is designed to ease what he sees as the adjustment process of "old line basic industries," commonly called "sunset industries," and to facilitate the emergence of small high-tech firms in what are described as "sunrise industries."

The Reich Proposals

Robert Reich believes that the key to revitalizing the American economy is "adaptation" to the new economic realities of production. These he defines as flexible production processes, highly skilled workers (the presumed source of America's comparative advantage in international commerce), and "precision, custom, and technology-driven products." Such adaptation, for Reich, requires a number of policies similar, but not identical, to those of Senator Hart:

- To reduce structural unemployment and to speed the "adjustment process," Congress would enact an unemployment voucher system by which the federal government would pay half of firms' costs for training people unemployed for longer than three months. Even larger subsidies would go to those firms training workers in areas of high unemployment. Retraining vouchers for those unemployed for more than two years would be redeemable at universities and technical colleges. In addition, companies could establish "human capital reserves"—funds set aside to reflect the depreciation of the skills of the company's employees. These reserves would lower corporate profits and would be used to upgrade worker job-related skills, just as similar reserves now are used to replace worn-out equipment.

- To reduce the "inequity" of the current disparity in tax treatment of human and physical capital and the inclination of physical capital to move, a "human capital tax credit" in connection with training costs similar to the investment tax credit on physical capital, could be instituted, which would lower the after-tax training and retraining costs incurred by businesses.

- To reduce forms of "paper entrepreneurship" (specifically, mergers and acquisitions and tax avoidance), the tax code

[7]Hart, pp. 1–35.

5

could allow an interest deduction only for purchasing new or modernizing old plants and equipment.

- To reduce cyclical unemployment, unemployment insurance taxes would be more directly related to the unemployment experience of firms.

- To ease the decline of decaying industries, such as textiles, steel, automobiles, and rubber, "regional development banks," along the lines of the Reconstruction Finance Corporation of the Great Depression era, would be organized to provide low interest rate, subsidized loans to companies promising to retool and retrain workers or, in Reich's words, "to restructure themselves to become more competitive."[8] With their federal subsidies, such banks could redistribute investment funds among regions, urban and rural areas, and industries with the intent of enhancing social justice and job security and facilitating the adjustment process.

- To reduce the adversarial relationships that now presumably exist among businesses, labor groups, and government, tripartite councils would be organized. Such councils would seek consensus (which Reich acknowledges may be difficult to achieve) on how capital investment would be allocated differently than it is in free capital markets.

- To relieve unemployment and other social problems, the federal government would offer grants to entice firms to hire the unemployed, handicapped, or other groups subject to discrimination and unfortunate circumstances. Washington would also fund, through firms, such social services as "health care, social security, day care, disability benefits . . . and relocation assistance."[9] In short, "firms will become the agents of their employees, bargaining for different packages of government-supported social services."[10]

- To ensure that the programs negotiated by firms with government are run with the workers in mind, a form of "industrial democracy" would be imposed. The employees

[8]Reich, p. 243.
[9]Ibid., p. 248.
[10]Ibid.

will elect representatives who will select the combination of benefits and choose the providers. Through labor-management councils, also including worker representatives, workers will participate in company decisions about physical capital, helping to choose the direction and magnitude of new investment in research, plant and machinery.[11]

In summary, Reich starts with the propositions that the economy, as now organized, is insufficiently adaptive and that even now there is no "free market" due to extensive federal subsidies to businesses and to government protection from domestic and international competitors. In Reich's view, the federal government already has an "industrial policy," but it lacks sufficient coordination to serve the broad general public. No expanded involvement in the economy by the federal government is necessary, says Reich. He maintains that Washington could simply use the subsidy and protection resources already at its command to extract public benefits from businesses.

The Mondale Proposals

Having acclaimed Reich's book as "one of the most important works of the decade," former vice president Walter F. Mondale has not sketched in the details of his own brand of industrial policy. Instead, he complains that the country's industrial policy is "destroying industry—not building it."[12] The broad outlines of his NIP include five strategies:

- First, he believes something must be done to reduce "wasteful mergers and acquisitions."

- Second, he suggests altering the antitrust laws to allow more joint research and development ventures to "enhance international competitiveness without reducing domestic competition."[13]

- Third, "we've got to shape a policy to keep high technology here at home" because companies are shipping high-tech-

[11]Ibid.

[12]Walter F. Mondale, address to the Twenty-First Constitutional Convention of the United Steel Workers of America, September 11, 1982, p. 5.

[13]Idem, excerpts from speech to the Industrial Union Department Legislative Conference, May 4, 1983, p. 2.

nology production jobs abroad and "leaving the lower-end jobs here at home."[14]

- Fourth, he endorses the call of others for the creation of an "Economic Cooperation Council," with functions similar to those of the old Reconstruction Finance Corporation. Such a council, composed of representatives from labor, management, and government, would establish national economic goals for industry and make use of a wide range of federal incentives to influence the allocation of capital.

- Fifth, he wants federal aid directed to "those communities and regions hit hardest by economic change," which for him means "targeting infrastructure programs and impact aid—automatically triggered by measures of distress" and adopting plant-closing restrictions. The prototype industrial policy is the Chrysler bailout, which, founded on federal loan guarantees for Chrysler bonds, saved hundreds of thousands of jobs in the automobile industry, according to Mondale.

Though insisting that he is a "profound believer in our free enterprise system," Mondale hastily adds that "government must work in partnership with the market."[15]

The Rohatyn Proposals

Felix Rohatyn is a New York investment banker who wants to revitalize the national economy by applying principles he learned while heading the New York Municipal Assistance Corporation, the agency established to prevent New York City's bankruptcy. Like other NIP enthusiasts, he wants to expand the economic role of government. Examples:

- Along with Reich, Rohatyn advocates establishing a reinvigorated Reconstruction Finance Corporation (RFC) to allocate capital as directed by a council of labor, business, and government leaders. The bank's activities would be financed by a higher gasoline tax. The central task of the council would be to "allocate sacrifice."

- To reduce problems caused by unexpected inflation and to

[14]Ibid.
[15]Ibid., p. 4.

moderate competing claims on the national income realized in strikes, "annual negotiations resulting from one year contracts with no cost-of-living escalators" would be institutionalized.

- To improve labor-management relations, a "larger share of the compensation package [would be] in the form of profit sharing."
- To better coordinate U.S. domestic policies with Western Europe and Japan, the United States would consider re-creating "something like the Bretton Woods agreements," providing for central bank intervention within certain bands of exchange rates, like the European monetary system.
- To permit underdeveloped countries to develop, to "avoid enormous distress in those countries," to enable underdeveloped countries to repay their loans, and to avert protectionist measures, the International Monetary Fund would be "reliquified." This means increasing U.S. contributions to the IMF.[16]

Rohatyn admits that he tends to "look at money as a tool or weapon . . . to leverage concessions from unions, suppliers, banks, management, legislatures."[17] He justifies this by arguing that "the basic issue to me is whether we have a government with a philosophy that will look upon intervention as a philosophical imperative when disparities in the country become too great, or whether government's philosophy is simply to take its hand off the steering wheel and let the market work its will."[18]

The Thurow Proposals

MIT economist Lester Thurow bases his prescriptions on his diagnosis "that our economy and our institutions will not provide jobs for everyone who wants to work" and that "we have a moral responsibility to guarantee full employment."[19] To him, the federal government must be employer of last resort, paying wages above

[16]These positions are discussed in Jeremy Bernstein, "Profiles: Allocating Sacrifice," *New Yorker*, January 23, 1983, pp. 45–78.

[17]Ibid., p. 78.

[18]Ibid.

[19]Lester C. Thurow, *The Zero-Sum Society: Distribution and the Possibilities for Economic Change* (New York: Penguin Books, 1981), pp. 203–4.

the minimum and (in agreement with other NIP advocates) expanding training and retraining programs. He acknowledges that this would "create a socialized sector of the economy."[20] Quips Thurow: "Major investment decisions have become too important to be left to the private market alone. . . . Japan Inc. needs to be met with U.S.A. Inc."[21]

Seconding Reich, Thurow wants to use the government to accelerate the transition from sunset to sunrise industires.[22] To the extent that government helps people make the transition, the risk of economic change is "spread" among all citizens—a point also emphasized by Reich above and in the Bluestone-Harrison proposals considered below.[23] He believes that private investment banking should once again be made legal and that public investment banking, such as Rohatyn's new Reconstruction Finance Corporation, could be organized to lengthen private managers' time horizons that, according to Thurow, "are too short to encompass projects that will not pay off for a decade and [in cases where] too many benefits cannot be captured by the firm making the initial investments."[24] Thurow advocates the establishment of a "Ministry of Technology" to encourage civilian industrial research.[25]

The Ford Proposals

Practically every two years for the past decade, Rep. William Ford (D-Mich.) has introduced a bill to restrict plant closings. The first such proposal, which was introduced in the Senate in 1974 by Walter Mondale, concentrated primarily on the problem of the "runaway shop"—those firms that pull up stakes in one locality and reestablish themselves elsewhere. More recently, Ford has been attacking plant closings in general, even those resulting from firms going out of business altogether. Closed plants cause unemployment, says Ford, and create many economic and social problems for the workers and communities involved. As such, he wants to restrict closings to ameliorate these problems. At issue is the basic

[20]Ibid., p. 206.

[21]Ibid., p. 192.

[22]Ibid., pp. 191–93.

[23]Lester C. Thurow, testimony prepared for the House Subcommittee on Economic Stabilization, June 14, 1983, p. 2.

[24]Ibid., p. 3.

[25]Ibid., p. 4.

right of firms to open and close, expand and contract their businesses.

Ford's current proposal, called the National Employment Priorities Act of 1983, embodies a number of industrial policy concepts:

- To remedy the social and economic problems felt by workers and their communities when plants close, Congress would require firms that close plants (1) to give up to one year's notification of a pending closing; (2) to provide severance pay equal to 85 percent of one week's average pay for up to 52 weeks, not to exceed $25,000; (3) to continue the employer's contribution to employee benefit plans for up to 52 weeks; and (4) to provide restitution payments to the communities where plants are closed equal to 85 percent of the average tax payments of the three years prior to closing.

- To discourage firms from moving outside the United States, firms moving abroad would have to pay community restitution of 300 percent of the average tax payments of the three years prior to closing.

- To prevent plants from closing, the federal government would provide (1) technical assistance helpful in avoiding closure; (2) aid to firms in the form of "loans, loan guarantees, interest subsidies, and the assumption by the Secretary [of the Treasury] of any outstanding debt of such concern"; (3) subsidies to employee groups interested in buying their plants and keeping them open; and (4) targeted procurement plans that would save faltering industries.

- To ease the adjustment process when plants do close, federal assistance would be provided workers to cover training programs, job placement services, and job search and moving expenses.[26]

The Bluestone-Harrison Proposals

Economists Barry Bluestone (Boston College) and Bennett Harrison (MIT), in their book *The Deindustrialization of America*, accept the contention of Representative Ford that plant closings cause

[26]National Employment Priorities Act, H.R. 2847, House, 98th Cong., 1st sess., May 2, 1983.

11

social problems that extend beyond the private spheres of managers, workers, and even the immediate community. They believe also that private firms, interested almost exclusively in making profits, are recklessly "deindustrializing" the country. Many of these problems could be remedied, according to Bluestone and Harrison, by increasing the cost of closing via closing restrictions, since closing restrictions convert into operating costs and make continued operations relatively less costly than closing for many firms. Though Bluestone and Harrison endorse the basic precepts of Ford's National Employment Priorities Act, they have advocated even tougher restrictions on plant closings.[27]

What Bluestone and Harrison explicitly want is radical changes in, if not outright socialization of, the U.S. economy. Their panacea is called national economic democracy and planning, in which "*a rising standard of living for working people, more equally shared*" would be substituted for private profit as the guiding criterion for economic decisions and in which "*humanization* of the workplace should be the major objective of any truly democratically planned restructuring of the economy" (emphasis in original).[28] Their industrial policy would entail worker buyouts, government bailouts, and "selective" nationalization of industries. Central to their NIP scheme are " 'planning agreements' between the public and private 'partners,' on policies concerning pricing, location (and relocation), sourcing, automation, affirmative action in hiring and promotions, health and safety, environmental protection, and the maintenance of the workplace environment conducive to greater experimentation with new forms of internal economic democracy."[29]

Bluestone and Harrison conclude that the principles of any newly established industrial policy should include, at a minimum:

- spreading the burden over *all* the citizens of the society;
- public disclosure of company data to enable democratically

---

[27]The National Employment Priorities Act of 1979 required firms to give up to two years' notice of a pending closure. The length of notice then depended upon the number of employees affected by the closure, as it does today.

[28]Barry Bluestone and Bennett Harrison, *The Deindustrialization of America: Plant Closings, Community Abandonment, and the Dismantling of Basic Industries* (New York: Basic Books, 1982), pp. 244, 245.

[29]Ibid.

12

constituted bodies to decide whether and to what extent assistance is needed;

- research by and consultation with workers in the affected plants and advisors of their own choosing;
- planned agreements with companies receiving bailouts, specifying a *quid pro quo* with respect to increased democratic management of production, restrictions on the subcontracting of components or supplies to nonunion or foreign shops, the phasing in (and control over the use) of new technology, new plant location, and product pricing; and
- some government ownership of the subsidized corporation.[30]

More explicit than other NIP proponents, Bluestone and Harrison chart a course for centralized economic planning, tempered by the demands of active participation by workers in the decision making of their firms.

The Bluestone-Harrison proposals are not the most extreme in the industrial policy movement. Professors Samuel Bowles (University of Massachusetts), David Gordon (New School for Social Research), and Thomas Weisskopf (University of Michigan) advocate "An Economic Bill of Rights" that includes the right to

> a decent job, . . . public child care and community service centers, a shorter standard workweek and flexible hours, flexible price controls, . . . public commitment to democratic trade unions, . . . democratic production incentives, . . . democratizing investment, money, and foreign trade, . . . environmental democracy, . . . conservation and safe energy, . . . good food, a national health policy.[31]

The Hollings Proposals

Drawing on his experience as governor of South Carolina from 1958 to 1962, Sen. Ernest Hollings sees expanded educational opportunities, especially technical and science education, as a central ingredient of any industrial policy recipe. This implies, how-

[30]Ibid., p. 256.

[31]Samuel Bowles, David M. Gordon, and Thomas E. Weisskopf, *Beyond the Waste Land: A Democratic Alternative to Economic Decline* (Garden City, N.Y.: Doubleday, Anchor Press, 1983), p. 270.

ever, a return to past policies—more federal money for nutrition, child care, community health centers, student loans, science and math education, and on-the-job training. He would also grant a $5,000 across-the-board federal pay hike for all teachers in the country (which would add $14 billion to the federal budget, virtually doubling federal outlays on education).

At the same time, Hollings wants to freeze aggregate spending and opposes the individual income-tax reductions. He argues that the federal deficit must be cut to make more private savings available for investment. He also strongly supports greater protection from imports, especially textiles, a dominant industry in his home state. Although his program lacks specifics, Hollings talks of government becoming involved in "planning" and acting as a "catalyst in bringing business, labor and agriculture into partnership." He says: "We would not have a fixed industrial policy. But the many facets would amount to the best industrial policy."[32]

The Wirth "Yellow Brick Road" Proposals

After months of hearing proposals for industrial policy, the House of Representatives Democratic Caucus Committee on Party Effectiveness issued a wide-ranging report that, because of the color of its cover, is known as "The Yellow Brick Road."[33] It is packed with platitudes and vague generalities. Rep. Timothy Wirth (D-Colo.) is emerging as the primary spokesman for the package. According to Wirth the "Yellow Brick Road" rests on five propositions:

- boosting the level of gross national product spent on research and development to a goal of 3 percent, providing new incentives to entrepreneurs, helping universities upgrade their research equipment, and encouraging innovation in the economy;

- improving the education and training needed to compete in the world economy, including making computer literacy a goal for all students, and attracting talented teachers and professors in areas of special needs such as science, mathematics, and foreign languages;

[32]Hollings, p. 3.

[33]Democratic Caucus Committee on Party Effectiveness, *Rebuilding the Road to Opportunity: A Democratic Direction for the 1980s* (Washington: Committee on Party Effectiveness, September 1982).

14

- a major public-private effort to train and retrain workers in sectors of declining employment so they can become productive in areas of increasing employment;
- rebuilding the decaying public infrastructure; and
- investing in energy resources with the goal of becoming a net exporter by 1990 through expanding coal exports, building on solar technologies and conventional and unconventional drilling techniques, and returning to an aggressive energy conservation effort.[34]

These programs would be funded by higher taxes for segments of the population and by shifting a greater share of the burden of defending the West to our allies. They would be coordinated by an "Economic Cooperation Council to help our country gather the right information and improve our ablity to make long-term economic decisions—not as a centralized monolithic planning agency, but as a national arena to clarify complex choices and build broad support for national initiatives."[35]

Other Proposals

Among the less ambitious industrial policy proposals suggested is that of Joel Kotkin and Don Gevirtz, who focus on policies designed to encourage entrepreneurship. They suggest that the federal government (1) eliminate the capital gains tax, (2) dispense with the corporate income tax on profits of less than $500,000, (3) relax the unwritten but enforced formula relating bank loans to firm equity that banks must follow in making loans to emerging companies, (4) expand the research-and-development tax credit to offset the implied

[34]Timothy E. Wirth, "A Democratic Policy Agenda for the Future," *Wall Street Journal*, October 19, 1982.

[35]Ibid. We must assume that the Council would be composed of interest groups, such as the AFL-CIO, the National Association of Manufacturers, and the Chamber of Commerce. It would raise legitimate fears of economic policies being guided in the interests of the established "corporate state." Suggestions in the proposal that the Council would seek and recommend a consensus by those in the assembly imply that Congress would, if the bill were passed, delegate a portion of its policymaking duties to the interest groups fortunate enough to be represented on the Council (which would necessarily exclude the interests of many groups). And it means that the resolution of economic issues, like the allocation of capital or which industries will "win," would depend upon the consensus, which would reflect "truth" as seen by the political power structure. Economic behavior would be further standardized in a very large nation noted for diversity.

tax bias in favor of larger companies involved in the current investment tax credit, and (5) launch a major federal effort to train workers for new industries.[36]

Former governor of Florida Reubin Askew, on the other hand, flirts with centralized planning. He calls for "government policies, especially targeted tax policies, which give direction to the pattern of investment by making full use of market forces in a constructive way. We need a conscious, concerted, coordinated, and comprehensive policy for economic growth in the United States."[37]

George Hatsopoulos, founding member of the American Business Conference and chairman of Thermo Electron Corporation, argues that the critical difference between economic growth in the United States and Japan is that in the United States the real rate of interest (the nominal market rate of interest minus the current inflation rate) is three times higher than in Japan. To narrow this gap he suggests that (1) the federal government revamp the tax code to allow cumulative preferred stock dividends to be treated the same for tax purposes as interest on debt so that equity capital can flow into companies, and (2) the federal government restore the benign macroeconomic conditions of the 1960s, which included a 4 percent inflation rate and low equity risk.[38]

A number of giant firms seem tempted by NIP. Edward Jefferson, chairman of E. I. DuPont de Nemours Company, recommends a "cherry-picking" (i.e., selective) approach to industrial policy, one providing special tax incentives, loans, and loan guarantees for research and development efforts.[39] Believing that the promise of high-tech jobs will not replace the need for jobs in basic industries, Jefferson maintains that such subsidies would "shore up your industrial base and ease the unemployment problem at a time when the economy is in transition."[40] He adds, "The kind of government involvement I'm talking about should be highly selective, limited

[36]Joel Kotkin and Don Gevirtz, "Why Entrepreneurs Trust No Politician: Who Needs Friends Who Ruin Your Business While Aiding Corporate Dinosaurs?" *Washington Post*, January 16, 1983, pp. B-1, B-2.

[37]Reubin Askew, "The Democratic Alternative," speech prepared for presentation at the Democratic Business Council, French Lick, Ind., April 24, 1982, p. 12.

[38]*Economist*, April 30, 1983, pp. 118, 119.

[39]"How to Turn Recovery into Long-Term Prosperity," *U.S. News and World Report*, May 2, 1983, pp. 51–52.

[40]Ibid., p. 52.

16

to asserting the national interest on behalf of our declining industries. That's no different from the concern we expressed for agriculture when it was in great difficulty."[41]

The Premises of NIP

Proposals for a national industrial policy rest on three common premises, explained in the following section.

Premise One

The first premise is that the U.S. economy is in a serious decline, which will remain unchecked unless America changes the way it does business.

Reich, for example, begins *The Next American Frontier* with a depressing and very questionable observation:

> Since the late 1960's America's economy has been slowly unraveling. The economic decline has been marked by growing unemployment, mounting business failures, and falling productivity. Since about the same time America's politics have been in chronic disarray. The phenomena are related. Economics and politics are threads in the same fabric. . . . This link is perhaps stronger today than at any time in America's past because we are moving into an era in which economic progress depends to an unprecedented degree upon collaboration in our workplaces and consensus in our politics.[42]

Similarly, Bluestone and Harrison open *The Deindustrialization of America* by approving *Business Week's* conclusion that "the U.S. economy must undergo a fundamental change if it is to retain a measure of its economic viability, let alone leadership in the remaining 20 years of this century. The goal must be nothing less than the reindustrialization of America," a feat that would require "a conscious effort to rebuild America's productive capacity."[43] Lester Thurow maintains that "interest in industrial policy springs from a simple four letter word—fear. American industry is being beaten up by its international competition and business and labor are both afraid that American industry is going down for the count."[44]

[41]Ibid.

[42]Reich, p. 3.

[43]"The Reindustrialization of America," *Business Week* special issue, June 30, 1980, p. 58. Quoted in Bluestone and Harrison, p. 3.

[44]Thurow, testimony, p. 1.

17

The perceived causes of the decline vary. Gary Hart is convinced that government policy efforts have been misdirected because "we have remained mired in an irrelevant debate about the wrong issues" while the U.S. economy has been going through an industrial transformation, inspired to a major extent by the emergence of a global economy.[45] While agreeing with Hart and others that "false choices" have been addressed, Reich focuses on the extent to which American management has remained wedded to highly structured, mass production processes of the past.[46] Senator Hollings, meanwhile, blames Reaganomics, Carternomics, and the failure of presidents to "build and head a consensus of Americans for the common good."[47]

Bluestone, Harrison, Thurow, and Reich, among others, believe that the acceleration in technological change, the growing mobility of capital on a world scale, and the profit motive are key sources of what they insist is U.S. economic decline. Almost all NIP advocates believe that foreign imports, based in part on low wages and protectionist policies of other countries, have narrowed markets for many American goods. According to them, the downward trend of the economy that became evident in the early 1980s, especially in the industrial Frostbelt, will continue unabated unless measures are taken to protect basic industries from foreign competition. Crystallizing the sentiments of many industrial policy advocates, Wolfgang Hager, visiting professor at Georgetown University's School of Foreign Service, writes:

> Without trade barriers rich countries are bound to suck in cheap imports from low-wage countries, destroying the domestic industries that used to make those products. There will never be enough 'high tech' jobs to employ those who lose more traditional jobs. Therefore, unrestricted trade would eventually destroy the economies of all high-wage, developed countries.[48]

Premise Two

A second premise is the notion that other countries have charted the industrial policy course that should be followed, with modifications, by the United States.

[45]Hart, p. 1.

[46]Reich.

[47]Hollings, p. 2.

[48]Wolfgang Hager, "Let Us Now Praise Trade Protectionism: It's Free Trade That Would Bring Disaster Today," *Washington Post*, May 15, 1983, p. B-1.

Virtually all NIP backers cite Japan as a model. Hollings argues that 12 million Americans are out of work in part because other countries "are using government as an active partner in coordinating business and labor, agriculture and science to compete in the international marketplace."[49] Reich concludes, "The recent progress achieved by Japan and several other European countries, and America's relative decline, require no convoluted explanations. . . . These countries are organized for economic adaptation. . . . America is not."[50]

Ford, Bluestone, and Harrison argue that European countries that have plant closing restrictions have grown more rapidly than the United States. This, they say, proves that such restrictions have no negative effects on the economy. Thurow adds, "In Japan the banking system is heavily influenced by decisions of the government. MITI (Ministry of International Trade and Industry) tries to develop a consensus for its industrial policies, and 'administrative guidance' is a way of life."[51] Other advocates use the Chrysler bailout and American agriculture programs as quintessential examples of the kinds of industrial policies that can be pursued.[52]

Premise Three

A third premise is the assumption that through the democratic process, a consensus on the industrial makeup of the country can be achieved.

To NIP's champions, the culprit today is, to a large extent, the profit motive. It mistakenly focuses firms' attention, it is argued, on their individual circumstances and diverts their concern for "a broader economic perspective"—meaning the community's interests. Profit-making firms, according to this perspective, systematically close plants and ignore the effects such shutdowns have on workers' investment in their jobs, the community's tax base, home prices, and the viability of other businesses in the community and country.

For reasons not always clear, NIP advocates possess a nearly religious faith in the sobering effects of public discussions on industrial issues, in the extent to which the ballot box rather than con-

---

[49]Hollings, p. 2.

[50]Reich, p. 17.

[51]Thurow, testimony, p. 1.

[52]Bluestone and Harrison, pp. 74–75.

sumer and investment choices reveals community preferences, and in the willingness of people to set aside private interests when asked to vote on policies reflecting the national interest. Reich writes that government should not necessarily be asked to become larger (although it is difficult to understand how that can be avoided), only "more open, more explicit, and more strategic."[53]

The Evidence

Industrial policy proposals are founded on a variety of empirical claims:

- that the private sector of the economy is calcifying, due mainly to attitudes and inclinations of private profiteers;
- that the decline in many industries is due to an unprecedented rate of technological change;
- that without governmental direction the economy, especially the manufacturing sector, will continue its decline;
- that supply-side economics or, more generally, Reaganomics has failed, thus requiring new institutional relationships;
- that industrial policy programs in Japan and elsewhere have contributed significantly to the economic success of those countries;
- that low wages and foreign subsidies of industries explain the loss of markets for U.S. firms in basic industries;
- that industrial policy efforts of the past, specifically the Reconstruction Finance Corporation, the wide range of agricultural programs, and the Chrysler bailout, clearly indicate the potential success of an expanded industrial policy;
- that the government actually can "create" jobs by enacting additional money bills, designed to rebuild, for example, the nation's "infrastructure," or that an industrial policy can be instituted without increases in the government's budget and regulatory authority; and
- that expanded governmental efforts to enhance economic security can contribute to social justice and economic growth.

[53]Reich, p. 14.

Discussions of industrial policies generally start with the reasonable observation that several important industries—steel, rubber, textiles, and automobiles, among others—have experienced serious difficulties in recent years. Virtually no one denies this. It is quite another matter, however, to maintain that these difficulties are symptoms of structural rigidities that can be remedied only by government initiatives. Such a conclusion dissolves when the premises upon which NIP rests are scrutinized. A growing body of literature suggests that these premises reflect half-truths and massively distorted interpretations of what is actually happening in the economy. Consider the following points, which are developed more carefully and in greater detail in the chapters that follow.

Brookings Institution Senior Fellow Robert Crandall notes, in his review of Robert Reich's book, that the presumed demise of the manufacturing sector in the United States is based on selective analysis:

> German and French readers of his book will be amazed to read of their governments' success in industrial policy. Since 1975, industrial production has grown even more slowly in France and West Germany than in the United States.
>
> The industrial sector of the United States did not decline markedly from the mid-1960s to 1980. In fact, basic industry accounted for roughly 22 percent of our GNP in 1980, precisely the same share as in 1947. Our output per person remains above that of all but a few countries, such as Sweden and Switzerland (which have not exactly been refuges for the world's dispossessed over the 20th century). Reich's contrary conclusions are drawn from a period ending in 1979. Were he to extend his calculations to 1981, he would find that the United States has outperformed every major industrial country in the world except Japan since 1975.[54]

Few NIP proponents even note the upturn in U.S. manufacturing jobs, even in Frostbelt states, during the late 1970s before the 1980–83 recessionary period. With little attention to what is happening to jobs in other industries, proponents of new industrial policies, intent upon making their case as dramatic as possible, conclude that the relative growth in the service sector must mean that high-paying jobs of automobile and steel workers are rapidly being sup-

[54]Robert W. Crandall, "Can Industrial Policy Work?" *Washington Post,* Book World section, May 22, 1983, p. 8.

planted by low-paying jobs for janitors and fast-food waiters. This simply is not the case.[55]

Newsweek columnist Robert Samuelson questions, as does Crandall, whether or not countries with industrial policies have actually, on average, done any better in terms of employment and economic growth over the last two decades than the United States. Several countries with industrial policies may well have performed much worse because of their industrial policies.[56]

Former Council of Economic Advisers chairman Herbert Stein contends that Reich's conclusions concerning the economic decline of the United States relative to other countries are based on calculations Stein published in 1982. Observes Stein:

> I saw the evidence as saying that what has been happening to the U.S.—the slowdown in growth of output and productivity and the rise of unemployment—has been happening in other industrial countries as well—Reich uses the figures from my article to show that "other nations are gaining at a rapid clip." But the rate at which they are gaining on us is also declining rapidly. Take Japan. Between 1960 and 1970 Japanese real per capita output rose from 31.5% of ours to 70.2%. But the rate of gain on us fell sharply. If it continues to fall at the same pace, Japan's real per capita GNP would still be only about 74% of ours in 1983.[57]

George Mason University economist Dwight Lee explains how Reich and others are able to discount the lack of private investment as a source of deteriorating growth in the U.S. economy and then to claim that the slowdown is due in substantial measure to the inability of U.S. businesses to adapt and to totally avoid government tax and regulatory policies.[58] Lee points out that Reich focuses on gross private investment, which as a percentage of GNP has changed little over the last two decades. However, net private investment (that is, gross investment minus replacement investment) as a percentage of GNP has declined by over 40 percent during the same

[55]This point is developed at length in Richard B. McKenzie, "National Industrial Policy: Six Major Myths," *Policy Review* (Fall 1983): 75–79.

[56]Robert J. Samuelson, "The Policy Peddlers," *Harper's*, June 1983, p. 62.

[57]Herbert Stein, "Industrial Policy, a la Reich," *Fortune*, June 13, 1983, p. 202.

[58]Dwight R. Lee, "What's Wrong with Reich's Industrial Policy," Heritage Foundation Backgrounder (Washington, October 1983), pp. 5–6.

period, and much of this decline can be explained by past government policies.[59]

David Henderson, former senior economist at the Council of Economic Advisers; Philip Trezise, senior fellow at the Brookings Institution; and Katsuro Sakoh, policy analyst at the Heritage Foundation, writing independently of one another, question the extent to which Japan's MITI has been responsible for Japan's economic success.[60] Most Japanese government investment funds go to urban and regional development, environmental protection, and infrastructure, causing economist Sakoh to conclude, "There is no evidence that manufacturing industries, in general, or any particular manufacturing sector, have been targeted by the JDB [Japanese Development Bank]. In fact, the share of loans that manufacturing industries have received is negligible."[61] Much of Japan's public funds, moreover, were wasted on supporting "losers."

Even more telling is that a major part of Japanese government industrial policy efforts has subsidized coal mining, agriculture, and public railways, hardly examples of success. In fact, in the 1960s the Japanese government attempted to discourage the emergence of a competitive automobile industry in Japan on the grounds that it did not believe the industry would be a "winner" in international competition. Had Japan truly had a NIP, it probably would not be much of a threat to the U.S. economy today.

Attorney James Hickel argues in *Reason* magazine that the Chrysler bailout has not saved jobs or even averted Chrysler's bankruptcy. Chrysler has, for all practical purposes, gone bankrupt. Over 60,000 jobs at Chrysler have been eliminated since the bailout, and Chrysler has been allowed to discard $600 million of its debt at 30 cents on the dollar.[62]

The arguments underpinning proposed restrictions on plant clos-

[59]See John W. Kendrick, "International Comparisons of Recent Productivity Trends," in *Essays in Contemporary Economic Problems*, ed. William Fellner (Washington: American Enterprise Institute, 1981), pp. 125–70.

[60]David Henderson, "Behind the MITI Myth: The Real Japanese Miracle," *Fortune*, August 8, 1983, pp. 113–16; Philip H. Trezise, "Industrial Policy Is Not the Major Reason for Japan's Success," *Brookings Review* (Spring 1983): 13–18; Katsuro Sakoh, "Japanese Industrial Policy," Heritage Foundation Backgrounder (Washington, July 13, 1983).

[61]Sakoh.

[62]James Hickel, "Lemon Aid: Debunking the Case for the Chrysler Bailout," *Reason* (March 1983): 37–39.

ings are so flawed, from both empirical and conceptual perspectives, that they cannot be fully considered here.[63] Because restrictions on closings would add to the costs of doing business in the United States, investment and growth would be impaired, meaning that they would likely on balance destroy and jeopardize more jobs than they saved or made more secure.

The factual case for a national industrial policy will be critically explored further in the next chapter. We stress here in passing that no one seriously denies that the U.S. economy suffered from high unemployment and virtually zero productivity growth in the late 1970s. Yet the rise in unemployment and the slowdown in productivity growth occurred simultaneously with dramatic increases in government intervention in the economy in the form of higher taxes and regulation. This should be a danger signal for those who now call on Washington to "guide" free enterprise or to "manage" capitalism. It would seem that remedies for cyclical and structural economic problems are not to be found in the institutional changes in private-public relationships envisioned in many venturesome programs offered by industrial policy advocates, unless, at least, the conceptual arguments undergirding the national industrial case are compelling.

NIP's Conceptual Problems

The Fallacy of Good Intentions

Advocates of industrial policy romanticize the democracy of economics, maintaining that the results of a democratically determined industrial policy would be superior to the results of the democratic market system. They see the market system as founded on "greed and fear" rather than on "equity, security, and participation."[64] NIP advocates also tend to describe the nation as suffering from economic rigor mortis brought on by entrenched monopolists protected from market competition by government franchises, regulations, tariffs, and subsidies. They tend to believe that the political process that has served these special interests (also a major concern of NIP

---

[63]See Richard B. McKenzie, *Restrictions on Business Mobility: A Study in Political Rhetoric and Economic Reality* (Washington: American Enterprise Institute, 1978); idem, ed., *Plant Closings: Public or Private Choices?* rev. ed. (Washington: Cato Institute, 1984); and idem, *Fugitive Industry: The Economics and Politics of Deindustrialization* (San Francisco: Pacific Institute for Public Policy Research, 1984).

[64]Reich, p. 20.

opponents), when given more authority, somehow could be restricted from being used to provide even more special-interest benefits. The dismal history of government aid to business teaches—or should teach—that government rarely accomplishes the noble goals that often originally prompt such policies.

The case for an industrial policy is founded in part on the belief that motives and results form a logical link: "good" motives (i.e., concern for the community, equity, and fairness) necessarily inspire "good" results, whereas "bad" motives (i.e., concern for profits and self-interest) often, if not always, give rise to "bad" results. Dismissed by NIP backers is the historically confirmed central point of the market system: that even in the worst of worlds, one driven exclusively by greed (and no real-world society even approximates such a condition), good results can be expected as long as property rights are respected and enforced.

The drive for profits induces people to produce what others want at the lowest possible price, hence serving the community interest. Even if raw greed dominates private-sector behavior—and no convincing case has been made that it does—such greed is contained and directed by competitive market forces toward a commonly shared goal: the production of goods and services that people, not government agencies, want. At the same time, a market system ensures individual freedom, for individual behavior remains largely undirected by government.

Cases made for an industrial policy are replete with horror stories of market system performance. These are contrasted with visions of how a collective of well-meaning people would handle economic tasks. The word "cooperation" is used loosely, as if the presumed lack of cooperation in the market system could be expunged simply with good intentions. Little is said of the waste and corruption in government and the extent to which government "industrial policy" in the past has been shaped by the political imbalance between, on the one hand, the private interests that seek protection, subsidies, and special privileges and, on the other, the general public that must pay the bills through price increases and taxes. Furthermore, virtually nothing is said about the resources tied up in the lobbying efforts of the 15,000 or so registered lobbyists in Washington and the thousands of other unofficial lobbyists who regularly ply the streets of Washington and the halls of Congress. NIP advocates do not explain how these private interests will be made less harmful. If greed is the root problem even in an unfettered market system, as NIP advocates argue, then this root will not vanish by assuming it away. Yet this is precisely what is done by NIP backers when they propose political institutions as market substitutes.

Industrial policy proponents seem to understand that the three arbitrary divisions of the electorate—workers, managers, and government officials—have competing interests: each wants a larger share of a growing economic pie. But they still perceive politics as a civilizing or harmonizing process, one in which such competing interests can be reconciled through reflective and sober discussions concerning their common interest, which is to increase the size of the economic pie and to modulate the "adversarial relationships" that exist among them in market settings. NIP proponents seem to believe that social welfare is an objective truth that can be deduced by well-meaning people through the voting process. The implicit assumption is that Americans operating in their political capacities are different from Americans operating in their market capacities. Given the extensive use of porkbarrel politics, their claims remain unconvincing. Furthermore, competitive markets are a system for picking "winners," and there is no reason to believe NIP advocates would be satisfied with the economic system until "their winners" are picked.

The Information Problem

Centralized planning, whether called industrial policy or industrial democracy, is bound to fail to produce what people want because it cannot obtain the information needed to make those calculations without the markets it seeks to supplant. The fact is, information on what people want is not objective or determinable outside the market process.

Adam Smith noted in his *Theory of Moral Sentiments* more than two hundred years ago that "the man of system . . . seems to imagine that he can arrange the different members of a great society with as much ease as the hand arranges the pieces upon a chess board."[65] Smith would recognize today's industrial policy advocates, who claim that they can rearrange the "smokestacks" of American industries across the industrial matrix of the country. All they need, they say, is to collect "good information" on what people can produce, feed the data into a "properly" constructed computer

---

[65]Adam Smith, *The Theory of Moral Sentiments* (Indianapolis: Liberty Press, 1976), pp. 380–81.

program, and then hold votes on what particular configuration of industries should be developed. NIP advocates ignore what Smith explained: that chess pieces have "no other principle of motion than that which the hand impresses upon them," whereas "in the great chess board of human society, every single piece has a principle of motion of its own, altogether different from that which the legislature might choose to impress upon it."[66]

Supply and demand identify the limits of what producers and consumers, respectively, are willing to do in markets. Suppliers will hardly reveal they are willing to accept as little as $50 for a widget if, in the absence of competition, they can get by with offering it for $100. Similarly, buyers will rarely voluntarily offer to pay $100 for a widget if they can get it for $50. Perhaps more than anything else, the competitive market is a process for revealing people's limits.

Aside from suggesting that reputable people would discuss the issue, perhaps from the banks of the Potomac, and then vote on it, NIP advocates say little about how industrial policy engineers would secure the information they need to achieve the goals of what must be construed as "plans." To simply talk of improved statistics, as is done in proposed legislation for an Economic Cooperation Council, is to beg the question; it assumes that the statistics gathered outside of markets overcome people's inclination to hide their true economic limits until forced to reveal them when striking a bargain. To assume that government officials can, with reasonable clarity, assess wants and needs and calculate acceptable trade-offs for those living across this enormous nation is to assume cognitive skills so far undemonstrated by any group of people or cluster of computers. At the very least, industrial policy advocates should acknowledge, as government intervention in the economy mounts—and industrial policy proposals are not modest on this count—that the cognitive skills of government officials are bound to wane because prices will become progressively distorted and, accordingly, less useful in guiding policy. Industrial policy proposals will drastically distort the economic data that are needed to undertake the government guidance that is tendered.

With limited information at their disposal and a limited capacity to handle it, how then are NIP advocates to pick and favor those industries destined to emerge in the intermediate future, much less

[66]Ibid.

the distant future? How are they to identify the industries that will "win" the competitive struggle for resources and for the pocketbooks of consumers? The managers of NIP could only subsidize "winners" after they have been picked by the market or, even worse, impose their own vision of who should "win." A national industrial policy would thus discriminate against firms not "chosen" by the political process. Like any centralized planning process, NIP would limit the "plans" to the mental acuity of the planners and, in the process, limit economic growth.

If votes are to be taken on the allocation of capital, then NIP advocates must make the case not merely that the market has defects, but that industrial democracy and central planning are *less* defective. Proponents of an industrial policy ought to recognize by now that government imposes considerable costs and that greater foul-ups invariably follow extension of government authority. They should also recognize that democracy, important as it is in the political arena, has crucial limits in determining economic processes.

The Result: Inequity, Waste, and Decline

National industrial democracy would not alleviate but only exacerbate America's economic difficulties.

The historical record reveals a strong coincidence of growth in government economic intervention and growing severity of inflation, unemployment, and lagging productivity improvements. While this statistical fact may prove little, it does suggest strongly that new government efforts to manipulate the economy should be viewed with suspicion.

Industrial democracy would introduce new layers of bureaucratic obstacles for firms seeking to adapt to economic changes.

Decisions made on the allocation of capital would be subject to the influence of politically powerful interest groups. Established firms would tend to be treated favorably because they exist, have supporting votes from their laborers and suppliers, and have the profits available to sway allocation decisions. Because many new companies have only limited constituencies, they would tend to bear the burden of the subsidies given to established firms. Many potentially profitable firms would be thwarted by the potentially heavy tax burden imposed on them if or when they emerged.

Advocates of industrial policy earnestly believe that the burden of economic change should be shared across the country. When a

28

plant shuts down, for instance, people other than the workers and community residents directly affected should pay part of the cost of helping the plant reopen or retraining the workers. Such forced subsidies would encourage workers, especially the politically powerful, to get their wages raised in the knowledge that if their firms fail, they will be helped by government through the problems of adjustment. In other words, an industrial policy that "spreads the risk" would allow workers and firms to impose their production costs on others just as polluters do, thus encouraging failure and waste of the nation's resources.

A central lesson of environmental economics is that a stream will be used and abused, i.e., polluted, when property rights to it are not defined and people are allowed to use it free of charge for waste disposal. In the vernacular of the environmental literature, the stream is a "common access resource." The cost of the waste is "externalized" to others—those who have to clean the water before it can be reused. In the same way, industrial policy proposals designed to "spread the risk and cost of social adjustment" make the national income stream a common access resource and would effectively allow people by their own private decisions to tap into other people's income—hardly a democratic means of decision making.

To ensure over time that people did not externalize their production costs, the controls envisioned under various industrial policy proposals would in turn spawn their own controls. This is why Nobel laureate economist F. A. Hayek has called efforts toward even limited national planning the "road to serfdom" in a book by that title.[67] The trip down this road has already begun. A major argument offered in support of industrial policy has been that, if the federal government does not engage in buyouts, bailouts, and selective nationalization, it will have to provide unemployment compensation and welfare benefits. Buyouts and bailouts are seen as cheaper public policy substitutes. Of course, such controls will foster other unforeseen consequences that must be controlled if NIP goals are to be realized. Because costs can be externalized when government buys or bails out firms, failure is encouraged. Additional controls can then be justified on economic efficiency grounds, just as the initial forays into industrial control were justified on efficiency grounds.

[67]F. A. Hayek, *The Road to Serfdom* (Chicago: University of Chicago Press, 1944).

Concluding Comments

Several of the policies included in the spate of industrial policy reforms warrant further and serious consideration. Shifting current income taxation to consumption taxation, changing to a flatter tax-rate structure, treating preferred stock dividends as interest, reducing or eliminating the corporate income tax, expensing capital expenditures, and replacing current government employment retraining programs with a retraining voucher program—all merit study.

In looking at such proposals, however, Congress should be vigilant against policies that disproportionately and unknowingly benefit some industries at the expense of others, choke off entrepreneurial efforts that might make U.S. industries more competitive in international markets, and shorten the investment time horizons of businessmen. Much that is vaunted as national industrial policy translates into more of the same sort of government policies that have given rise to America's current economic difficulties—more protection of domestic industries from foreign competition, more subsidies for failing businesses, more welfare benefits for workers whose wages have been raised far above the national average, more spending on social services, and more proposals for the federal government to centralize control of the economy.

The industrial policy movement should be watched carefully because NIP advocates are also seeking many profound changes in the structure of the U.S. economy itself. This alone requires that their conceptual framework be scrutinized for consistency and cogency. They must be confronted with their factual errors and internal contradictions, and their perception of the current state of economic affairs and their vision of America's economic future must be challenged.

Reich, Bluestone, Harrison, Hart, Hollings, Mondale, Askew, and many others contend that the American economy is in the midst of an agonizing industrial transformation, spurred by an accelerating rate of technological change and capital mobility, which supersedes the Industrial Revolution in impact on people's livelihoods. One must wonder how standards of logical consistency can be met when the solution—changeability—is also believed to be the problem.

Reich, for example, maintains that a major source of U.S. economic difficulties lies in the inability and/or unwillingness of U.S.

businesses to adapt to new realities of a world economy. At the same time, he and others propose to democratize workplaces and the allocation of capital. Given the difficulties Congress has in voting on the budget—the inability of the government bureaucracy to carry out its assigned tasks efficiently—the worry becomes that the proposed solution, industrial democracy, would do nothing but further reduce the capacity of U.S. industry to adapt and to meet demands of the changing world economy.

As Dwight Lee has observed, "in dismissing the obvious [explanation of our economic difficulties, faulty government policies, which, if acknowledged, would have drawn into question his solution], Reich has substituted the absurd argument that the creativity behind paper entrepreneurialism is explained by the inability of American businessmen to adapt."[68] If businessmen are willing and quite capable of creating a "paper economy," why are they not equally able to adapt their production techniques? What seems to concern Reich and others is that businessmen *have* adapted to obvious incentives built into the tax code and to a political system that allows government to cater to special interests, but not in ways that he and others would prefer.

Industrial policy advocates appear to be proposing more of the same "adaptation." At the very least, they fail to tell us how the political system can be enlarged and, at the same time, closed to further exploitation. A government with enlarged powers to allocate the nation's capital stock—with the selective capacity to aid some industries at the expense of others—would likely be viewed by entrepreneurs as a valuable resource (incorporating coercive powers) that could be enlisted through the political process in pursuit of their narrow private interests.

Finally, proponents of industrial policy presume an immense stupidity on the part of profit-maximizing entrepreneurs, workers, and consumers. NIP advocates contend that entrepreneurs are systematically willing to close profitable plants; that they grossly mistreat workers, who are needed for production and profits; and that they are unwilling to adapt when adaptation would mean survival, if not substantial profits. Workers are unable or unwilling to make tolerably intelligent decisions regarding training and retraining, and consumers are poorly informed about many of the decisions they make daily. At the same time, advocates of a national industrial

---

[68]Lee, p. 13.

policy call for the democratization of industrial decisions, which in the end would have to rely not on the advertised wisdom of the self-appointed industrial policy sages but on citizens presumed inept at handling their private affairs.

The rhetoric of the debate is enticing. There is much talk of "cooperative efforts of labor, business, and government leaders to pick winners," suggesting that markets, which political institutions organized under a national industrial policy would supplant, are devoid of cooperation and fail to pick winners. Nothing could be further from the truth. The purpose of markets is to do both: to further cooperation among people with compatible interests and to pick winners through competition. Given the insistence of industrial policy advocates that we need additional means of picking winners, we must be concerned that they possess a preconceived view of which firms or industries *should* be winners.

Under private market arrangements, NIP advocates and others already have an excellent opportunity for ensuring that "their" chosen industries can be winners—by using their own resources to invest in selected companies or (if they happen to be workers or suppliers) by keeping their costs competitive and attracting investment. A national industrial policy would tend to replace such voluntary arrangements, constrained by the sobering effects of competition, with political institutions that have at their disposal the coercive taxing and regulatory authority of government. The real dispute is over visions of what is possible in the industrial sector through government: whether or not industrial development and stability can—and should—be attained and enhanced through private or collective institutions.

II. The Deindustrialization Hoax

As is evident from our discussion in the first chapter, many proponents of a national industrial policy seek not a mere extension of the welfare state, but rather a transformation of it into a loosely conceived centralized industrial democracy. No longer are they willing to argue simply that more federal dollars would serve their purposes. No longer are they willing to accept the philosophy of our Founders, which was that government should restrict its role in the "economic game" to that of rule-maker and rule-enforcer. Rather, they advocate, sometimes with considerable zest, that government should become an active participant, willing to alter the rules in the middle of the game in order to adjust the game's *content* to their preconceived notion of what it should be. They seek governmental authority to "pick the winners" and "protect the losers," phrases that should raise suspicions regarding the fairness of the political game they wish to play.

The review of NIP positions in chapter 1 revealed that an economic policy founded on what advocates call "equity, security, and participation" would require a restructuring of public and private decision making in the economy. The list of proposals may be usefully summarized as including the following:

- greatly increasing federal expenditures on education, retraining, health care, child care, unemployment compensation, research and development, relocation expenses for displaced workers, and disability benefits;

- imposing additional rigidities on American industries, for example, mandating the "domestic content" in domestically produced automobiles and the percentage of our foreign-traded bulk cargo that must be carried on U.S. ships (20 percent under current proposals in Congress);

- reregulating the domestic transportation industry—specifically, airlines and trucking—in the interest of promoting market stability and "rationalizing" otherwise destructive competitive pressures;

- expanding protection of domestic firms from foreign imports that are cheaper and sometimes of higher quality;

- making firms the social agents of a wide range of welfare services, presumably supplanting government welfare offices with corporate personnel offices;

- giving workers the "right" to participate in many management decisions, including investment, disinvestment and reinvestment decisions;

- instituting a modern-day Reconstruction Finance Corporation (renamed "Industrial Development Bank" or "Bank of Industrial Competitiveness"), which would, based on democratic votes, "allocate sacrifice" through subsidies, low-interest-rate loans, grants, and loan guarantees;

- restricting the right of firms to close down plants by imposing substantial prenotification, severance pay, and community restitution payment requirements on firms that wished to discontinue unprofitable operations; and

- providing worker groups with federal subsidies to buy out their closed plants (thereby giving firms a means of unloading unprofitable plants at public expense).

All of these efforts would be "rationalized" (along with the structure of industries) through the establishment of tripartite councils (called "Economic Cooperation Councils" or "Councils of Industrial Competitiveness"), which would be federally funded and composed of representatives from interest groups (perhaps the AFL-CIO, the Chamber of Commerce, and Nader's Raiders) in labor, government, and management that would guide economic planning. Presumably, there would be central control of these councils through some Washington-based planning board that would, in the minds of many national industrial policy proponents, be guided by a breathtaking "Economic Bill of Rights."[1]

The Decline of America

In titling this chapter "The Deindustrialization Hoax," the words were carefully chosen. As the chapter and, indeed, the entire book

[1]Samuel Bowles, David M. Gordon, and Thomas E. Weisskopf, *Beyond the Waste Land: A Democratic Alternative to Economic Decline* (Garden City, N.Y.: Doubleday, Anchor Press, 1983), p. 270.

will show, the empirical case for national industrial policy is nothing short of a hoax. A gross misconstruction of the economic circumstances of and policy options for this country is not only intended by many (though by no means all) of the proponents of a national industrial policy, but it is absolutely necessary for pulling off the dramatic changes in policy that they seek. After all, the public would not likely consider seriously the NIP economic game plan unless it were led to believe that the present economic system is in crisis and can't accomplish the goals that so many of us—opponents and proponents of government intrusion in the economy—share with conviction. These shared goals include a return to economic prosperity, greater economic growth through expanded investment opportunities, and better paying and more secure jobs.

In their writings NIP proponents exude pessimism, if not a sense of crisis, for the future of our economic system. The media rhetoric started several years ago with "economic malaise" and has advanced to the point that "deindustrialization," a word that had to be defined when first used several years ago, has become worn. Robert Reich's solemn pronouncements on the "unraveling" of the U.S. economy,[2] meaning primarily the closing down of the manufacturing sector due, according to Barry Bluestone and Bennett Harrison, to the growing mobility of capital, the expanding competitiveness of the world economy, and the increasing pace of technological change, are now echoed by many NIP advocates.[3]

MIT economist Lester Thurow suggests that proposals for industrial policy are founded on a pervasive fear that American industries will be unable to meet the competition from countries that have "some mechanism for strategic coordination of their industries."[4] In arguing for the development of a "new social contract" built around a "new economic democracy," Martin Carnoy, Derek Shearer, and Russell Rumberger assert forthrightly that "there is a crisis in America." As a consequence, we must urgently move to erect a "new social arrangement between all of us living here—employees and employers, women and men, white and nonwhite, those with

[2]Ibid., p. 3.

[3]Barry Bluestone and Bennett Harrison, *The Deindustrialization of America: Plant Closings, Community Abandonment, and the Dismantling of Basic Industries* (New York: Basic Books, 1982).

[4]Lester C. Thurow, testimony prepared for the House Subcommittee on Economic Stabilization, June 14, 1983, p. 1.

high and low incomes, young and old, working and retired"—one that "must reaffirm and energize the fundamental dynamic of our history: democracy—a democracy where individuals working together politically make government extend their economic and social rights."[5]

Professor George Lodge of the Harvard Business School opens his book *The American Disease* with a discomforting reminder:

> The cold winter of 1982 brought home to America the realization that our economy, once the wonder of the world, was failing. The power and efficiency of the industrial system, which since World War II had been taken for granted, was eroding. The United States was aware, for the first time, of losing ground in the competitive race with other developed nations.[6]

Lodge stresses the special difficulty we have encountered with Japan, which has prospered supposedly because of government coordination of the Japanese industrial structure, and he tells us that "the symptoms of the American disease" had become painfully evident in the early 1980s, as measured by slow economic growth, falling real incomes, rising interest rates, plunging corporate profits, and lagging business investment. "In fact," Lodge tells us, "every indicator, social as well as economic, revealed sickness."[7]

The Empirical Hoax

The details of the story may change with the current state of the economy and with the particular industrial policy advocate, but the theme remains consistent: We are haphazardly heading to economic ruin. Past policies have failed to revitalize the economy; indeed, they have contributed to economic decline. We can be saved only by a radical redirection in our economic relationships.

Admittedly, advocates of a national industrial policy have some of the facts straight; no one would give them much attention if they were all wrong. We have had, and continue to have, economic difficulties, especially given the severity of the recent recession, and government policies have been a contributing factor. The problem

---

[5]Martin Carnoy, Derek Shearer, and Russell Rumberger, *A New Social Contract: The Economy and Government After Reagan* (New York: Harper and Row, 1983), p. 1.

[6]George C. Lodge, *The American Disease* (New York: Alfred A. Knopf, Inc., 1984), p. 3.

[7]Ibid., p. 5.

with the case made for a national industrial policy is its warped interpretation of many of the facts and the failure of advocates to tell us, as Paul Harvey might say, the "rest of the story"—that is, those parts of the story that, if told, would make the case for industrial policy and economic democracy suspect. Much of the rest of the story will be presented here.

Job Losses

Professor Bluestone tells us that between 1969 and 1976 22 million jobs were destroyed as a consequence of plant closings and relocations and that the pace of job destruction is accelerating: between 1978 and 1982, 31 million jobs in the country were destroyed. Indeed, Bluestone points out that "fully one-third of all private sector jobs in 1978 had disappeared by 1982."[8] He notes, citing the work of Duke University professor Roger Schmenner,[9] that between 1970–72 and 1978 the 410 largest manufacturing firms divested themselves of "over 21 percent of the 12,000+ establishments they owned and operated at the beginning of the period," while they opened over 1,600 new plants and bought 3,400 others in new industries and different regions during the same period.[10]

One might get the impression from reading such accounts of contemporary economic history that the American economy is rapidly eroding, which is hardly the case. What Bluestone and others who follow his lead do not tell us is that between 1965 and 1980, before the advent of the recent recession, employment increased in the United States by 30 million, or by about 50 percent. During the previous 15-year period, employment rose by only 35 percent.[11] None of the European countries that are supposed to have, in Thurow's words, "some mechanism for strategic coordination of their industries" can match the employment record of the United States during the 1970s, and neither can Japan.

[8]Barry Bluestone, "Industrial Dislocation and the Implications for Public Policy," paper prepared for the third annual policy forum on employability development, "Displaced Workers: Implications for Educational and Training Institutions," National Center for Research in Vocational Education, Ohio State University (Washington, September 12–13, 1983), p. 3.

[9]Roger W. Schmenner, "The Location Decisions of Large, Multiplant Companies" (Cambridge: MIT-Harvard Joint Center for Urban Studies, September 1980).

[10]Bluestone, pp. 3–4.

[11]Richard B. McKenzie, *Fugitive Industry: The Economics and Politics of Deindustrialization* (San Francisco: Pacific Institute for Public Policy Research, 1984).

The Decline of Manufacturing

Even in the manufacturing sector the presumed general "deindustrialization" can only be construed as a misreading of the facts. True, manufacturing employment has always exhibited cyclical swings that are more pronounced than the up-and-down movements in general economic activity, and manufacturing employment was on a downturn during the early 1980s, reflecting the two successive recessions in those years. Hence, one can show that over an appropriately selected period of years (say, 1969–76 or 1980–83) manufacturing employment was on the decline. However, it should be stressed that during the 1965–80 period, manufacturing employment remained more or less constant at about 20 million. The computed trend in manufacturing employment at that time rose at a compound rate of 0.4 percent, not much admittedly, but not negative either. During the last half of the 1970s—specifically, 1976–80—manufacturing employment was on the rebound, rising at a compound rate of 2.36 percent.[12] Furthermore, advocates of an industrial policy fail to tell us that the decline in manufacturing employment as a percentage of the labor force was due primarily to the relatively faster rate of productivity growth in the manufacturing sector.[13]

But what of the claims of NIP proponents that manufacturing production is declining? Table 2.1 contains the industrial production index for all American industries taken together and broken down into manufacturing sectors. It reveals that industrial production in the aggregate expanded by 24.5 percent between 1975 and 1980, whereas it expanded on average by 21.6 percent for the five-year periods between 1960 and 1980. Most manufacturing sectors grew over the period covered by the table, a fact that led George Mason University economist Thomas DiLorenzo, who made these calculations, to conclude: "The one thing missing from the 'decline of the manufacturing sector,' therefore, is any evidence of a decline. It might have been expected that the rate of growth of industrial production would decline during the past decade—as it did—in

---

[12]For more on this point, see idem, "NIP in the Air: Fashionable Myths in Industrial Policy," *Policy Review* (September 1983): 75–87.

[13]Charles Schultze, "Industrial Policy: A Dissent," *Brookings Review* (October 1983). Reprinted in *Plant Closings: Public or Private Choices?* ed. Richard B. McKenzie, rev. ed. (Washington: Cato Institute, 1984).

Table 2.1

Industrial Production Indexes, by Industry, 1960–82*

Major Industry Group	1960	1965	1970	1972	1973	1974	1975	1976	1977	1978	1979	1980	1981	1982 Jan–May
Industrial production	66	90	108	120	130	129	118	131	138	146	153	147	151	140
Manufacturing	65	90	106	119	130	129	116	130	138	147	154	147	150	138
Durable goods	63	89	102	114	127	126	109	122	130	140	146	137	141	127
Primary metals	72	102	107	112	127	123	96	110	111	120	121	102	108	86
Fabricated metal products	71	91	102	112	125	124	110	124	131	142	149	134	136	119
Electrical machinery	52	82	108	122	143	144	117	135	145	159	175	173	178	170
Nonelectrical machinery	57	85	104	116	134	140	125	135	144	154	164	163	171	155
Transportation equipment	65	95	90	108	118	109	97	111	122	133	135	117	116	106
Instruments	58	83	112	120	138	144	132	147	156	167	175	171	170	161
Clay, glass, stone products	79	98	106	121	134	133	118	136	146	157	164	148	148	125
Lumber and products	75	96	106	121	126	116	108	123	131	136	137	119	119	104
Furniture and fixtures	72	95	108	131	144	138	118	137	145	156	162	150	157	150
Miscellaneous	71	94	111	127	138	138	128	145	149	151	154	148	155	141
Nondurable Goods	69	91	112	127	134	135	126	142	151	157	164	161	165	154
Textile mill products	69	93	112	133	143	133	122	135	134	138	145	139	136	123
Apparel products	82	97	101	109	117	114	108	126	134	134	134	127	120	NA
Leather and products	90	98	90	88	83	78	77	77	74	74	72	70	69	64
Paper and products	68	92	115	129	137	135	116	133	138	145	151	151	155	153

Table 2.1 (continued)

Major Industry Group	1960	1965	1970	1972	1973	1974	1975	1976	1977	1978	1979	1980	1981	1982 Jan–May
Printing and publishing	71	88	107	113	118	118	113	123	128	132	137	140	144	137
Chemicals and products	56	88	120	144	155	159	147	171	186	197	212	207	216	196
Petroleum products	77	92	113	122	129	125	124	134	143	145	144	133	130	118
Rubber and plastics	52	86	132	172	184	195	167	200	232	254	272	256	274	255
Foods	79	92	109	117	121	124	123	133	139	143	148	150	152	140
Tobacco products	91	100	102	106	112	110	112	117	113	118	118	120	122	121
Mining	80	93	112	113	115	115	113	114	118	124	126	133	142	137
Utilities	63	89	125	139	145	144	146	152	157	161	166	168	169	171
*Energy***	70	89	117	125	128	126	126	129	133	135	138	138	137	138

SOURCE: Board of Governors of the Federal Reserve System, *Federal Reserve Bulletin* (monthly).
*1967 = 100. Based on *1967 Standard Industrial Classification Manual*. See also *Historical Statistics, Colonial Times to 1970*, series P 13 and P 18–39.
**Production of energy is represented by output energy, such as crude oil, natural gas, and coal mining, and by the conversion of primary energy to other energy forms for final consumption.

light of the vastly expanded costs of regulation and the inflation of the 1970s."[14]

Granted, using current dollar estimates, the value of manufacturing output in the United States as a percentage of GNP declined between 1950 and the beginning of this decade from about 29 percent to 22 percent. (See Table 2.2.) However, the relatively faster rate of productivity growth in manufacturing during that period translated into a relative decline in the prices of manufacturing output. As a result, the percentage drop in manufacturing goods noted above reflects the relative price decline, as well as any drop in the share of real production. When the relative price change is extracted from the analysis and real manufacturing output is measured as a percentage of real GNP, a different picture of "decline" in the manufacturing sector is obtained. DiLorenzo estimates that real manufacturing output as a percentage of real GNP remained at about 25 percent during the 1950–81 period, with cyclical swings that are evident in Table 2.2. The table also shows that contrary to popular belief, the service sector has grown only slightly over the last three decades.

Care must obviously be taken in using real dollar calculations. With such figures one could argue that the United States has remained an agrarian society, since the relative decline in agricultural production over past decades is attributable to a significant degree to relative price decreases in agricultural goods. While recognizing this pitfall, however, we must also remain aware of the problems of using current dollar production figures alone. During a congressional hearing in 1984, Rep. John LaFalce (D-N.Y.), a major sponsor of legislation that would authorize an "Industrial Competitiveness Council" and a "Bank of Industrial Competitiveness," recounted data on the relative decline of the manufacturing sector and asked one witness how the United States could expect to provide manufacturing consulting services to the world if the country allows its manufacturing sector to dwindle away.[15] Obviously, if the manufacturing sector did not continually improve its productivity at faster rates than experienced in other countries and if, accordingly, manufacturing prices did not decline relatively, we could not hope to provide consulting services in manufacturing.

[14]Thomas J. DiLorenzo, "The Myth of America's Declining Manufacturing Sector," Heritage Foundation Backgrounder (Washington, January 13, 1984).

[15]As recalled by the author, who was, at the time, waiting to testify.

Table 2.2

MANUFACTURING AND SERVICE OUTPUT, 1950–81 (% OF GNP)*

Sector	1950	1955	1960	1965	1970	1975	1977	1978	1979	1980	1981
Manufacturing	25	25	23	25	24	24	25	18	25	24	24
Services	11	10	11	11	12	12	12	12	12	13	13

SOURCE: Thomas J. DiLorenzo, "The Myth of America's Declining Manufacturing Sector," Heritage Foundation Backgrounder (Washington, January 13, 1984), p. 5. Calculated from Bureau of the Census, *Statistical Abstract of the U.S.* (Washington: Government Printing Office, 1982–83).

*Calculated using constant 1972 dollars.

Regional Decline

National industrial policy proponents lament the regional disparity in economic growth. They point out that the decline of manufacturing is a regional problem, confined almost exclusively to the Frostbelt, which has had to suffer disproportionately over the past decade under escalating energy costs. What they fail to tell us is that New England, which is very much part of the Frostbelt, has been dubbed the "Sunbelt of the North" in recognition of the strong revival of its manufacturing sector. Indeed, the trend in manufacturing employment in New England during the last half of the 1970s grew at a compound annual rate of 3.46 percent, a growth rate 50 percent higher than that experienced in the South Atlantic states, the author's area of the country. Furthermore, the growth rate in manufacturing employment in Massachusetts was more than twice the rate in South Carolina, a state believed to be an industrial seedbed.[16]

Many are worried that the South is growing at the expense of the North and is "robbing" the North of its economic birthright to manufacturing jobs. In assessing such claims, we should not forget three important points.

First, because of differences in workers' education and skills, the jobs created in the South through the relocation of industries from the North (which is not nearly as big a problem as many people seem to think) are not always the type of jobs lost in the North. Firms often move in order to take advantage of differences in worker skills because different skills are needed at different stages in the development of products and production processes.

Second, we should not assume that jobs lost by the North to the South can be reclaimed by restrictions on the regional movements of firms. Firms move so as to take advantage of profitable opportunities or to avoid losses and being driven out of business by more cost-effective firms. If northern firms are restricted from taking advantage of profitable opportunities elsewhere, then other firms will do so themselves. As a result, northern firms will be outcompeted, and northern jobs will be lost anyway.

Finally, we should not forget that, contrary to common assumption, shifts of industries from the North to the South and West can, on balance, be beneficial to the North. The goods produced in the

---

[16]For further development of the points made in this section, see McKenzie, *Fugitive Industry*, chap. 2.

South and West at lower cost can be purchased in the North at lower prices, and the potential for industry movements keeps the prices of northern goods competitive.

Granted, between the end of 1980 (the peak of a business cycle) and the end of 1984 (still in the recovery that began in late 1982), manufacturing employment was in serious decline in all regions of the country except one, the Mountains. Twenty-eight states had a compound rate of decline in the trend of manufacturing employment of more than 1 percent. The trend in manufacturing employment in Louisiana and West Virginia declined at a compound annual rate of more than 5 percent, a disheartening statistic by any measure. While manufacturing employment declined more seriously in Frostbelt states, about half these states were in the South and West, suggesting that the problem has been national in scope, with differences in degree among regions.

Still, for two important reasons, we should not be so distressed by the manufacturing decline in recent years that we change our vision of the country's economic future and seek a new future through national industrial policy corrections, such as the ones we have reviewed. First, it cannot be stressed too much that during the 1980–84 period, in spite of serious recessions and the accompanying declines in manufacturing employment, the trend in total nonagricultural employment in 43 states was more or less flat or positive, meaning that in most states the nonmanufacturing sectors were either offsetting or more than offsetting the employment losses in manufacturing.[17] And the economy was still in the midst of its recovery in late 1984, with total and manufacturing employment expanding in virtually all states. The growth in nonmanufacturing employment was due partially to the fact that during the recessions that extended over much of the 1980–84 period many factory workers who had been laid off from their jobs sought temporary or second-best employment in nonmanufacturing sectors. However,

[17]The compound rates of growth in the trend of nonagricultural employment was greater than 1 percent in 19 states and between minus 1 and plus 1 percent in 24 states. The 7 states with compound rates of decline greater than 1 percent in the trend of their total nonagricultural employment between 1980 and 1984 were Montana (−1.1 percent), Wyoming (−2.0 percent), Ohio (−1.1 percent), Illinois (−1.7 percent), Michigan (−1.2 percent), Iowa (−1.5 percent), and West Virginia (−2.5 percent). Five additional states had rates of decline of between .5 and 1 percent: Mississippi (−.69 percent), Louisiana (−.86 percent), Oregon (−.67 percent), Pennsylvania (−.78 percent), and Indiana (−.76 percent).

44

many manufacturing jobs were also lost because of expansions in the nonmanufacturing sectors. The nonmanufacturing sectors in many states have expanded, have pushed up the prices of labor and other resources, and have competitively nudged many manufacturing firms out of business or into less labor-intensive (more capital-intensive) and more productive methods of manufacturing.

Second, the relatively high rate of decline of manufacturing employment in the Northeast and North Central regions of the country should not be particularly disturbing, since manufacturing dominates the non-agricultural economies of many of the states in those regions. And, most importantly, the general decline in manufacturing employment during most of the first half of the 1980s can be chalked up as the normal, expected consequence of recessions, especially severe ones like the one that ended in late 1982. Historically, recessions have been most accurately reflected in declines in manufacturing employment. Robert Z. Lawrence, a senior fellow at the Brookings Institution who has studied manufacturing employment trends and cycles in considerable detail using econometric techniques, concludes that "contrary to the recent fears, America is not deindustrializing"[18] and that manufacturing employment will return to its long-run trend with the general economic recovery:

> The demand for manufacturing goods is very sensitive to the growth rate of the overall economy. If GNP grows above its long-run trend, manufacturing growth will outstrip it; if GNP grows below its long-run trend (which it did from 1973 through the early 1980s), manufacturing employment will lag behind.[19]

Lawrence adds that despite problems of an inflated value of the dollar on international markets (which makes imports cheaper and exports more expensive and more difficult to sell abroad), "U.S. manufacturing output and employment between 1979 and 1983 have conformed with their historical patterns given overall growth of the economy."[20] The recent problems faced by the manufacturing sector can be attributed primarily to problems of demand manage-

---

[18]Robert Z. Lawrence, *Can America Compete?* (Washington: Brookings Institution, 1984), p. 8.

[19]Ibid., p. 6.

[20]Ibid., p. 8.

ment, meaning an inappropriate mix of fiscal and monetary policies, not to the lack of a national industrial policy like the ones in Europe.

The extent to which the recovery still underway in early 1985 was compatible with past experience is evident in Figure 2.1, which compares the gains in various macroeconomic measures for the recovery that began in 1982 with the average gains achieved in five other "long" post–World War II recoveries. As the figure reveals, the recent gain in real gross national product, far from being unusual, was in line with past experience. The same general observation is applicable to improvements in employment, real personal income, industrial output, real consumer spending, housing starts, factory workweek, and consumer prices—a revelation that should greatly comfort the prophets of gloom and doom. Only the change in industrial materials prices varied significantly from past experience.

America's International Competitiveness

Advocates of a new industrial policy often base their pessimistic assessments on the failure of American businesspersons to "adapt"— that is, to innovate and compete effectively with our international competitors who, presumably, have captured our competitive edge through government guidance of their economies. Again, the inability of American business to adapt is the theme of Reich's *The Next American Frontier*, in which he writes:

> By and large, America's transition to flexible-system production continues to be halting, painful, and fraught with inequities. Managers' attention continues to be fixed on rearranging industrial assets and on manipulating abstract numbers and rules.[21]

Industrial policy advocates stress that the inability of American business to adapt is hurting our international competitiveness, and they remind us repeatedly of the number of jobs destroyed because of imports. What they do not tell us is that over 5 million jobs in this country are tied directly to exports and that our ability to export is tied directly to our willingness to import (and so our ability to export will be restricted by restrictions on imports). As evidence of a presumed deteriorating competitiveness of U.S. producers in the international economy, industrial policy advocates point to the growing merchandise trade deficit, meaning the increasing degree to which our imports are exceeding our exports.

[21]Reich, pp. 224–25.

46

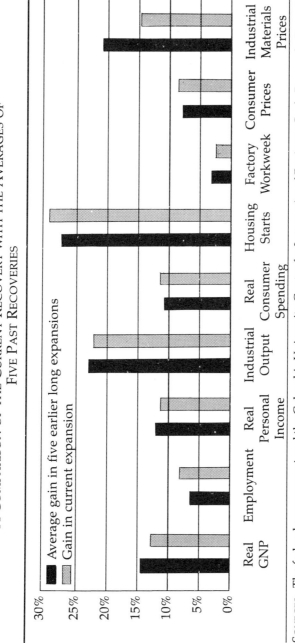

Figure 2.1

A COMPARISON OF THE CURRENT RECOVERY WITH THE AVERAGES OF FIVE PAST RECOVERIES

■ Average gain in five earlier long expansions
▨ Gain in current expansion

Real GNP | Employment | Real Personal Income | Industrial Output | Real Consumer Spending | Housing Starts | Factory Workweek | Consumer Prices | Industrial Materials Prices

30% — 25% — 20% — 15% — 10% — 5% — 0%

SOURCES: The federal government and the Columbia University Center for International Business Cycle Research. Reported in Alfred L. Malabre, Jr., "Current Expansion Takes Well-Worn Path," *Wall Street Journal*, April 15, 1985, p. 6.

47

But concentrated focus on the merchandise trade balance is deceptive for three reasons. First, it does not consider our trade balance in services, where we continue to have a surplus.

Second, the trade deficit says nothing of the growth in our exports, which is a useful measure of our ability to compete and sell in foreign markets. Between 1964 and 1970, when the country generally had merchandise surpluses, our constant-dollar exports grew at an annual rate of 4.9 percent; between 1976 and 1982, when the country had consistent deficits, our constant-dollar exports grew at an annual rate of 5.8 percent.[22] The deficit problem the country has had to face is, accordingly, due largely to a growth in imports, which has been caused partially by faster growth in the U.S. economy compared with other industrial countries and by the rise in the international value of the dollar (which itself could be construed as a measure of strength in the U.S. economy).

Third, many of the deficits over the past decade have been due to the dramatic rise in the price of oil on the world market. Table 2.3 shows in the column "Balance of Trade" that during the last 13 years, the merchandise trade balance was, indeed, negative, reaching more than $60 billion in 1983. However, those deficit figures mask the impact of our petroleum imports. If petroleum trade is subtracted from total exports and imports, as in the column "Non-Petroleum Balance of Trade," the deficit for 1983 is a far more modest $2.2 billion. And it should be noted that the non-petroleum balance of merchandise trade was positive in every year between 1973 and 1982.

Has the United States over the long run seen its dominance in manufacturing trade deteriorate? Given the wholesale destruction of the economies of Japan and many European countries during World War II, it would be amazing to find that the U.S. share of manufacturing goods in all, or even most, industries had grown or held steady since that war. When foreign countries recovered from the war, it was only natural that they would no longer be as dependent upon the United States for many of their industrial needs. In addition, it is not even necessarily the case that the U.S. economy

[22]U.S. International Competitiveness: Perception and Reality (New York: New York Stock Exchange, August 1984), p. 9. See also William H. Branson, "Trade and Structural Adjustment in the U.S. Economy: Response to International Competition," paper prepared for the conference "Structural Changes in the World Economy," American Enterprise Institute and Institute for Economic Studies at Clark University (Washington, September 22–23, 1983).

Table 2.3
U.S. MERCHANDISE TRADE BALANCE, 1970–83 ($ BILLIONS)**

	Total Exports	Petroleum Exports	Non-Petroleum Exports	Total Imports	Petroleum Imports	Non-Petroleum Imports	Balance of Trade	Non-Petroleum Balance of Trade
1970	42.5	*	42.5	39.9	2.9	37.0	+ 2.6	+ 5.5
1971	43.3	*	43.3	45.6	3.6	42.0	− 2.3	+ 1.3
1972	49.4	*	49.4	55.8	4.7	51.1	− 6.4	− 1.7
1973	71.4	*	71.4	70.5	8.4	62.1	+ 0.9	+ 9.3
1974	98.3	*	98.3	103.8	26.6	77.2	− 5.5	+21.1
1975	107.1	*	107.1	98.2	27.0	71.2	+ 8.9	+35.9
1976	114.8	*	114.8	124.2	34.6	89.6	− 9.4	+25.2
1977	120.8	0.3	120.5	151.9	45.0	106.9	−31.1	+13.6
1978	142.1	0.3	141.8	176.0	42.3	133.7	−33.9	+ 8.1
1979	184.5	0.3	184.2	212.0	60.5	151.5	−27.5	+32.7
1980	224.2	0.3	223.9	249.8	79.3	170.5	−25.6	+53.4
1981	237.0	0.2	236.8	265.1	77.8	187.3	−28.1	+49.5
1982	211.2	0.2	211.0	247.6	61.2	186.4	−36.4	+24.6
1983	200.2	0.2	200.0	260.8	58.6	202.2	−60.6	− 2.2

SOURCE: *U.S. International Competitiveness: Perception and Reality* (New York: New York Stock Exchange, August 1984), p. 59.

*Less than $0.1 billion.

**Data are on an international transactions basis and exclude military shipments.

49

would have been better off if U.S. dominance had been maintained; revival of our allies and international competitors has meant increases in productivity abroad and in the U.S. economy, since the greater competition from abroad has forced U.S. producers to watch their costs and productivity improvement more carefully.

It should also be stressed that U.S. manufacturing exports as a share of world trade can deteriorate in what may be considered relatively prosperous times in the domestic economy. A study by the New York Stock Exchange makes this point with unusual clarity:

> Let us look at the period 1962–1972. By almost any and all standards this was a period of superior U.S. economic performance. Real economic growth averaged 4% per year; inflation, 3.3% per year; and unemployment, 4.7% per year. Yet during this period one could have pointed to distressing statistics in the international trade arena. Of the 40 U.S. industry groups in our analysis, 12 had at least 20% share of world exports in 1962, but only six did in 1972! In total, 37 of the 40 industries had a lower market share in 1972 than in 1962![23]

As evident in Table 2.4, U.S. manufacturing exports as a percentage of world manufacturing exports were lower in 1972, 12.1 percent, than in 1962 or 1982, which were 14.8 percent and 12.3 percent, respectively. However, two points made clear by the data in this table are especially noteworthy.

First, U.S. manufacturing exports as a percentage of world trade have cycled over the last two decades, and the recent downturn in the U.S. share may be mostly temporary, due to factors relating to the world-wide recessions of the early 1980s. Second, the share of world manufacturing exports for the European Economic Community, composed of countries that have reputedly tried to follow the centralized industrial policy route, also trended downward, from 44.5 percent in 1962 to 40.7 percent in 1982.

The presumed broad-based decay of U.S. international competitiveness is further drawn into question when the manufacturing sectors are broken down into industries, 40 in the case of the New York Stock Exchange study. In Table 2.5 we can see that 15 of those industries in the United States actually gained in terms of world export share, while 25 lost world export share. The industries that had "superior" (15 percent or more), "intermediate" (7½ percent

---

[23]Ibid., p. 10.

Table 2.4

WORLD SHARE OF MANUFACTURING EXPORTS: U.S. vs. EEC vs. REST OF THE WORLD (%)*

Year	U.S.	EEC**	Rest of the World***
1962	14.8	44.5	31.0
1967	14.1	44.8	28.9
1972	12.1	46.3	27.5
1977	12.6	44.1	28.7
1979	14.0	42.3	30.0
1980	14.7	40.7	29.6
1981	13.9	40.2	30.2
1982	12.3	40.7	31.2

SOURCE: *U.S. International Competitiveness: Perception and Reality* (New York: New York Stock Exchange, August 1984), p. 12.

*Based on constant dollar data.

**Belgium, France, Italy, Germany, Netherlands, U.K.

***Total world exports less those of Canada, Belgium, France, Italy, Germany, Netherlands, Japan, U.K., and U.S.

Table 2.5

GAINS AND LOSSES OF WORLD EXPORT SHARES, 1972–82
(NUMBER OF INDUSTRIES BY COUNTRY)

	Gained*	Lost**	Held Even
Italy	26	14	0
Japan	25	15	0
France	18	20	2
Belgium	17	20	3
U.S.	15	24	1
Germany	13	26	1
Canada	12	27	1
U.K.	3	37	0
Netherlands	3	35	2

SOURCE: *U.S. International Competitiveness: Perception and Reality* (New York: New York Stock Exchange, August 1984), p. 14.
*Higher share in 1982 than 1972.
**Lower share in 1982 than 1972.

to 15 percent), and "inferior" (0 to 7 ½ percent) world export shares in 1982 are listed in Table 2.6. Granted, as evident in Figure 2.2, a number of U.S. industries have seen imports take a larger share of their domestic market, but, to accurately assess the deindustrialization claims, we must remember the following:

> Twelve industry groups have actually seen imports account for a smaller proportion of domestic output in 1982 than in 1972 [see Figure 2.2]; in 9 others penetration increased by one percentage point or less. More importantly, in only 17 of the 40 do imports account for more than 10% of the domestic market and in only six [TV and radios, shoes and leather, office equipment (except computers), motor vehicles, special industry machinery, and miscellaneous manufacturing] do they account for more than 20%.[24]

Of course, using 1984 figures, steel could be added to these 6 industries that now account for more than 20 percent of domestic industry output.

The economic difficulties key industries have faced in international markets are in part a reflection of the relative success of other

[24]Ibid., p. 20.

Table 2.6

U.S. WORLD EXPORT SHARE, BY INDUSTRY, 1982 (%)*

Superior (15 +)	
Computers	35.8
Aerospace	30.9
Other office equipment	29.8
Agricultural machinery	21.1
Engines, turbines	21.0
Household appliances	19.3
Agricultural fertilizers	19.2
Communications equipment, electrical components	17.2
Construction mining, oilfield equipment	16.9
Electrical lighting, wiring equipment	16.8
Other transportation equipment	16.4
Service industry machinery	15.7
Special industry machinery	15.6
Electrical and industrial appliances and distribution equipment	15.3
Intermediate (7½–15)	
Miscellaneous non-electrical machinery	14.9
Other chemicals	14.0
Metal products	13.2
Food, tobacco	12.8
TVs, radios, phonographs	12.1
Instruments	11.8
Plastic products	11.6
Printing, publishing	10.7
Paper	10.1
Metalworking machinery	9.6
Lumber	9.4
Textiles (excluding knits)	9.1
Miscellaneous manufacturing	9.0
Stone, clay, glass	8.7
Motor vehicles	8.2

Table 2.6 (continued)

Inferior (0–7½)	
Other non-ferrous metals	7.4
Rubber products	7.2
Ships, boats	6.2
Furniture	6.1
Petroleum refining	5.6
Fuel oil	5.1
Shoes, leather	4.7
Copper	4.6
Apparel, household textiles	4.0
Knitting	3.0
Ferrous metals	3.0

SOURCE: *U.S. International Competitiveness: Perception and Reality* (New York: New York Stock Exchange, August 1984), p. 17.
*Percentages based on constant dollar data.

U.S. industries. Successful U.S. industries are pushing up the prices of U.S. resources and thus making success less possible for other industries, especially the "sick six": textiles, knitting, apparel, shoes and leather, motor vehicles, and iron and steel. Because resources are limited, as a practical matter not all industries can always be expected to expand; the expansion of some often forces others to contract. (More will be said on this point in chapter 8.) The important point to remember here is that a number of U.S. industries *have* remained competitive internationally; there are firms even within "sick" industries that hold their own in open competition with anyone in the world.[25] These facts suggest that many of our industrial problems are not national, subject to a national remedy, but rather are managerial problems that must be faced largely by individual firms and industries.

Industrial policy advocates have frequently touted the "Japanese economic miracle" on the presumption that all Japanese industries have registered successes, which is simply not the case. In its study, the New York Stock Exchange found that while 25 Japanese indus-

[25]For example, see an article on very successful textile companies in Martinsville, Va.: William Baldwin, "Golden Fleece," *Forbes*, August 1, 1983, pp. 110–16.

Figure 2.2
IMPORT PENETRATION OF U.S. INDUSTRY, 1982 VS. 1972
(% CHANGE IN U.S. IMPORT/OUTPUT RATIO)*

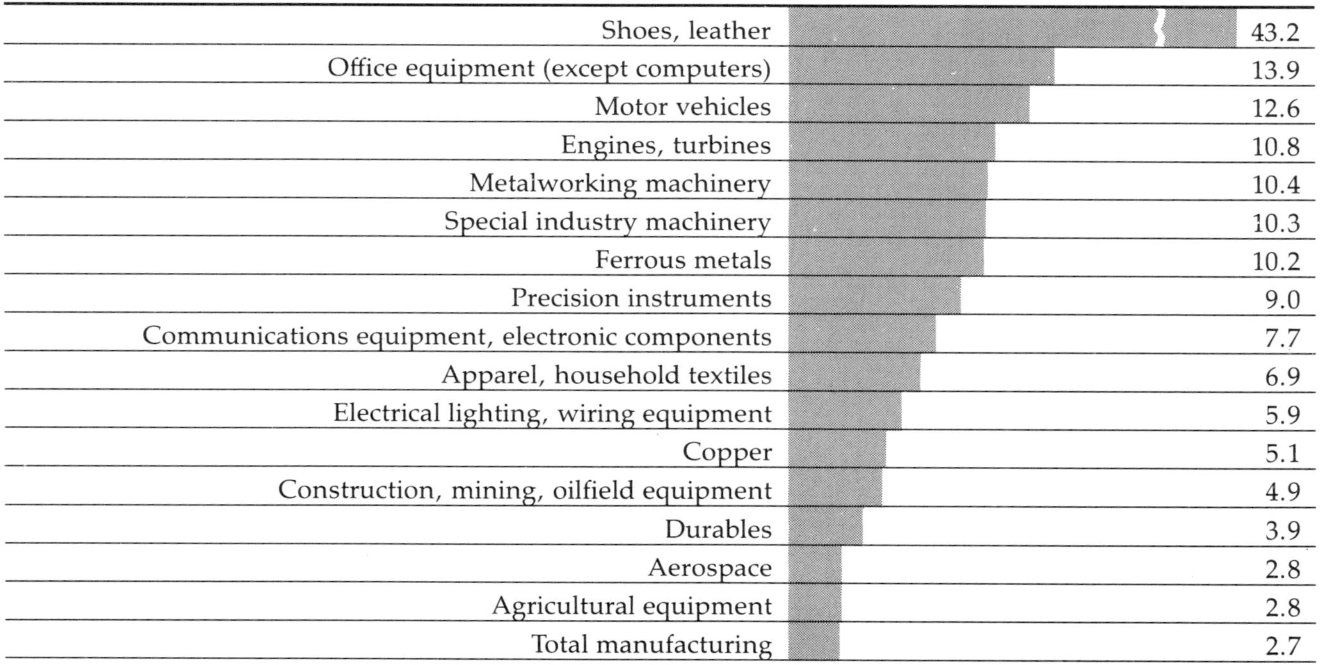

Shoes, leather	43.2
Office equipment (except computers)	13.9
Motor vehicles	12.6
Engines, turbines	10.8
Metalworking machinery	10.4
Special industry machinery	10.3
Ferrous metals	10.2
Precision instruments	9.0
Communications equipment, electronic components	7.7
Apparel, household textiles	6.9
Electrical lighting, wiring equipment	5.9
Copper	5.1
Construction, mining, oilfield equipment	4.9
Durables	3.9
Aerospace	2.8
Agricultural equipment	2.8
Total manufacturing	2.7

Figure 2.2 (continued)

Miscellaneous non-electrical machinery	2.7
Miscellaneous manufacturing	2.6
Furniture	2.1
Service industry machinery	1.1
Paper	1.0
Lumber	1.0
Household appliances	1.0
Non-durables	1.0
Electrical and industrial appliances and distribution equipment	0.8
Metal products	0.8
Plastic products	0.7
Stone, clay, glass	0.4
Chemicals	0.3
Food, tobacco	0.2
Printing, publishing	– 0.1
Agricultural fertilizers	– 0.2
Ships, boats	– 0.8

− 1.4	TVs, radios, phonographs
− 1.4	Knitting
− 1.5	Rubber products
− 1.5	Non-ferrous metals (except copper)
− 1.8	Textiles (excluding knits)
− 1.8	Petroleum refining
− 2.8	Computers
− 8.8	Transportation equipment
−27.8	Fuel oil

SOURCE: *U.S. International Competitiveness: Perception and Reality* (New York: New York Stock Exchange, August 1984), p. 19.

*Import/output ratio = U.S. imports ÷ U.S. domestic production.

57

tries had higher shares of the world manufacturing market in 1982 than in 1972, which is important, 15 had lower shares.[26]

Many, though not all, industrial policy advocates talk glowingly of the social good that import protection will bring, but they do not tell us that our system of tariffs and quotas cost Americans in 1983 in excess of $71 billion in lost current income and much more in lost competitive drive of American firms that are able to hide behind the security of government protection.[27] This estimate is divided among five industry groups in Table 2.7. Industrial policy advocates do not remind us that protectionism, perceived as an important industrial policy tool, is a drag on U.S. business competitiveness in domestic and world markets because the $71 billion in added cost will ultimately feed into the prices of American products. They fail to see that the cost of saving jobs through tariffs and quotas is often enormous, several times the pay of workers whose jobs are supposedly saved. For example, in 1980 the annual cost of saving one job through trade restrictions on television receivers was $74,155; footwear, $77,714; steel, $110,000; and autos, $85,400.[28] (See Table 2.8.)

Table 2.7

COSTS OF PROTECTIONISM TO U.S. CONSUMERS
(1980 $ BILLIONS)

Product	Tariffs	Quantity Limitations, Other Barriers	Total
Textiles, apparel	15.0	3.4	18.4
Machinery, transport equipment	15.9	—	15.9
Metals, minerals	7.3	2.8	10.1
Other manufactured products	5.5	2.6	8.1
Agricultural	2.1	3.9	6.0
Total	45.8	12.7	58.5

SOURCE: Murray Weidenbaum and Michael Munger, "Protection at Any Price?" *Regulation* (July/August 1983): 17.

[26]Ibid., p. 14.

[27]Murray Weidenbaum and Michael Munger, "Protection at Any Price?" *Regulation* (July/August 1983): 15.

[28]Ibid., p. 16.

Table 2.8

ESTIMATED ANNUAL COSTS TO CONSUMERS PER JOB PROTECTED

Product	Average Compensation (1980 $)	Consumer Cost per Job (1980 $)	Cost to Compensation Ratio
Televisions (tariffs, quotas)	12,923	74,155	5.7
Footwear (tariffs, quotas)	8,340	77,714	9.3
Carbon steel (tariffs, quotas)	24,329	85,272	3.5
Steel (trigger price mechanism)	24,329	110,000	4.5
Autos (proposed "domestic content" bill)	23,566	85,400	3.6

SOURCES: Murray Weidenbaum and Michael Munger, "Protection at Any Price?" *Regulation* (July/August 1983): 14. Compensation figures are from the Department of Labor, *Labor Force Statistics Derived from the Current Population Survey: A Databook,* vol. 1 (September 1982), adjusted to include fringe benefits. Estimates of the consumer cost per job created in television, footwear, and carbon steel are derived from Robert Crandall, in *Brookings Papers on Economic Activity,* 1978; the estimate for steel comes from Crandall, in *Regulation* (July/August 1980), and that for autos from a Council of Economic Advisers staff study.

International Comparisons

Those who urge us to follow the path of righteousness toward a new industrial policy do not tell us that in this country the number of total jobs and the number of manufacturing jobs both grew at a faster clip than in any of the major industrial countries with advertised industrial policies, Japan included, during the 1970s.[29] And while private research-and-development spending as a percentage of U.S. GNP rose irregularly during the 1970s, ranging from 1.11 to 1.31 percent (Table 2.9), it was higher in the United States than

[29]Robert Z. Lawrence, "Change in U.S. Industrial Structure: The Role of Global, Secular Trends and Transitory Cycles," paper prepared for the symposium "Industrial Change and Public Policy," Federal Reserve Bank of Kansas City (Jackson Hole, Wyo., August 25–26, 1983). See also Schultze.

Table 2.9

SOURCES OF RESEARCH AND DEVELOPMENT EXPENDITURES
FUNDS BY SECTOR, 1953–83 (% OF GNP)

Year	Federal Government	Industry and Other	Total
1953	0.75	0.65	1.39
1968	1.71	1.11	2.82
1975	1.17	1.10	2.27
1976	1.16	1.11	2.27
1977	1.13	1.11	2.24
1978	1.11	1.13	2.24
1979	1.12	1.16	2.28
1980	1.13	1.24	2.37
1981	1.13	1.26	2.39
1982	1.14	1.31	2.45
1983	N.A.	N.A.	2.51

SOURCE: John W. Kendrick, "Productivity, Costs, and Prices: Outlook for 1983–1984, *AEI Economist* (January 1983): 9.

in many other countries (Table 2.10).[30] Furthermore, the average annual rate of increase in real plant and equipment spending in manufacturing rose from 2.4 percent in the 1947–72 period to 6.9 percent in the 1972–80 period (Table 2.11).[31] Charles Schultze, Brookings Institution scholar and economic adviser to Democratic presidents, has written:

> The United States does have some old-line heavy industries with deep-seated structural problems—especially the steel and automobile industries. But they are not typical of American industry generally. There is *no evidence* that in periods of reasonably normal prosperity American labor and capital are incapable of making the gradual transitions that are always required in a dynamic economy, as demand and output shift from older industries to

[30]John W. Kendrick, "Productivity, Costs, and Prices: Outlook for 1983–1984," *AEI Economist* (January 1983): 9. See also Bruce Yandle, "Jobs, Peace, and Freedom: A Search for Industrial Policy," paper presented at Montana State University (Bozeman, Mont., September 15, 1983).

[31]Richard R. West and Dennis E. Logue, "The False Doctrine of Productivity," *New York Times*, January 9, 1983, p. F-3. Cited in Yandle, p. 22.

Table 2.10

RESEARCH AND DEVELOPMENT, 1960–79 (% OF GNP)

Year	U.S.	Canada	Japan	U.K.	France	West Germany	Italy	Sweden	Belgium
1960	2.67	0.83	1.36	2.52	1.30	0.96	0.48	1.45	—
1973	2.34	1.03	1.95	1.97	1.78	2.23	0.49	1.68	1.30
1979	2.32	0.92	1.94	1.83	1.74	2.39	0.86	1.80	1.48

SOURCE: John W. Kendrick, "International Comparisons of Recent Productivity Trends," in *Essays in Contemporary Economic Problems*, ed. William Fellner (Washington: American Enterprise Institute, 1983).

Table 2.11

AVERAGE ANNUAL RATE OF INCREASE IN PLANT AND EQUIPMENT SPENDING*

	1947–80	1947–72	1972–80
Total nonfarm business	3.8	3.9	3.6
Manufacturing	3.5	2.4	6.9
Durable goods	4.4	3.5	7.3
Nondurable goods	2.7	1.5	6.5
Nonmanufacturing	4.1	4.6	1.9
Mining	3.8	2.6	7.6
Transportation	0.8	1.4	1.1
Public utilities	4.8	6.1	0.9
Trade and services	4.4	5.1	2.1
Communications, other	4.8	5.7	2.1

SOURCE: Richard R. West and Dennis E. Logue, "The False Doctrine of Productivity," *New York Times,* January 9, 1983, p. F-3.
*Figures are percentages, based on 1972 dollars.

newer ones at the forefront of technological advances [emphasis added].[32]

In addition, the proponents of industrial policy who beat their chests about the successes of industrial policy in Japan do not tell us that while the Japanese government spent $80 billion in 1980 on what are presumed to be industrial development projects (through the Fiscal Investment and Loan Program), 50 percent of those funds went for local government and public investment purposes. Seventy to 80 percent of the rest was loaned to small businesses, homeowners, farmers, and "others." In short, a minor share was available for "targeting" the type of industries that have supposedly been helped so much by Japan's industrial policy, and 72 percent of *those* funds was used for nonmanufacturing purposes, principally gas, water, transport, and communications facilities.[33] Such observations have caused Philip Trezise, a senior fellow at the Brookings Institution, to observe, "Effectively, the bulk of the post-1972 lend-

[32]Schultze, p. 5 (1983), p. 160 (1984).

[33]Katsuro Sakoh, "Industrial Policy: The Super Myth of Japan's Super Success," Heritage Foundation Asian Studies Center Backgrounder (Washington, July 13, 1983).

ing program was for infrastructure and improvements in the quality of life [in Japan]. . . . If all the JDB [Japan Development Bank] lending had been left to the private capital market, the economy would not have developed differently."[34] After observing that Japan has a smaller share of its income going to government than do other countries (Japan, 23 percent; United States, 28 percent; West Germany, 32 percent; United Kingdom, 41 percent), Katsuro Sakoh, an economist at the Heritage Foundation, concluded that Japan's recent economic success is "based not on how much it [the Japanese government] did for the economy, but on how much it restrained itself from doing."[35]

This is not to say that Japan's government hasn't had successes with its industrial policy. Indeed, the Japanese government has poured money into the successful semiconductor industry, but it has also poured money into steel, shipbuilding, and agriculture—not notable successes. The objective of propping up such industries has been accomplished through the imposition of a tax burden greater than what it would otherwise have been on other industries in the Japanese economy, retarding their development. And it is a well-known fact that the Japanese government attempted to discourage automobile production in Japan in the 1960s on the grounds that the country could never develop an international comparative advantage in that industry, a point U.S. automobile workers now find hard to accept.

Reevaluation

Proponents of industrial policy, who calculate the breadth of job destruction, must understand that their figures are distorted, if not downright phony. They must realize that any calculation of the number of jobs destroyed between, say, 1978 and 1982, is inflated by the impact of the worst post–World War II recession this country has experienced (which they should know was brought on by deliberate anti-inflationary policy and by major changes in government regulatory and budget policies that imposed significant demands for adjustment on the economy). They must realize that the burgeoning federal deficits, which many advocates see as a tool for securing jobs, have destroyed jobs directly through the crowding

[34]Philip Trezise, "Industrial Policy Is Not the Major Reason for Japan's Success," *Brookings Review* (Spring 1983): 15.

[35]Sakoh, p. 14.

out of private investors in the bond markets and indirectly through upward pressures on interest rates. Higher interest rates, in turn, have placed upward pressures on the international value of the dollar, which has worsened the international competitive position of many U.S. industries.[36]

NIP advocates must also understand that many of the country's lost jobs were destroyed because of the jobs that were created— that many jobs are lost simply because workers prefer other and better employment and that it is ludicrous to argue that greedy, profit-maximizing capitalists systematically develop jobs that are incompatible with the desires and skills of the bulk of the labor force, when such workers are strategic to the profits that are sought. Indeed, proponents of a national industrial policy must realize that the interdependence of job creation and job destruction is so complete that we might just as well use the rate of job destruction as a sign of economic vitality rather than as a sign of economic distress. They must comprehend that the history of progress is a record littered with destroyed jobs that resulted from created jobs, a subject to which we will return in the next chapter.

Concluding Comments

By itemizing the industrial myths that have been purveyed by the proponents of a national industrial policy, we do not mean to suggest that the country does not have problems; continued government growth, an expanding federal deficit, lagging productivity, high unemployment rates, and the continuing threat of inflation are just a few. We mean simply to argue that the case for a national industrial policy is replete with empirical inaccuracies. Before we buy into such a dramatic shift in policy, we had better carefully scrutinize the case for it. As mentioned at the start, competitive capitalism, as we have known it, hangs in the balance.

---

[36]C. Fred Bergsten, "What Kind of Industrial Policy for the United States?" testimony before the Subcommittee on Economic Stabilization, House Banking and Urban Affairs Committee, June 9, 1983.

III. The Displaced Worker Mythology

> We've been running up the white flag, when we should be run-
> ning up the American flag! . . . What do we want our kids to do?
> Sweep up around Japanese computers?
> —Walter F. Mondale[1]

National industrial policy enthusiasts are concerned that the United
States is in the process of being transformed into a nation of ham-
burger cooks and computer jocks—that middle-skilled industrial
workers will go the way of stagecoach drivers as their jobs are
pulled from underneath them. Indeed, MIT professor Lester Thurow tells us that high-technology industries such as microelectron-
ics tend to have two levels of income distribution—high and low—
as opposed to the smokestack industries, like machine tools, with
their high-wage, skilled blue-collar workers. There is usually a large
group of low-wage assemblers, but not many middle-income jobs.[2]
Bob Kuttner, a frequent economic writer for the *Atlantic Monthly*,
warns that

> There is a good deal of evidence that job opportunities in the
> United States are polarizing, and that, as a result, the country's
> future as a middle class society is in jeopardy. What the decline
> of the middle class would mean to the country can only be guessed
> at, but it presumably would be unwelcome to the millions of
> parents who hope their children can move up the economic ladder;
> to American business, which needs a middle class to consume its
> products; and to everyone who is concerned about fairness and
> social harmony.
>
> As the economy shifts away from its traditional manufacturing
> base to high-technology and service industries, the share of jobs
> providing a middle-class standard of living is shrinking. An indus-
> trial economy employs large numbers of relatively well-paid pro-

---

[1]Martin Schram, " 'Big Fritz': Tough Talk And a Flag," *Washington Post*, October
7, 1982, p. 1.

[2]As reported by Peter Behr, "This Idea's Time Hasn't Come," *Washington Post*,
April 16, 1984, p. 16.

duction workers. A service economy, however, employs legions of keypunchers, salesclerks, waiters, secretaries, and cashiers, and the wages for these jobs tend to be comparatively low.[3]

Nothing could be more farfetched.

According to the scenario laid out by industrial policy advocates, the growing "dualism in the labor force" (meaning many workers with very low- or very high-level skills and few workers with medium-grade skills) will force traditionally well paid production workers to (1) accept low-skill and low-paying jobs, (2) become wards of the welfare state, or (3) retrain for high-skill jobs at great personal expense. As a result, they predict, American competitive capitalism will be without a large middle class to consume its product; workers will be easily exploited by their employers, since many of the "old jobs" are union and many of the "new jobs" will be nonunion; the nation will gradually become peopled with the "permanently displaced"; and the citizenry will have to shoulder a progressively greater tax burden to finance training and retraining programs.

Before Congress jumps on the retraining bandwagon, it should carefully reevaluate the economics of federally funded retraining programs directed not at the hardcore unemployed (traditionally the object of federal aid), but mainly at the hard-working, reasonably paid Americans who find themselves in what are thought to be declining industries, for example, steel and automobiles. Our purpose here is to question the wisdom of further federal government intrusion into the retraining process of workers—not to argue, as some may imagine, that no retraining problem exists when millions of people during any period of time may be unemployed. Both proponents and opponents of national industrial policy agree that unemployment is a serious social problem and are equally concerned about people who have to suffer through recessions and industrial transformation, especially when the suffering is the purposeful product of public anti-inflationary policy, as the two recessions in the 1980–82 period were.

Where proponents and opponents of national industrial policy generally do disagree is over the solution. Being long on emotion and short on appreciation for the needs and consequences of markets in a free society, proponents tend to assert that social justice can be pursued directly through the passage of enabling legislation

---

[3]Bob Kuttner, "The Declining Middle," *Atlantic Monthly*, July 1983, p. 60.

and the spending of more federal dollars. As a general proposition, opponents contend that such a policy course will most likely achieve its contradiction: more injustice and social mischief than relief, especially in the long run.

In making the argument against industrial policy, references will be made to data on displaced workers. However, the focus of the chapter will be on the conceptual arguments underpinning the current political drive for more federal taxes and expenditures to retrain displaced workers. This approach is taken mainly because the debate, at its core, is not over numbers. The debate over what to do about displaced workers would probably have been joined if the problem were half what it is or if federal funding of retraining programs were doubled or quadrupled. Rather, the debate is fundamentally philosophical: it is over the assignment of responsibility for relief of social ills, the needs of a free society, and the escalating tendency of people to seek public as opposed to private relief for perceived social ills.

The debate, in other words, is basically concerned with the broader issue of how much government, in the aggregate, can be expected to accomplish in relieving a broad range of social ills, including unemployment. If the problem of displaced workers were the only issue on the social agenda, there is little doubt as to what we would all agree to do: we would willingly appropriate money for retraining programs, for we would have a lot of dollars to appropriate. The problem of displaced workers, however, does not stand alone. The social agenda is, indeed, very crowded with competing claims on the limited capacity of government to extract revenue from the citizenry's income. Any argument for government action that does not recognize these competing claims and the limited coercive capacity of government to do good is hardly worthy of sober reflection. However, interest groups continue to meet all over Washington to discuss in some detail the social distress caused by the failure of the federal government to spend more money on their causes. With their narrow focus, these groups fail to acknowledge that recognition of a social ill is not all that is necessary to lay claim to federal government revenue. The case for federal action must ultimately be made in the context of competing claims, and interest groups must ultimately show that their claims on government revenue are more worthy than the claims of others.

The case for more federal government involvement in worker

training and retraining programs can be attacked on both empirical and conceptual grounds. Let us look first at the empirical case.

The Displaced Worker as an Empirical Problem

As proof of the decaying job structure in the United States, statistics are often cited on the hundreds of thousands of jobs for salesclerks, cashiers, janitors, typists, and stockhandlers that are predicted to come into being during the 1980s. Kuttner tells us that

> According to the most recent comprehensive forecasts of the Bureau of Labor Statistics, released in 1982, the economy will generate some 19 million new jobs between 1980 and 1990, about 3.5 million of which will be "professional and technical." Low-wage service and clerical work will account for almost 7 million new jobs.[4]

The presumed decay of skilled employment is further illustrated by the list of job openings in Table 3.1, which appears in Kuttner's

Table 3.1
JOB OPENINGS IN 1980

Job	Openings
Retail salesclerk	757,750
Manager, administrator (not elsewhere classified)	711,793
Cashier	617,973
Secretary (not elsewhere classified)	599,216
Waiter, waitress	465,628
Cook (except private-household)	437,341
Stockhandler	358,393
Janitor, sexton	333,309
Bookkeeper	304,789
Miscellaneous clerical	299,940
Nursing aide, orderly	284,332
Child-care worker (private-household)	277,525
Building-interior cleaner	259,528
Typist	250,276
Truck driver	245,377

SOURCE: Bob Kuttner, "The Declining Middle," *Atlantic Monthly*, July 1983, p. 62.

[4]Ibid., p. 62.

article. If so many menial jobs are going to be created, then American workers must be turning into a low-skilled work force—or so we are led to believe.

Boston College economist Barry Bluestone, on whom Kuttner relies for scholarly support, compounds the confusion over the future job structure by asserting, "A dramatic transformation in the structure of the entire national job distribution is responsible for an *extreme mismatch* between the skills and income needs of displaced workers and the skill requirements and wage levels of the new jobs" [emphasis added].[5] Circumstances are so "extreme," according to Bluestone, that only government expenditures on worker training can pull us back from the brink of economic disaster.

Such a solution, however, is based on a warped perception of reality. Advocates of greater government expenditures, like Kuttner and Bluestone, fail to tell us that the hundreds of thousands of new jobs for clerks and janitors would be added to an already large work force of clerks and janitors, meaning that the rate of change in the work force over time would not be very significant and that people in the future would be no more forced to become clerks and janitors than they are now. NIP advocates also fail to tell us that over the past couple of decades, manufacturing employment in the United States has remained more or less level, after adjusting for cyclical swings in the economy, at about 20 million. Not only that, but manufacturing employment will grow—not decline—at an average annual rate of 0.8 percent a year during the 1980s, according to the Bureau of Labor Statistics.

As a consequence, and as is evident in Table 3.2, the structure of the U.S. labor force in 1990 will be only marginally different from what it was in 1980. Granted, 2–3 million manufacturing jobs were "lost" during the recent recession. However, as reported in the preceding chapter, dips in manufacturing jobs have historically been more severe than the recessions they accompany.[6] Further-

[5]Barry Bluestone, "Industrial Dislocation and the Implications for Public Policy," paper prepared for the third annual policy forum on employability development, "The Displaced Workers Problem: Implications for Educational and Training Institutions," National Center for Research in Vocational Education, Ohio State University (Washington, September 12–13, 1983).

[6]Robert Z. Lawrence, "Changes in U.S. Industrial Structure: The Role of Global, Secular Trends and Transitory Cycles," paper prepared for the symposium "Industrial Change and Public Policy," Federal Reserve Bank of Kansas City (Jackson Hole, Wyo., August 25–26, 1983); idem, *Can America Compete?* (Washington: Brookings Institution, 1984). See also Charles Schultze, "Industrial Policy: A Dissent," *Brookings Review* (October 1983). Reprinted in *Plant Closings: Public or Private Choices?* ed. Richard B. McKenzie, rev. ed. (Washington: Cato Institute, 1984).

Table 3.2
DISTRIBUTION OF THE WORK FORCE, 1979 AND 1990 (%)

	Average Annual Change 1979–90	Actual Distribution 1979	Projected Distribution 1990
Total employment	1.4	100.0	100.0
General government	0.6	15.9	14.8
Federal	0.3	4.1	3.6
Military	0.0	2.0	1.7
Civilian	0.7	2.0	1.9
State and local	0.7	11.8	11.2
Education	0.5	6.4	5.3
Noneducation	1.8	5.4	5.9
Total private	1.5	84.1	85.2
Agricultural	2.3	2.7	1.9
Nonagricultural	1.6	81.4	83.2
Mining	1.5	0.7	0.8
Construction	0.5	5.8	5.7
Manufacturing	0.8	20.6	19.2
Durable goods	1.0	12.5	11.9
Nondurable goods	0.3	8.1	7.3
Transportation, communications, public utilities	1.1	5.3	5.1
Wholesale, retail trade	1.7	21.5	22.2
Finance, insurance, real estate	2.8	5.3	5.7
Other services	2.7	19.4	21.8
Government enterprise	1.8	1.4	1.4
Private households	0.1	1.7	1.3

SOURCE: Bureau of Labor Statistics, *Economic Projections to 1990*, Bulletin no. 2121 (Washington: Government Printing Office, 1982), p. 31.

more, manufacturing employment will, as it did in the 1984 recovery period, rebound more rapidly than general economic activity.

An important worry of the supporters of the "dualistic labor force" hypothesis is the high-tech sector, dominated by the growing computer industry. Supposedly, the computer industry has a sizable number of jobs for hardware and software developers and a large number of low-skill jobs possibly suitable for people no more skilled than monkeys. To evaluate such claims, the Computer Business Equipment Manufacturers Association surveyed its 18 member firms in early 1984, including most of the large computer manufacturers such as IBM and Digital. The survey covered over 600,000 employees and focused on the problem of how employees are distributed statistically around the mean annual average-worker income. The detailed results are contained in Table 3.3 and Figure 3.1. While the distribution in Figure 3.1 is skewed slightly to the left, an important conclusion is readily apparent: the computer industry does not have a "bimodal" labor force distribution. The "middle" is not missing.

Advocates of expanded government involvement would have us believe that the problem of permanently displaced workers, most of whom have long years of service, engulfs the economy and

Table 3.3

CBEMA WAGE AND SALARY FREQUENCY DISTRIBUTION SURVEY, MARCH 1984

Class	Number of Employees	% of Total
0.00–0.20	2,057	0.3
0.21–0.40	11,018	1.8
0.41–0.60	81,439	13.4
0.61–0.80	154,333	25.4
0.81–1.00	127,374	20.9
1.01–1.20	90,918	15.0
1.21–1.40	56,619	9.3
1.41–1.60	34,737	5.7
1.61–1.80	20,792	3.4
1.81–2.00	13,417	2.2
2.01–2.20	9,394	1.6
2.21–2.40	3,436	0.6
2.41–2.60	1,750	0.3
2.61 +	732	0.1
Total	608,016	100.0

SOURCE: Computer and Business Equipment Manufacturers Association, "CBEMA Wage and Salary Frequency Distribution Survey" (Washington, March 9, 1984).

Figure 3.1

WAGE DISTRIBUTION IN COMPUTER AND BUSINESS EQUIPMENT MANUFACTURING

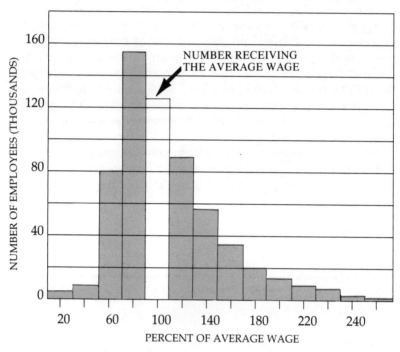

Chart shows number of workers in 15 pay categories based on the average pay in the industry. For example, 127,374 employees received the average wage and 154,333 employees received 80 percent of the average wage.

SOURCE: Computer and Business Equipment Manufacturers Association.

threatens to stifle growth and prosperity. While no one can deny the hardship experienced by the millions of workers unemployed as a result of the recent recession, the number of workers with considerable job tenure in declining industries who are suffering from long-term unemployment represents a relatively minor proportion of the labor force. The Congressional Budget Office estimates that of the 8 million unemployed workers in January 1983, only 1.6 million (20 percent) were in declining industries and most of these were the victims of recession, not structural change. Of the unemployed workers in the declining industries, only 240,000 out of work for 26 weeks or more had 10 or more years on the job.[7] If we define "dislocated worker" in less restricted terms to include workers in "declining industries" unemployed for 8 or more weeks in 1980, the number of dislocated workers rises to 412,000, 3 percent of the labor force in declining industries and less than 0.4 percent of the total labor force.[8] The data suggest that the displaced worker problem exists, but hardly on an overwhelming scale.

The Conceptual Case

The case for government aid to displaced workers is replete with appeals to social compassion. We will consider below four major conceptual reasons why our enthusiasm for expanding federal aid to displaced workers should be tempered.

The Beneficiaries of Aid Programs

Many, though by no means all, backers of expanded aid for retraining seem to harbor the notion that workers are the object *and* the beneficiaries of that aid, whereas in fact much of it is pocketed by the workers' firms, which as a result do not themselves have to cover the costs of training and retraining their own workers. Indeed, much of industry support for federal retraining programs is founded upon the strictly business proposition that lobbying for training programs is profitable—that is, more profitable than alternative productive activities. Businesses understand that if more federal monies are passed to states and communities for retraining programs, then competition among the states and communities for industries, through government defraying of the industries' training costs, will be enhanced. They recognize that the more federal money there is to be allocated, the greater the competition among governments to subsidize industries, and the greater the proportion of the subsidies intended for workers that will be passed on to their firms.

It is grossly naive for industrial policy advocates to assume that politicians, who are dependent upon industries for campaign funds, are as concerned about workers as they profess to be. It is equally

---

[7]As reported in A. F. Ehrbar, "Grasping the New Unemployed," *Fortune*, May 16, 1983, p. 108.

[8]See Marc Bendick, Jr., and Judith Radlinski Devine, "Workers Dislocated by Economic Change: Do They Need Federal Employment and Training Assistance?" in *The Federal Interest in Employment and Training*, 7th annual report (Washington: National Commission on Employment Policy, 1981).

naive to assume that the effectiveness of expanded aid programs can be judged by the effectiveness of previous programs. The limited funding of past programs has restricted competition among governments for industries, thus limiting the effective subsidies channeled to firms from government.

The Stock of Retrained Workers

Proponents of federal programs appear to believe that federal expenditures on retraining would result in an *increase* in the stock of retrained workers equal to the number of people who are retrained. Even if the retraining programs were perfectly effective in retraining workers (and there are good reasons to assume otherwise), nothing could be further from the truth. Many of the workers retrained through government programs would have been retrained by their firms, at their firms' expense, or would have retrained themselves, at their own expense.

In addition, many proponents fail to comprehend the two-edged sword of government expenditure policies. They appear oblivious to the negative effects on employment that result from the government taxes and deficits used to finance expenditures. From experience it is all too clear that greater government taxes destroy jobs just as surely as expenditures create them. Thus, expenditures targeted for retraining workers in identified sectors of the economy also create a need for more retraining, whereas the taxes necessary to fund retraining programs destroy jobs in other sectors.

Further, deficits are as damaging as tax increases. For years, economists have focused their professional attention on the extent to which federal expenditures "crowd out" private producers and investors from resource markets. We should learn a simple point from their research: efforts to pay for the retraining of displaced workers by way of federal deficits will create a need for worker retraining in those industries that are crowded out of the market through government credit demands.

We should also recognize that jobs have recently been destroyed indirectly by the impact of federal deficits on international money markets. Those deficits, now projected to be in the range of $200 billion for the next several years, are contributing marginally to abnormally high real interest rates in the United States, which in turn are attracting capital from abroad, driving up the international value of the dollar, and reducing the international competitiveness of many basic industries. Additional deficits to fund expansive new government training programs will, through greater pressure on international exchange rates, destroy and jeopardize more jobs and exacerbate any retraining needs.

In the context of the total federal government budget, retraining expenditures may continue to amount to the proverbial drop in the bucket. But the negative consequences of a "little more" in federal expenditures cannot be cast off so easily, since the route to the $200 billion deficits has been paved by a-little-more-won't-hurt arguments from virtually every interest group. Such arguments, made with conviction, also assume that the political process can be extended to include additional aid for retraining and, at the same time, that the process can be closed off to supporters of so many other programs lobbying with equal justification for government to increase expenditures for their own programs. In other words, additional aid for retraining can give rise to additional expenditures for a host of other programs and to a significant expansion of future federal deficits, if not taxes.

Before we accept the argument that the proposed industrial policies would advance social welfare, it would appear reasonable to require proponents of reform to support their policy recommendations with "economic impact statements" that would do three things: (1) provide estimates of the jobs saved and/or created in identified industries, (2) provide estimates of the jobs destroyed and/or jeopardized in identified industries, and (3) provide compelling reasons why the jobs of workers in identified "losing industries" should be destroyed and/or jeopardized for the benefit of other workers.[9] Such impact statements are necessary if public debate of retraining proposals is to be open, honest, and truly democratic.

Proponents of retraining displaced workers argue that commonly accepted ethics and a sense of social priorities dictate that more federal funds be allocated to retraining displaced workers in manufacturing sectors—automobile and steel, for example—where jobs are supposedly being destroyed by technological advance, growing competitiveness in world markets, and the economy's presumed transformation from manufacturing to service industries. This argument is worrisome because many of the workers in manufacturing have for years enjoyed above-average wages and fringe benefits.

[9]For details of the proposal, see Richard B. McKenzie, "Name Winners, Losers of Industrial Policy," *New York Times*, October 31, 1983, p. 25.

In fact, the wages of many of these workers have been inflated in part by the growing risk that their jobs would be eliminated and that they would have to retrain themselves. By covering the current retraining cost of these workers with federal funds, the general public would be paying double for retraining: once through higher prices for products the workers produce, and again through higher taxes. We must question the social ethics of those who contend that workers who have earned far less over the years and who have covered their own retraining needs should now be asked to help pay for the retraining of higher-paid workers, especially when a portion of such payment would go to the firms of the subsidized workers.

Federal retraining assistance would also have perverse effects on the incentives workers have to remain alert to their continuing employment prospects with their current skills and to remain abreast of the many opportunities for self-improvement. Workers' incentives would be redirected marginally toward maintaining and negotiating noncompetitive wages in the knowledge that they can fall back on government-subsidized retraining when their firms are forced out of business. In short, federal retraining subsidies can give rise to worker displacement. On the margin, such subsidies would induce workers to take greater risks in raising their wages and to shift to riskier employment. Greater risks imply more frequent business failures—more worker displacement. Similarly, additional federal subsidies for retraining would, on the margin, temper employers' interest in keeping their workers' skills current. After all, the responsibility and cost of retraining workers would be shifted to taxpayers.

Market Failures

Much is said of how markets presumably "fail" in the area of worker training as a result of the "externalities" to education. That is, proponents contend that people other than the employer and employee benefit from retraining and that these benefits are not captured by the pricing system. Few human activities are totally devoid of "externalities." Even the clothing we wear affects others, some positively, others negatively. By the same token, because the type of education—vocational—that is the subject of the displaced worker debate is designed largely, if not exclusively, to produce jobs and income for workers, the presumed "market failure" justification for retraining programs should be questioned. After all, the National Commission on Employment Policy tells us that "employment and training programs are intended to raise the earnings of those who participate."[10] The technological barriers that prevent, to any significant extent, the benefits of retraining programs from being captured through the pricing system by either employees or employers are certainly not obvious, and such technological barriers must be present if one is to make the externality case for retraining programs.

Even if externalities were shown to exist, federally financed retraining would not be fully justified. The externalities must be sufficient to justify the cost of having government do something about them, which is no trivial concern. In addition, negative, as well as positive, externalities exist. Some people are harmed by the retraining of others; indeed, many people for purely personal reasons do not like to see others, the beneficiaries of welfare, retrained. Others object to paying taxes to retrain competitors for their own jobs. This is not to suggest that people should not be helped by government because other people personally object to relief. Rather, the point is, consistency in the externality argument—which is a question of efficiency, not equity—requires that the people harmed by the retraining of others be compensated for that harm. Such compensation, if paid, would greatly increase the cost of retraining. As detailed elsewhere, the collectivization of such a service as retraining does not necessarily imply the provision of more of that service than would be provided privately—that is, if everyone's likes and dislikes were counted.[11] Proponents of federal retraining programs do not appear willing to give everyone's likes and dislikes equal treatment in their conceptual framework. To the extent that is the case, their arguments reduce to a set of assertions, not logically deduced conclusions.

The Externality Argument Evaluated

The whole of the externality argument suggests that, left to private markets, worker retraining would be "suboptimal" and that

---

[10]Steven G. Cecchetti, Daniel H. Saks, and Ronald B. Warren, Jr., "Employment and Training Policy and the National Economy," in *The Federal Interest in Employment and Training*, p. 12.

[11]For further details on this argument, see Richard B. McKenzie, "The Construction of the Demand for Public Goods and the Theory of Income Redistribution," *Public Choice* (1981): 337–44.

there are definite limits to the amount of government involvement in the educational process. For all we know, the present level of federal funding may have surpassed the funding requirements to achieve the elusive goal of economic efficiency.

In addition, it should be stressed that those making the externality argument should realize that the argument for additional federal retraining programs can be self-defeating. Because of the subsidies and the incentive effects, federal retraining programs can create "externalities" of their own. By failing to retrain themselves, workers can impose a heavier tax burden on the rest of the tax-paying population. From the perspective of market failure economics, therefore, no one can guarantee that social efficiency will be enhanced by retraining programs. Again, from the externality perspective, economic efficiency may be worsened.

The case for reliance on markets in establishing the retraining needs of our country is, indeed, a case for minimizing externalities. By holding workers and firms responsible for their own retraining needs, we impose the costs on those who benefit from the retraining. As responsibility for keeping worker skills current is transferred from the worker to the community, then to the state, and finally to the federal government, the potential for externalizing the costs of retraining is expanded; that is, we tend to increase the extent to which government intervention itself gives rise to a form of "social pollution" (or to an externality problem). From this perspective, the externality argument for *federal* retraining is largely self-defeating.

The concept of "externality" has been greatly expanded over the last two decades. Proponents of government retraining (and many other social programs) contend that if retraining is not provided for unemployed workers, the unemployed will be forced onto the welfare rolls. In the words of the National Commission on Employment Policy, "Once again, the policy-relevant question is the long-term cost effectiveness of this approach [meaning a particular retraining program] versus a program of income redistribution."[12] Hence, so the argument goes, retraining reduces the externality of taxes collected to pay for welfare expenditures. The argument has an appealing ring and is not altogether an easy one to answer, especially in the absence of empirical data. It should be understood, however, that such an argument is not based on some presumed "market

[12]Daniel H. Saks and Ralph E. Smith, "Overview," in *The Federal Interest in Employment and Training*, p. 31.

failure." Indeed, if there is a "failure" to be contemplated, it is the failure of government policy and an admission of the tremendous disincentive effects of welfare.

There are several other reasons to be unimpressed by the externalities argument. First, it implies that the cost of social welfare or transfer programs is substantially greater than one might think by counting only those funds that are spent exclusively on welfare. A measure of total cost should include expenditures on retraining and on a host of other programs designed to prevent people from making use of welfare. But including in the welfare budget the cost of all the programs that could be federally funded just to prevent direct welfare expenditures could make welfare prohibitively expensive. If the argument were taken seriously, the expanded calculation of welfare costs could perhaps encourage voters to re-evaluate the appropriate level of welfare, in turn leading to a reduction in public assistance to the truly needy.

Furthermore, those who use this revised externality argument are frequently unwilling to generalize it and, to that extent, are not articulating a logical principle for policy formulation but rather an ad hoc rationalization for personal preferences. One could just as easily argue that poor people's procreation has an impact on the population of welfare recipients and the budget for welfare. Would anyone be willing to argue that the policy-relevant question is the long-term cost effectiveness of government control of poor people's fertility versus a program of income redistribution? If it could be shown that abortions were cheaper than welfare payments, would advocates of retraining aid be willing to argue seriously that government ought to get into the business of mandating abortions on the grounds that the policy-relevant question is the cost effectiveness of mandated abortions?

Of course, simply posing such questions and generalizing the externality argument advanced by the proponents of government retraining is not to be interpreted as advocating the extension of government powers—hardly. It simply stresses the obvious, that more than cost-benefit questions comes into play over the issue of retraining. One such issue is the extent to which we intend to make government every worker's caretaker.

Second, the assumption behind the externality argument—that any additional federal expenditure on retraining would be a net addition to the total welfare budget—is unfounded, for part of the expenditure may come from the welfare budget already, implying in some cases a transfer from lower-income people who would have received welfare benefits to the higher-income people who receive the retraining benefits.

Third, as noted earlier, any additional expenditures on retraining would imply greater taxes and deficits and the destruction of some people's jobs, meaning a greater welfare problem for others.

Finally, the acceptance of the externality argument obliterates limits on government intervention in the economy. A whole host of other programs, from child care to medical care, could be justified on similar grounds and expanded without limit. Nobody concerned about the welfare of future generations should feel comfortable with any government that is not bounded in what it can do.

Concluding Comments

In summary, the arguments that net social benefits would result from expanded federal government efforts to retrain displaced workers in targeted industries such as steel and automobiles are unconvincing. The efficiency of such efforts is highly questionable because it appears that the market is tolerably well equipped to handle the nation's retraining needs. Wages can adjust upward, as they do, to reflect the retraining costs incurred by workers. To say that retraining costs are "high" is not to say that the market cannot adjust, especially when nonpoor workers are the object of the retraining programs. If there exists a need for government action, that action should be taken by local governments, not the federal government—that is, by those governments that are closest to the problem and that can therefore most rationally choose the appropriate level of retraining.

The ethics of many of the current proposals for retraining should be reevaluated as well. Such proposals appear to be just another political scam designed to use the fate of the unfortunate poor, who would probably not benefit to any great degree from government retraining programs, to generate political support for programs that would transfer income, under the cloak of the educational system, from lower-income to higher-income workers—in many cases from workers who have kept their wages competitive to workers who have not.

IV. The Reconstruction of the Reconstruction Finance Corporation

During recent years, at least half a dozen bills have been introduced in Congress that would, in one form or another, establish (or reestablish) a Reconstruction Finance Corporation (RFC).[1] The common objective of the pending legislation is commendable: "to rebuild the national infrastructure and restructure and revitalize basic industries; and ensure the ability of the United States to compete in the world economy."[2]

The broad political appeal of the RFC legislation is indicated by the array of business and labor leaders who support the concept and by the fact that the bills introduced to date have broad geographic support, sponsored by members of Congress from Florida, Mississippi, Michigan, New Jersey, New York, South Carolina, and Pennsylvania. More RFC bills will likely be introduced as the years pass.

In introducing his bill, South Carolina senator Fritz Hollings commented,

> The purpose of the RFC would be to provide limited, temporary, and repayable assistance to cities and businesses to help them rebuild, repair, and remodel, so that our businesses can become competitive again and our cities can function efficiently again. . . .
>
> We cannot afford to let the situation continue. We must not permit our basic industries—the foundation upon which we have built the world's dominant economic power—to wither and die. To abdicate the role we have established, to let it pass to the hands of other nations because we made a conscious decision to let it

---

[1]These bills include House, 98th Cong., H.R. 134 (January 3, 1983, Rep. Frank Guarini); H.R. 1480 (February 15, 1983, Rep. Claude Pepper); H.R. 1827 (March 1, 1983, Rep. Jamie Whitten); H.R. 2612 (April 12, 1983, Rep. John Murtha); H.R. 2847 (May 2, 1983, Rep. William Ford; it is not specifically an RFC bill, but incorporates the main thrust of RFC legislation); H.R. 4360 (November 10, 1983, Rep. John LaFalce); and Senate, 98th Cong., S. 265 (January 27, 1983, Sen. Fritz Hollings).

[2]S. 265, pp. 1–2.

happen would mark one of the sorriest episodes in our economic history.[3]

Rep. Frank Guarini adds, by way of introduction to his proposed legislation, that

> Our economic problems are very severe. They defy quick-fix solutions. This is why we need to approve the time-tested approach by establishing a Reconstruction Finance Corporation as the central feature of our economic development plans in the 98th Congress. The original RFC, created in the Depression, helped boost American productivity and employment for nearly two decades. It also returned a profit to the Government.[4]

Contrary to the admirable intentions of its sponsors, the establishment of an RFC would not likely reinvigorate the economy as predicted. Rather, the reconstruction of the RFC would have the effect of institutionalizing the Chrysler bailout of the early 1980s and imposing yet another government drag on economic development. In short, as argued in detail below, the case for an RFC is greatly flawed from both empirical and conceptual perspectives. Called by any other name, the RFC is a very foolish concept.

The RFC Proposal

Typically, the RFC legislative initiatives—the centerpieces of the Democrats' national industrial policy—call for the creation of a government agency that would be capitalized to the tune of $5–$8 billion from general federal revenues. This agency would be authorized to make loans at below-market interest rates to, and to guarantee the loans of, private firms and local governments. An early RFC proposal, tendered in 1982, called for a capitalization of $20 billion. The RFC would be directed by a board of seven trustees, each appointed by the president for three-year terms. Depending on the exact proposal, the RFC board might automatically include specified government officials, for example, the secretary of the treasury, the chairman of the Federal Reserve, and/or the chairman of the Council of Economic Advisers.

Under Senator Hollings's proposed RFC, a business would be eligible for aid as long as the governing board of the RFC would

---

[3]Senate, *Congressional Record*, January 27, 1983, p. S454.
[4]House, *Congressional Record*, January 3, 1983.

certify that it was "likely to become insolvent without such assistance, that its closure would adversely and severely affect the economy, and that credit is not otherwise available to the concern on terms and conditions that are conducive to its survival."[5] Furthermore, to be eligible, a business would be required to submit a "plan of reorganization and recovery which, in the judgment of the Board, is reasonably certain to restore such concern to profitability within the period for which credit or other assistance is extended."[6] The Hollings RFC apparently would permit the making of loans to firms that were expected to fail; the purpose would be to ease the transitionary pain felt by workers and communities when plants close in a restructuring economy.[7]

The amount of aid given any one firm could be restricted, for example, to 5 percent of the "sum of (i) the authorized capital stock of the Corporation [the RFC], plus (ii) the aggregate amount of the bonds of the Corporation authorized to be outstanding when the capital stock is fully subscribed" or to 50 percent of the amount of aid required in the firm's "reorganization and recovery plan."[8] And the loans could be restricted to, say, 10 years and carry interest rates no less than the average market yield on U.S. government bonds and notes that have the same remaining period until maturity.

The economic power of an RFC, however, would greatly exceed its capitalized value. Because the RFC's capital would be used to leverage private investment, the amount of private capital directed by a new RFC would be several times its own capital. Manuel Johnson, undersecretary of the treasury for economic affairs in the Reagan administration, estimates that the "Bank of Industrial Competitiveness," proposed by Rep. John LaFalce (D-N.Y.) and capitalized at $8 billion, could affect upwards of $140 billion of private capital.[9]

The proponents of an RFC—also variously labeled "Economic Development Bank," "Bank of Industrial Competitiveness," "Regional Development Bank," and "Technological Development

---

[5]S.265, p. 5.

[6]Ibid., p. 6.

[7]Ibid.

[8]Ibid., p. 10.

[9]As reported in oral testimony before the Economic Stabilization Subcommittee of the House Banking Committee, February 1, 1984.

Bank"—differ over the emphasis to be placed on aid going to sunrise (high-tech) industries versus sunset (smokestack) industries. A common theme is that government should intervene in the investment and reinvestment process. As investment banker Felix Rohatyn, a leading advocate of an RFC, has been quoted as saying, "I'm not sure there is any one blueprint. There are many roads that lead to Rome—as long as you're willing to intervene."[10] However, the diversity of views over exactly how the RFC should be constituted may be the Achilles' heel of the movement. Rep. Richard Gephardt (D-Mo.), an outspoken leader in the national industrial policy movement, has noted,

> To come in with a bill for an RFC, that's a fifth step. An RFC may be okay, but I think it's putting the cart before the horse. If you don't have a basic understanding that we want to starve these industries and nurture those, then the RFC will be a group without a consensus, a group without a mandate. And it won't work.[11]

Harvard University economist Robert Reich, who originally strongly supported the RFC concept in his widely read book,[12] now questions its political viability. He frets that, "In many respects, the [RFC] bank conjures up the wrong image. It plays into the hands of those who say industrial policy is a disguised form of central planning. It sets up a straw man."[13] But when RFC proposals are predicated on the view that private markets have inadequately allocated capital, that the federal government must become involved in investment and reinvestment decisions for the purpose of altering the flow of capital across regions and industries (and in the process "pick winners and losers"), and that the efforts of the RFC would be guided by national economic goals established by a "tripartite council" (composed of labor, government, and business leaders), what else can be deduced other than that the RFC is part and parcel of a central, albeit limited, planning process? When proponents of an RFC are actively promoting central planning, the construction of a straw man is unnecessary: to judge only by the widely disseminated

[10]As quoted in Randall Rothenberg, "An RFC for Today: A Capital Idea," *Inc.* (January 1983): 48.

[11]Ibid.

[12]Robert Reich, *The Next American Frontier* (New York: Times Books, 1983).

[13]As quoted in Peter Behr, "Industrial Policy is a Knot in the Democrats' Economic Plank for '84," *Washington Post Weekly*, November 7, 1983, p. 12.

arguments of RFC advocates, it is evident that the RFC concept is, of itself, full of straw in any case.

Problems with the RFC

The RFC concept is founded on a number of contentions that need to be questioned.

The State of the Economy

As evident in the comments of Representative Guarini, proponents of an RFC are concerned that "our economic problems are severe," so severe that normal market processes cannot handle them. We are supposedly going through a major restructuring of industry. That is, we are moving rapidly, if not haphazardly, from a manufacturing-based economy to a service-based economy. As demonstrated in some detail in chapters 2 and 3, the empirical case undergirding this claim is fatally flawed. An RFC could not stand upon the factual foundation laid for it, since the empirical case made on its behalf presumes—falsely—that we are going through this general "deindustrialization." The political appeal of the RFC must be due to other arguments.

The RFC in History

Backers of an industrial redevelopment bank contend that all they seek is a revival of the Reconstruction Finance Corporation of the past, implying that the history of the original RFC can and should be duplicated. For this reason, a brief review of the first RFC's experiences cannot be avoided.[14]

Although proposals for an RFC in contemporary times come mainly from Democrats, the original RFC was a Republican idea, having been promoted by President Hoover in 1931 and passed into law in 1932, before Franklin Roosevelt brought his New Deal to Washington. Hoover viewed his RFC as a decendant of the War Finance Corporation, which had been organized to handle the economic emergencies created by World War I. Similarly, the RFC was Hoover's answer to the ravages of the Great Depression that were beginning to be keenly felt in the country in the early 1930s.

Although Roosevelt had originally opposed the RFC, he quickly incorporated the agency into the grand design of his New Deal

---

[14]This brief history is based on Clark Nardinelli's excellent review of the RFC's history in "The Reconstruction Finance Corporation's Murky History," Heritage Foundation Backgrounder (Washington, December 21, 1983).

antidepression strategy. The RFC became involved in organizing or supporting the organization of the Commodity Credit Corporation, the Federal National Mortgage Association, the Electric Home and Farm Authority, the Export-Import Bank, the Disaster Loan Corporation, the Federal Deposit Insurance Corporation, and the Small Business Administration.

Most importantly, however, the RFC devoted its lending capability to bailing out the banking and finance industry, which was in a state of disarray during many of the Great Depression years. As evident in Table 4.1, a major share of the loans and investments made by the RFC in its early years, 1932–41, were directed to banks and other financial institutions, with the next largest shares going to agriculture and self-liquidating construction projects. The revival of the banking industry during the period that RFC loans were being made to banks was, according to Clemson University's economic historian Clark Nardinelli, probably coincidental for several reasons.

First, the actual loans to and investment in banks during the 1930s were overwhelmed by the one-third contraction in the money stock engineered by the Federal Reserve between 1929 and 1933. The less than $1 billion lent by the RFC annually during the 1930s was a drop in the bucket when compared with the 50 percent contraction in gross national product between 1929 and 1933.

Second, to secure its loans, the RFC normally required banks to use their strongest assets as backing, denying banks the use of such collateral for obtaining loans and investment funds from other sources.

Third, the publication of RFC loans going to a bank was interpreted by the financial markets as a sign that the bank was in trouble. As Nardinelli notes, "The ensuing panic often put the bank in worse condition than before the loan was made. Indeed, many banks refused to apply for loans, believing the damage from publicity would outweigh the direct financial benefits of the loan."[15]

After the RFC was granted authority to make business and industrial loans in 1934, Jesse Jones, the RFC's first chairman, set out to make loans to business and industry that were expected to be profitable, a goal that often came into conflict with another, less openly professed objective: keeping people at their jobs in times of massive unemployment. "The result," according to Nardinelli, "was

[15]Ibid., p. 6.

86

Table 4.1

LOANS AND INVESTMENTS OF THE RFC
FEBRUARY 2, 1932–JANUARY 19, 1941

	Amount ($ Millions)	% of Total
Loans		
On cotton, corn, tobacco, other commodities	830.0	10.2
For distribution to depositors in closed banks	1,030.8	12.5
To railroads	795.7	9.7
To drainage districts	91.1	1.1
To public school authorities	22.9	0.3
To business	241.1	2.9
To banks, trust companies	1,138.4	13.8
To Federal Land Banks	387.2	4.7
To mortgage loan companies	519.0	6.3
To agricultural and livestock credit corporations	191.6	2.3
For disasters	12.0	0.1
For self-liquidating construction projects	463.1	5.6
To insurance companies	90.7	1.1
To joint stock land banks	24.7	0.3
To Rural Electrification Administration	150.5	1.8
On preferred stock in banks, insurance companies	79.8	1.0
To secretary of agriculture	37.0	0.5
To Export-Import Bank	25.0	0.3
Other	25.8	0.3
Purchases		
Of preferred stock, capital notes, debentures of commercial banks	1,197.8	14.6
Of securities from Public Works Administration	640.6	7.8
Other	11.1	0.1
Loans and purchases in aid of national defense	62.1	0.8
Total	8,220.5	100.0

SOURCE: Samuel I. Rosenman, ed., *The Public Papers and Addresses of Franklin D. Roosevelt*, vol. 2 (New York: Random House, 1938), pp. 403–4; vol. 7 (1941), pp. 99–100. From Clark Nardinelli, "The Reconstruction Finance Corporation's Murky History," Heritage Foundation Backgrounder (Washington, December 21, 1983), p. 5.

that the RFC avoided risky, potentially profitable investments but also avoided what Jones called the 'Santa Claus Giveaways' favored by some members of the Roosevelt Administration."[16]

After World War II, the RFC turned more and more to making

[16]Ibid., p. 7.

loans to firms that could not obtain credit in private markets except at high interest rates, and a professed objective of its loans was to close the "credit gap" that existed between the ability of "large" and "small" businesses to get needed funds. However, as shown in Table 4.2, the RFC's publicly articulated objectives and its lending record were at serious odds with one another. The 93 largest loans in 1949 accounted for 57 percent of the $349 million lent that year. In addition, while small business loans ($25,000 or less) represented over half of all loans made in 1949, they employed little more than 5 percent of the total funds lent. The $44 million loan received by Kaiser-Frazer automobiles in 1949 was greater than the combined total of all funds lent to small businesses in the two-year 1948–49 period.

The interest subsidies implied in RFC loans inevitably created a market shortage of such loans, requiring that some nonmarket, if not political, rationing mechanism be devised. While RFC officials claimed that the funds were lent with the "public interest" in mind, a 1951 Senate report concluded that

> many RFC loan applications in the past 2 years have been approved by the Board of Directors without any apparent affirmative reason. In fact, many applications have been approved by the board notwithstanding the existence of persuasive reasons why loans should not be made.

The report also stated that

> certain Washington attorneys and certain other people were unduly influential with officials of the RFC. In some instances the reports have been received in sworn testimony which asserts that for a sufficient fee these people would give assurance, where no one else could, that matters pending before the RFC would have a successful outcome.[17]

All in all, the original RFC seems hardly a model to be followed in establishing any new government agency to subsidize industrial renewal.

After years of scandals, the RFC was broken up. Its funds were too often allocated on the basis of political friendship and bribery

---

[17]*Favoritism and Influence: Interim Report of the Committee on Banking and Currency Pursuant to Senate Resolution 219*, 82d Cong. 1st sess. (Washington: Government Printing Office, 1951), p. 5.

Table 4.2

RFC Business Loan Authorizations, 1948 and 1949, by Size

Size ($)	Number	%	Gross Amount ($)	%	RFC Share ($)	%
5,000 and under	1,309	16.2	3,827,439	0.4	3,687,271	0.5
5,001–10,000	1,090	13.5	8,488,939	1.0	7,592,435	1.0
10,001–25,000	1,894	23.3	33,847,186	3.9	29,032,663	3.8
Subtotal	4,293	53.0	46,163,564	5.3	40,312,369	5.3
25,001–50,000	1,597	19.7	62,010,992	7.2	52,635,996	6.9
50,001–100,000	1,303	16.1	102,304,275	11.9	86,843,373	11.5
Subtotal	7,193	88.8	210,478,831	24.4	179,791,738	23.7
100,001–200,000	381	4.7	58,512,468	6.8	51,058,428	6.8
200,001–500,000	326	4.0	102,742,739	11.9	89,456,978	11.8
Subtotal	7,900	97.5	371,734,038	43.1	320,307,144	42.3
500,001–1,000,000	98	1.2	71,184,016	8.3	63,752,124	8.4
1,000,001 and over	102	1.3	418,453,702	48.6	372,980,638	49.3
Total	8,100	100.0	861,371,756	100.0	757,039,906	100.0

SOURCE: *RFC Act Amendments of 1951: Hearings before the Committee on Banking and Currency, United States Senate, 82d Cong. 1st sess.* (Washington: Government Printing Office, 1951), p. 340. From Clark Nardinelli, "The Reconstruction Finance Corporation's Murky History," Heritage Foundation Backgrounder (Washington, December 21, 1983), p. 10.

rather than sound economic factors or even congressionally man-dated national objectives. Any success the RFC may have enjoyed was probably a consequence of fortuitous circumstances and its initial resistance to risky investment ventures. As Herbert Stein, senior fellow at the American Enterprise Institute, has observed, the RFC of the 1930s operated at a time when business was so depressed that it could easily spot and promote profitable business ventures. Now the task of determining which industries should be aided and lifted to the status of "winners" is not nearly so simple. The success of any new RFC is not likely to mirror the limited success of the RFC of the 1930s.[18]

The activities of the original RFC were not terminated in 1953, but divided among several agencies. These included the Housing and Home Finance Agency, the General Services Administration, the Export-Import Bank, the Small Business Administration, and the Treasury Department. At one time or another, the Federal National Mortgage Association, the Electric Home and Farm Authority, the Disaster Loan Corporation, and the Commodity Credit Corporation had also been part of the original RFC. Most of these programs, in one form or another, still exist—and have been greatly expanded since the early 1950s. To establish another RFC would be to compound the efforts of the original RFC—and to compound the destructive consequences.

The Stock of Jobs

Proponents of an RFC contend that expanding the loans to tar-geted industries would add to the country's total stock of jobs. The underlying logic follows the simplistic line of all so-called jobs bills. For example, when Congress considered the $5.7 billion appropri-ations bill for roads and bridges in 1983 (under the Highway Rev-enue Tax Act of 1982), it calculated that 320,000 construction jobs would be "created." It failed to calculate the number of jobs that would be destroyed in the oil drilling industry, for example, by the added nickel-a-gallon gas tax that accompanied the jobs program. Contrary to proponents' claims, an RFC would merely redirect funds from taxpayers (who must ultimately finance the loans and cover the interest subsidies) and from non-favored businesses (which, because of RFC loans, would be less capable of borrowing in the

[18]Herbert Stein, "Don't Fall for Industrial Policy," *Fortune*, November 14, 1983, pp. 64–78.

open credit markets) to the favored firms that were the object of the RFC-camouflaged corporate welfare. There is no reason to believe that jobs would, on balance, be created.

Indeed, there is reason to presume that the employment consequences of an RFC would be perverse. Many of the companies that would seek government aid would be doing so because of the noncompetitive wage demands of workers. For example, the steel industry, a likely candidate for RFC assistance, saw the relative wages of steel workers rise during most years of the 1970s while their productivity, on average, fell or didn't rise at all. As a consequence, the effect of RFC loans in such cases would often be to redirect investment funds from industries whose wages were competitive and generally lower to industries whose wages were noncompetitive and generally higher. The result would tend to be a reduction in total jobs: employers in high-wage industries would not be able to add as many jobs to their payrolls with RFC subsidies as low-wage industries could have added with the money they had to pay in taxes to finance those subsidies.

In summary, loans and loan guarantees might create and save jobs of workers in targeted firms, but they would just as certainly destroy and jeopardize jobs of workers in other industries whose only public offense was that they remained competitive and, therefore, were not deemed needy of public assistance. Instead, they were found capable of assuming the tax burden accompanying RFC subsidies for others. Central to understanding the effect of an RFC is Representative Gephardt's declaration "that we want to starve these industries and nurture those."[19]

The Maybank Amendment

The efficacy of an RFC can be assessed, partially and indirectly, by past efforts to "target" defense expenditures. As with the RFC, proponents of a national industrial policy have sometimes advocated using defense expenditures to ease the pain of economic hardship felt by the unemployed. Specifically, they have recommended that perceived social problems caused by the growing mobility of capital, the lagging competitiveness of U.S. industries in world markets, and structural changes in the U.S. economy should be and have been solved in part by "targeting" defense procurements to contractors in "distressed areas" of the country.

[19]As quoted in Rothenberg, p. 48.

Contrary to what may be presumed, the Reagan administration has tested such an industrial strategy on a limited scale, and the results have been disastrous from both defense and employment perspectives.[20] Beginning in 1954, defense appropriation bills have included what has come to be known as the "Maybank Amendment," which specifically prohibits the Defense Department from using its funds to "relieve problems of economic dislocation." However, in 1981, with the acquiescence of the Reagan administration, Congress required the Defense Department to allocate up to $3.4 billion in contracts to producers in "labor surplus areas" (as designated by the Labor Department). The procurement limit was raised to $4 billion in 1982. Instead of taking the low bids in 1981 and 1982, the Defense Department was able to pay contractors in labor surplus areas a premium of up to 5 percent above the lowest bids from non–labor surplus areas.

The 1981–82 test of the "modification of the Maybank Amendment" covered nearly 36,000 contracts, worth a little more than $3 billion. Only 956 of these contracts, valued at approximately $88 million, were actually let to non–low bidders in labor surplus areas. However, those contracts cost the Defense Department $1.8 million in premiums and an additional $1.7 million in administrative costs due to the added complications of evaluating acceptable bids—or $3.5 million the Defense Department would not have had to spend had the Maybank Amendment been in full force. Given the magnitude of the defense budget, $3.5 million is the proverbial drop in the bucket. Still, this new industrial strategy meant that national defense suffered marginally as a consequence. The United States literally got less bang for the defense buck during the two-year test.

Admittedly, a major purpose of the Maybank modification was to create and save jobs. However, Defense Department analysis indicated that the test had a perverse effect: on balance, jobs were destroyed. The 956 contracts awarded to non–low price bidders in labor surplus areas increased employment in those areas by 3,207. But the low bidders in the non–labor surplus areas lost 3,335 jobs because they did not get the contracts. In short, the test program on balance *destroyed* 128 jobs at a cost to American taxpayers of $3.5 million, or $27,300 per job! The cost would have been substantially

[20]See Department of Defense, Defense Logistics Agency, *Report of Test on the Modification to the Maybank Amendment: FY 1981–FY 1983*, February 1981–December 1982.

greater (upwards of $24 million in procurement costs alone) had the 5 percent premium limit not been in force.

The net loss of jobs should have been expected. Firms in labor surplus areas unable to underbid competitors are often stuck with noncompetitive wages. As a consequence, they are less inclined to hire as many workers as are employers elsewhere.

The added costs of modifying the Maybank Amendment for a short, two-year period is in itself cause for concern. However, the long-run consequences of not having the Maybank Amendment in full force can be even more detrimental to the health of the nation's economy and defense posture. Competition among bidders and production efficiency can be seriously reduced by the continued application of the modification. When the Defense Department is forced to accept above–low bid contracts, efficient producers in labor surplus areas that would otherwise be low bidders have less incentive to keep their costs in check, and inefficient producers are rewarded with what are, effectively, political plums.[21]

The two-year test of using defense expenditures to pursue industrial goals reveals an important principle voters should never forget when assessing proposals from industrial policy enthusiasts: when government spends money to subsidize "winners" (under the guise of improving employment opportunities), it often helps "losers" (those firms that cannot compete). In the process, the government often makes efficient producers "losers" at considerable cost to consumer and taxpayer welfare.

The Political Bias of an RFC

As was true of the original RFC, any new RFC would tend to discriminate in favor of established industries, especially the larger ones, and against emerging industries. Proponents of an RFC advocate, in essence, substituting politics for markets in the allocation of investment funds; and votes, not future profitability, are what count in politics. Large established firms, through their workers and stockholders and network of suppliers and buyers, have the votes necessary to command the respect they need in the political arena. Small emerging firms in untested product lines, on the other hand, do not have enough votes to sway the decisions of an RFC,

---

[21]Fortunately, in 1983 the approved premium to non–low price bidders was lowered to 2.2 percent, but that is still unnecessarily high.

which, regardless of its ostensible "political independence," would have to remain in step with the political drummers in Congress.

Chrysler was bailed out in 1979—but not because it was the only employer teetering on the brink of bankruptcy that year. There were tens of thousands of other firms, whose total employment far exceeded that of Chrysler, that went under but whose fate was never considered by Congress. Rather, Chrysler was bailed out for one simple reason: it is a relatively large firm, with a relatively large number of votes represented in its workers, stockholders, customers, and suppliers, and these votes are strategically important to a number of members of Congress.

The proponents of an RFC attempt to comfort us by suggesting that safeguards would be devised that would make lending decisions immune to political tampering. However, there is nothing in the construction of an RFC that would appear to prevent the frequent intrusion of politics into the lending process. Certainly, the board of directors, responsible to the president or to Congress, would heed the political drummers. Moreover, the Hollings proposal makes a criterion of a firm's eligiblity for assistance the perception that "its closure would adversely and *severely* affect the economy." Few small emerging firms would, by their closing, "severely affect" the economy. As a general rule, therefore, an RFC would favor the status quo, sacrificing economic growth in the process.

As a final note on this issue, we must wonder how any bureaucratic construction emerging from the political process could rise above that process. If an RFC did not heed the political drummers, we would have to wonder why it was created or how it would be controlled, other than by the "good intentions" of those who ran it; and we have had too much experience with control mechanisms based on good intentions to have much faith in real control being exercised.

The Chrysler Mythology

The federal government's aid to the Chrysler Corporation in 1979 is touted as the quintessential example of what industrial policy, strategically aimed at helping firms out of financial crises, can accomplish through a renewed RFC. Former vice president Walter Mondale exhorted union leaders as follows:

> Look at Chrysler. I believe in a free market. Most decisions have to be made there. But there are times when things are so important

that that's why we have a government of the United States. If we had let Chrysler go down the drain, we would have lost a major competitor in the auto industry. We would have lost a major source of industrial productivity in our country. The federal government would have lost billions of dollars through the cost of unemployment and the collapse of the industry and the tax losses and all that went with it. . . . Many people, including the man who is now President, turned his back on Chrysler and said, "No help."

I'm proud of the fact that I worked for the auto workers and the auto industry to drive a quality recommendation through our administration to support that Chrysler loan and to help pass it in Congress. Three years later, the Chrysler Corporation is one of the success stories in America. It's starting to make progress. It's paying the federal government back. We're making money off the loan. The communities with plants are stabilizing. People have jobs. We've got more competition in the auto industry. What's wrong with using the government when it serves?[22]

If one judges the bailout in terms of whether Chrysler still exists, then the bailout worked. But Chrysler might have survived even if bankruptcy proceedings had begun in 1979. Indeed, attorney James Hickel declares that for all practical purposes "the Chrysler Corporation has gone bankrupt. Or, more accurately, in the past three years Chrysler has renegotiated its debt and restructured its organization in a way that greatly resembles a company that has gone through bankruptcy."[23]

Hickel points out that the bailout law required Chrysler's creditors to make "concessions," a provision pressed by then secretary of the treasury G. William Miller that enabled Chrysler to pay off more than $600 million in loans at 30 cents on the dollar and to convert $700 million in loans into a special class of preferred stock, a kind that according to Hickel, is

> relatively worthless in the financial markets, because the shares presently earn no dividends and are unredeemable for several years. Granted, these preferred stockholders were able to trade

[22]Walter F. Mondale, excerpts from speech delivered to the Industrial Union Department Legislative Conference, May 4, 1983 (Washington, Mondale for President Campaign), pp. 1–2.

[23]James K. Hickel, "The Chrysler Bailout Revisited," Heritage Foundation Backgrounder (Washington, July 1983), p. 2, a revised and expanded version of "Lemon Aid: Debunking the Case for the Chrysler Bailout," Reason (March 1983): 37–39.

their shares of preferred for common in early 1983, however, it is fair to believe that the market value of the newly acquired common stock will be less than the value of the original debt, plus lost interest.[24]

Had the company been allowed to declare bankruptcy, the changes in Chrysler's balance sheet might have been little different, except that stockholders and creditors would probably have taken a greater financial beating. But that is the risk of investing in private enterprise, a risk for which stockholders and lenders are compensated through dividends and interest rates.

Did the bailout save jobs? That is questionable for a number of reasons. First, the company could have started anew after bankruptcy proceedings, as many other companies do, and it could be employing today as many workers as the "New Chrysler Corporation" currently does. Second, other investors (including any number of other companies) could have purchased Chrysler's assets at the post-bankruptcy market price, and production could have continued, perhaps on a more modest but still profitable scale. Third, other car companies could have emerged or expanded, providing jobs in the process. Fourth, lendable funds were drawn away from other firms and other investment purposes. Some Chrysler jobs were saved, but jobs in other firms were just as surely destroyed. And finally, since Chrysler had by 1983 cut its white-collar work force by as much as 20,000 and its production work force by over 40,000, there was ample reason for Sen. William Proxmire and others to wonder whether the bailout actually saved any jobs at all.[25]

Certainly, if the government treated all firms the way it treated Chrysler, as industrial policy advocates suggest it should, Chrysler's workers would find the benefits of the bailout more questionable. Fortunately for Chrysler employees, the company's stockholders, suppliers, and customers did not have to carry the heavy tax burden of salvaging tens of thousands of other companies. Few Chrysler cars would have been bought if all firms had been given the same government attention and privileges that Chrysler was given. One objection to generalizing the Chrysler bailout through

[24]Ibid.
[25]Ibid., p. 3.

96

an industrial policy applicable to all firms is that a bailout for firms like Chrysler would have far less chance of success.

Hickel also questions whether Chrysler is actually recovering. Half of the company's reported profits of $170 million in 1983 came from large losses that were carried forward to 1983, reducing Chrysler's tax liability. Given its cutbacks in purchases of plant and equipment in the early 1980s, Chrysler may be forsaking long-term profitability for short-run profits, something that has not gone unrecognized by industry analysts. Chrysler managed to defer $220 million in pension fund contributions, and it negotiated $600 million in wage concessions for 1982 and 1983. Some of these concessions were canceled under threat of a strike in 1982, and more givebacks are at this writing expected to be negotiated.[26] The company can also thank "voluntary restrictions" accepted by Japan on the importation of Japanese cars between 1981 and 1985. Brookings Institution economist Robert Crandall attributes most of Chrysler's 1983 profits to these voluntary restrictions, which may have added substantially more than $280 to the average auto's sticker price since 1981.[27] Finally, any success Chrysler has in staying out of the red may be due more to the special entrepreneurial skills of its chairman Lee Iaccoca than to the bailout. Certainly, Iaccoca revalidated a well-worn principle of markets: any firm can be successful if it is subsidized and if its competition is shackled by government controls.

In short, there is every reason to believe that Hickel was right when he wrote:

> In reality, the primary difference between the actual bankruptcy that Chrysler faced in 1979 and the quasi-bankruptcy that Chrysler has gone through in the past three years, is that under this quasi-bankruptcy the federal government has accepted responsibility for guaranteeing over $1 billion in Chrysler loans. But if Chrysler's creditors and employees have already suffered through the debt negotiation and layoffs that typify reorganizations under the bankruptcy laws, who is benefitting from those loan guarantees? Primarily Chrysler's stockholders.[28]

---

[26]Ibid., pp. 9–11.

[27]Robert W. Crandall, "Import Quotas and the Automobile Industry: The Cost of Protectionism," *Brookings Review* (Summer 1984): 8–16; and "Carving up the Car Buyer," *Newsweek*, March 5, 1984, pp. 72–73.

[28]Hickel, "The Chrysler Bailout Revisited," pp. 3–4.

The Incentives of Firms

Because of the subsidies implied in financial aid from a newly created RFC, the incentives firms have to watch their costs and avoid financial distress would, on the margin, be lowered. As a consequence, a new RFC could lead to much economic waste and to a reduction in the long-run competitiveness of U.S. firms that believe they can secure federal aid when they need it. The growing demands that could be expected to be placed on RFC resources should at some point cause the system to become overloaded, if it were not overloaded at the start. Because of these growing demands, we would expect more and more of the nation's lending decisions to give way to the demands of politics, not economics. As a consequence, there is every reason to believe that the establishment of an RFC would have perverse effects on employment stability. Gradually, employment tenure would rely on political, rather than market, decisions; and Congress is notorious for changing its mind, contributing to economic instability in the private sector.

The Problem with "Conditionality"

A favorite argument of backers of an RFC is that the federal government already provides considerable benefits to industries in the form of protection from imports, direct grants, regulatory protection from domestic competition, and loan guarantees. The aggregate magnitude of several of these business benefits was estimated to be $100 billion in fiscal 1984.[29] This figure does not include loans and loan guarantees, protective regulation, and tariffs and quotas. However, the federal government and American people, so the argument is developed, get practically nothing in return for the benefits distributed. The benefits lack "conditionality." That is, they are not conditioned on the favored industry doing anything for the American public or government (aside from making campaign contributions to the political backers of the enabling legislation).

For example, the "trigger price mechanism" that automatically increases the tariff on protected steel when the price of imported steel falls below officially prescribed levels has provided billions of

---

[29]Congressional Budget Office, *Federal Support of U.S. Business* (Washington, 1984). Most ($81.6 billion) of the total benefits were tax expenditures, which disputably are subsidies to businesses. Calculations of "tax expenditures" implicitly presume that firms' sales revenues are actually the government's, which the government, through deductions and credits, allows firms to retain. Implicitly, the argument denies the income rights of private property.

dollars of income transfers, disguised in market prices, to steel producers. These billions, RFC advocates charge, are given to the steel industry literally free of charge: it has no future obligation but to continue to collect its greater profits (or to suffer lower losses) as a result of government-supplied protection. As a consequence, instead of using its greater profitability to rebuild its plants, U.S. Steel bought Marathon Oil in 1983.

RFC advocates maintain that the aid envisioned under a new RFC would be structured differently; indeed, the subsidies would be used, according to Robert Reich, to induce domestic industries "to restructure themselves" to become more competitive,[30] as well as to encourage them to modernize, avoid plant closings, and create and save jobs.

While appealing, the argument has two principal flaws. First, it suggests that even more federal subsidies, passed out to industries through an RFC, would be directed to firms that have gotten in economic difficulty partially because they had become noncompetitive. Such a subsidy arrangement represents a none-too-subtle transfer of purchasing power from firms that have remained competitive, and do not qualify for the subsidies, to firms that do qualify because they may have raised their costs (including wages) and prices above competitive levels. Reinterpreted, conditionality as a part of the subsidy process provides an incentive for industries to become noncompetitive. They would then escape the taxes imposed on competitive industries and would be able, instead, to collect subsidies passed along to noncompetitive industries. Contrary to what is sought, the net effect of conditionality would be to discourage industrial competitiveness in America.

Second, RFC backers apparently fail to see that the overall level and distribution of federal subsidies to businesses in this country is a consequence of real-world political power held by various industries. The steel industry, for example, is the beneficiary of protection largely because it is a very large industry with sufficient votes and political money to obtain (or "buy") the political support needed to transfer real purchasing power from the steel-using public to itself. Industrial policy advocates cannot simply wish away, by way of well-articulated and noble social objectives, the existing political power structure. Existing political power groups are interested mainly in the net benefits transferred to themselves. If a

[30]Reich, pp. 246–47.

protected or subsidized industry were required to incur costs from a conditionality or restructuring requirement, it would simply ask for more protection and/or subsidies to ensure that its *net* benefits remain more or less the same.

To change the level of *net* federal benefits going to industry, changes that lessen the political visibility of favored industries in fundamental political institutions would appear necessary. However, industrial policy advocates seem intent upon making darn certain that the level of net benefits going to protected or subsidized industries is increased, not contracted. They propose such institutions as tripartite councils, which would likely increase the political power of the industry and labor groups that are current beneficiaries of government largesse. This is because these groups would likely be heavily represented on the tripartite council. The result would be an increase in net benefits going to politically powerful business interests, not exactly what the proponents of a new RFC have in mind.

The Growth of Political Influence

Finally, the establishment of an RFC would increase the perceived relative profitability of political activity, i.e., lobbying for government handouts. It would, therefore, cause firms to divert their scarce resources from productive market purposes to largely unproductive political (or transfer) purposes. Growth in the nation's output would, again, suffer.

The Function of the Market

Advocates of an RFC fail to see that we already have a mechanism for allocating investment funds—the market, which is composed of millions of citizens who are constantly concerned with investing their funds where they will be the most productive. Industrial policy advocates do not understand, or do not want to see, that the market provides all firms a grand opportunity to secure the funds they need for innovation and expansion. All they have to do is convince investors that they are more worthy of credit or equity investment than other firms. Again, RFC advocates apparently do not understand that when funds are made available to one set of "targeted" firms, they are drawn away from other firms, those that in the absence of government intervention would have been judged more worthy.

A common presumption of RFC advocates is that politicians and government bureaucrats can choose "winners" more efficiently than can the market. As we argue in more detail in the next chapter, these advocates are in effect presuming that the corporate intelligence of a relatively few people in Washington is greater than the corporate intelligence of the millions of private citizens in the market who, through the pricing system, are constantly getting feedback information on how others assess their investments. Such a presumption has no basis in either historical fact or sound theory. In private markets and through changes in the value of their stock, firms receive continuous market assessments of how they are doing. The information flow in politics, dependent on votes taken only intermittently, is not nearly so clear and continuous.

RFC bills sometimes mention that loans would be made on the basis of a firm's prospective profitability. In considering such a contention, one must wonder how political operatives could more accurately assess the profitability of aid-seeking firms than could market operatives, especially if the political operatives' personal incentives were not tied to the firms' profitability.

Concluding Comments

In summary, few can dispute the need for more and better-paying jobs; and, admittedly, the notion of a Reconstruction Finance Corporation is a politically seductive means of achieving that end. However, it is a misguided means. An RFC would tend to centralize economic decisions and, to that extent, politicize them.

Adam Smith's discussion of the "man of systems," whose notion of arranging "the different pieces of a great society" fails to account for the fact that these "pieces," unlike those in a game of chess, have "principles of motion" of their own again comes to mind.[31] Proponents of an RFC have been seduced into believing that they, as "men and women of systems," can improve human welfare by simply rearranging the pieces of the industrial structure of the country. In effect, they think they are smarter than markets, that they are anointed with unusual powers to discern which of the many industries that could emerge and remain profitable is deserving of investment funds. They tend to believe that given the power of the purse as incorporated in an RFC, they could construct a "better" society.

---

[31]Adam Smith, *The Theory of Moral Sentiments* (Indianapolis: Liberty Press, 1976), pp. 380–81.

Their efforts would fail, however, not because their intentions are misplaced, but because they are simply not as smart as they think. In Smith's words, people have "principles of motion" altogether different from those that the RFC administrators might choose to impress upon them; and their efforts to reinvigorate the national economy by way of an RFC can only founder because they cannot know with any reasonable degree of accuracy what the "principles of motion" of others are. This is especially true when dealing with an uncertain future and with unborn people and technologies. These points will be further developed in the next chapter.

V. Managed Capitalism: "The Fatal Conceit"

Professor F. A. Hayek's writings span six decades and more volumes than anyone cares to count. He justly earned his 1974 Noble Prize in Economics, for his works have, through the years, contributed much to the intellectual development of hordes of economists and social philosophers. As may be obvious to devotees of Hayekian economics, threads of his thoughts weave their way through the chapters of this book.

While his work has for many years been very important to my own writings, the first chance I had to meet Professor Hayek was only recently during a hospitality hour before a conference on "Constitutional Economics." His advanced age and then recent illness were apparent from the uneasiness with which he walked, but even in casual cocktail conversation the brilliance of his printed word was evident. At that party, he outlined the themes of his current work, which he admitted was an extrapolation of his earlier writings and would likely be his last major effort, on the problems of planning any economy, much less a complex economy of diverse groups and individuals the size of one of the major industrial nations. From the twinkle in his eye, those of us around him could tell he was more than a little pleased to have already entitled his new book *The Fatal Conceit*, a turn of phrase that stands in sharp contrast to the truly gentlemanly and scholarly manner of Professor Hayek. His new book will probably finalize a peculiarly interesting riddle he noted in his formal conference remarks:

> In order to be a good economist you have to be a great deal more than an economist. . . . This is because the understanding of the extremely complex structure of society requires an insight into more than economic theory, which starts out on what is called *given data* and then presumes that it is data given to the organizers of society . . . [who may be charged with the responsibility of deriving] the proper order of society. To me it has become a standing joke that the old generation of economists, who believed

in a constructivist approach to the problem of the capacity of men to organize deliberately human cooperation, started out by reassuring themselves that the data were really given to them. I will even tell you that of course no data need be given, in particular for mathematical economics which starts out with the assumption of given data and then draws elaborate conclusions that are given to no one.[1]

Everywhere he went during the week following the conference—and he was interviewed by the media on a number of occasions and gave several speeches—he reminded his listeners that there are limits to human intelligence; that there is only so much that the *individual* mind can grasp; that "the fatal conceit" of the intellectuals, policymakers, and political leaders is the belief that a complex society can be effectively directed from the center, meaning a small number of people who are no more or less intelligent than the rest of us but who must set "national" goals and devise "national" plans. His essential message was an appeal for intellectual humility in policy formulation.

To one reporter's question on the efficacy of current efforts to formulate a national industrial policy, which was more in vogue at the time of the interview than it is now, he admitted that he had not been able to keep up with the particulars of the debate from his home in Zurich but that he could predict with tolerable confidence that such efforts might be well intended yet would be in vain. Why? "They just can't do what they want to do," he replied in a few incisive words that should be etched on the foreheads of every industrial policy advocate.

This chapter has as its overriding purpose unraveling the "Hayekian riddle" posed above and explaining the immensity of the conceit required on the part of those who think that industrial planning, even on a limited scale, can be effectively pursued.

The Economic Problem

Following the lead of the late British professor Lionel Robbins, economists have for decades defined their subject matter as a study of a "problem," called "*the* economic problem," of allocating scarce resources among competing ends with the intent of maximizing

---

[1]F. A. Hayek, "Reflections on Constitutional Economics," in *Constitutional Economics: Containing the Economic Powers of Government*, ed. Richard B. McKenzie (Lexington, Mass.: D.C. Heath and Company, 1984), p. 286.

people's welfare. Accordingly, like many other economists Robert Heilbroner, an advocate of industrial policy, characterizes economics as fundamentally concerned with "scarcity":

> To be sure, the economic problem itself—that is, the need to struggle for existence—derives ultimately from the scarcity of nature. If there were no scarcity, goods would be as free as air, and economics, at least in one sense of the word, would cease to exist as a social preoccupation.[2]

An important purpose of this chapter is to explore how this "economic" view of the world—and, indeed, economic pedagogy—has served the interests of industrial policy advocates and has misguided the policy debate.

According to the discipline's paradigm as repeatedly presented to beginning economics students, two immutable facts are deducible from the world in which we live. First, the resources available for producing the things we want are finite, limited by what is ultimately found in nature. There is only so much "land," "labor," "capital," and "entrepreneurial talent," to use four broad categories of resources defined by economists. For example, the limited number of trees, tons of iron ore, and barrels of oil found in nature impose a stringent discipline on our productive system. We can produce, during any defined period of time, only so many cars, boats, concerts, and tubes of toothpaste with our resources. Second, we want far more things than can be produced; our wants are, for all practical purposes, unlimited. If they are not unlimited during any *given* period of time, then they are certainly expandable in unlimited ways with the passage of time.

The economic problem is that of using the available resources in the best possible ways. Or, in Heilbroner's words, "Putting men to work is only the first step in the solution of the production problem. Men must not only be put to work; they must be put to work in *the right places.*"[3] Students are usually taught that the three fundamental questions at the foundation of economic science can be summed up in four words, "what?" "how?" and "for whom?": What are we as a country going to produce? How are we going to produce these goods? And for whom are these goods going to be produced?

---

[2]Robert L. Heilbroner, *The Making of Economic Society* (Englewood Cliffs, N.J.: Prentice Hall, 1962), pp. 4–5.

[3]Ibid., p. 7.

Although individual choices are sometimes considered, the emphasis of the ensuing analysis tends to be on "national" answers to those questions. Should the country produce more guns or more butter? Wheat or steel? Bicycles or matches? Should more or less capital (or labor or land) be employed to produce the guns and butter? Do the rich, poor, or middle classes get the benefits of the country's productive machine?

All these choice problems are typically presented to students in graphic form, with the goods subject to choice identified on the axes of the graphs. The "production possibilities" of a country (and the choices alternative production combinations represent) are seen as points on a "production possibilities curve" in a graph such as that in Figure 5.1. The curve is assumed to exist "out there" in the "macroeconomy" and to be known or, if not known, capable of being computed. The choices facing a country are analogous to A, many guns (G_3) and little butter (B_1); B, a moderate quantity of both guns (G_2) and butter (B_2); and C, a lot of butter (B_3) and few guns (G_1). These choices are assumed to be available (or else they would not qualify as choices) and independent of the institutional-government setting in which production and consumption occur.

The typical course in economics, therefore, begins (and ends)

Figure 5.1
PRODUCTION POSSIBILITIES CURVE

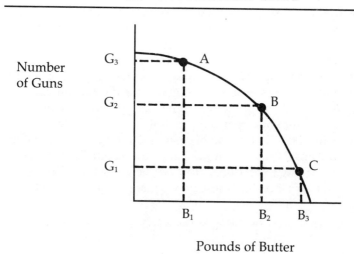

Number of Guns

Pounds of Butter

with the students instructed to assume an Olympian vantage point, one that will permit them to view their forthcoming study as a means of solving a problem: the allocation of scarce resources (which, presumably, are known) to their most productive uses (which, presumably, can also be identified). The students are asked, in effect, to imagine that they have been elevated to the role of social engineers whose assigned task is to take *as given* the known resources and wants and to evaluate the extent to which societal welfare is maximized. *The economic problem,* as generally presented, is perceived as *the problem* confronting the social analyst–student (at least for the duration of the course).

The concept of scarcity is further explored in the typical introductory economics class with the construction of "supply and demand curves" such as the ones in Figure 5.2. The curve sloping downward to the right is "demand," which depicts graphically the assumed inverse relationship between the price of a given product and the quantity consumers are willing to buy in a designated time period. The demand curve reminds us that consumers will buy more of the product in question (butter in our example) if the price falls, and vice versa. The upward-sloping curve is "supply," which repre-

Figure 5.2

SUPPLY AND DEMAND CURVES

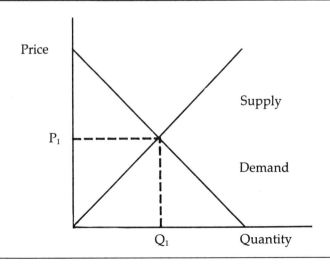

sents graphically the assumed direct relationship between the price charged by producers and the quantity they are willing to offer (or supply) on the market. The supply curve reminds us that producers are generally willing to offer more of a product at a higher price than at a lower price.

Obviously, what consumers and producers are willing and able to do is not always, under all prices, compatible. The market "solution" to the diverging views of buyers and sellers (meaning the way in which the competing interests of buyers and sellers are reconciled) is the intersection of the two curves, or a price of P_1 and a quantity of Q_1 in the figure. That is, a competitive market will move toward the price-quantity combination at the intersection of the supply and demand curves if it is not there already, and it will remain at that price-quantity combination when it is achieved as long as the economic forces underlying supply and demand remain unchanged. Competitive movements in the price will occur if the price is above or below P_1. There is one overriding virtue in the price-quantity combination at the intersection: at that price the market clears. In other words, producers offer for sale just as many units of a given product as consumers are willing to buy at a price of P_1.

Again, the message that must be readily inferred by many, if not most, beginning students is that supply and demand exist "out there" in the market and that they exist more or less independent of the competitive market process, which works to push the price and quantity toward the intersection of the *existing* supply and demand curves. Such a view is reinforced in mathematical and econometric extensions of supply and demand curve analysis. Students are then taught that supply and demand can actually be calculated, albeit imperfectly; and once the curves are known in mathematical form, the market-clearing price and quantity can be deduced by conventional mathematical procedures for finding solutions to any set of simultaneous equations.

Our purpose here in outlining introductory economics pedagogy is not to present the actual mechanics of classroom discussions; our discussion has been much too brief for that. Rather, our purpose is to emphasize that the way economics is often taught may partially explain the affection many intellectuals and policymakers have for planning. The unwary student is likely to come out of the course with a strong belief that the problem of allocating scarce resources that is accomplished through unguided markets, as represented by supply and demand curves, can be resolved just as readily and effectively by social analysts who can, with the aid of powerful computers, calculate market-clearing prices and quantities of the many goods and services people buy. Indeed, many students must conclude that competitive markets are largely a waste, since the essential tasks of markets can be accomplished with fewer resources. After all, if the products consumers want are known and the supplies and demands for the various products can be computed, we as a society can avoid the time and energy wasted in haggling over prices and in worrying about what market outcomes should be. We can pose such problems to a small number of reasonably intelligent "experts" steeped in the study of mathematics, economics, and econometrics. Furthermore, when we rely on the calculations of experts, we don't have to be subjected to the abuses of greed, which motivates people in an unfettered market process. From the Olympian perspective of the experts, profit serves no useful purpose. (It is "surplus value" and represents "exploitation" of workers, who may be viewed as the ultimate source of productive worth.) For that matter, competition serves no useful social function.

Perhaps the foregoing characterization of many courses in introductory (and advanced) economics presents an unfair generalization. There are, without doubt, many instructors who take a different tack in the presentation of their discipline's principles, and there is much more that is done in principles classes than has been outlined here. However, to the extent that our outline of introductory courses is descriptive of the pedagogy employed for principles of economics, as well as for introductory classes in other disciplines, we have a *partial* explanation for many people's confidence in the capacity of planners—e.g., industrial policy planners—to allocate the country's resources more effectively than markets.

Unfortunately, for several important reasons the capacity of people to plan economic systems is largely illusory. First, it might be conceded that if it were accurate to say that, during any given period of time, resources are *known*, wants are *known*, and the various supplies and demands could be reconciled through computations, then planning might be a highly attractive means of organizing human society. However, the deduction that planning is plausible is all wrong because the assumed "knowns" are "given to no one," as Hayek puts it. We really do not know very much at all about what people "want." Granted, they do buy cars; at any point in time the makes and models purchased can be identified by surveying car dealer lots. However, we can know that because markets have operated and have revealed certain information about past consumer preferences. Even if the problem assigned to planners were simply one of assessing what people have purchased in the past, it is doubtful that a handful of planners could do a very good job of planning an entire economy the size of a nation-state. While there are some very smart people in government, none of them are smart enough, even with the help of very large computers, to really *know* the billions of goods, virtually unlimited in color and form, that the millions of people in a country buy. There is simply too much information in the economy for a relatively small number of people to handle. A virtue of decentralized decision making is that no one, or no group of people, has to know what millions of people know. The market is a social device for dividing up the information requirements of effectively running a large, complex, and sophisticated economy. From this perspective, decentralized decision making (intrinsic to markets) that yields individual "plans" is not only a political nicety, because it affords people a great deal of freedom from the drives and whims of people in central authority, but it is a social necessity, if the wants of people, not their leaders, count for very much.

The economic problem is, accordingly, not a simple matter of overcoming scarcity, which seems to be a statement of how we must exist, but rather one of coordinating the use of information that is, in its entirety, given to no one, but is, in bits and pieces, known by everyone. We each know something about our wants, needs, desires, abilities, and resources that can be understood imperfectly only by ourselves or, at most, by relatively few others. The limitations we each have to comprehend, gather, and use information that others hold, virtually exclusively, impose strict limitations on our ability to engage in central planning—and make markets a social necessity.

Second, the problem of the central planner is enormously complicated when it is recognized that what people need and want is often not "given to anyone" in the sense of being identified long before the purchases are made. Many, if not most, individual consumers do not always know what they need and want until they enter the market to buy, and their purchasing plans are constantly being revised as they shop and buy. This is so because markets are valuable sources of information on what is available and what others are buying and because the preliminary plans with which people enter the market often conflict with the preliminary plans of others. It is very hard to see how central planning, if it intends to satisfy consumer wants as opposed to the wants of those in authority, can be very effective if the information that is needed to undertake planning is not readily apparent to anyone, if the information useful to planning constantly changes and emerges as a part and parcel of the competitive market process, and if the planners are not sufficiently intelligent even to handle information that is discernible.

Third, central planning requires an immense capacity to reconcile competing claims on resources. Planners may be able to establish that "cars" (let's ignore the problem of what color, model, and make) should be produced, but effective planning requires that arrangements be made to ensure that the necessary resources (i.e., steel, plastics, and cloth) be available in the right quantities, right places, and at the right times; otherwise, production bottlenecks can be expected to emerge and a lot of resources will be wasted. In turn, plans must be made to ensure that the resources employed in the production of the steel, plastics, and cloth used in the production of cars are available in the right quantities, at the right places, and at the right times, and so forth. Then the planners must ensure that income is distributed so that the cars can be purchased and that provisions are made for changes in consumer tastes and production technologies over time. Repeating a now familiar theme, one can well imagine that efforts to reconcile such planning problems for millions of goods and services can short-circuit the mental capacities of the most brilliant among us, much less the more ordinary people of modest talents who are likely to be saddled with the problem of centrally planning an industrial economy.

In choosing the title of his new book, Hayek was actually lamenting the extraordinary conceit required by proponents of central planning even when their intentions are to plan only a portion of the economy (the "industrial sector" or "basic industries"). These proponents must hold a romantic as well as unrealistic view of their own and others' capacities as social visionaries. The essential task of planners is to foresee the future, which is largely unknown because it is necessarily untested. The critical economic test of what people want is whether or not they buy a product. Seen this way, a plan must be a test, which is a task the market seeks to accomplish at the individual and firm level. If a plan is designed to give people what they want, it must be constantly revised in light of these tests.

The only difference between a "central plan" and the "market" is that a central plan is likely to be far more rigid than the market, since it is created out of a political and bureaucratic process noted for inflexibility. This is because so many people must agree before changes can be made. To presume, therefore, that planning would result in less "waste" than the market is to articulate a faith unlikely to be supported by experience.

Fourth, even though we may know what people buy, to the extent that we can count the number of cars of various makes and models, we will still likely know little of what people actually want and are purchasing. Products such as cars are used in individual and social contexts. Cars may represent a resource in the production of something else that consumers actually want, for example, social recognition or transportation of a certain style and amount; and these individual production processes that occur largely in the home will probably involve many other resources (i.e., many other goods and the consumer's time and energy) that are not readily counted by observers (planners) not directly involved in the use of the cars. Useful planning requires that the production of cars be planned along with the production of many other goods. Otherwise, the plan will result in too many or too few cars being produced.

In a static world, planning would be *relatively* easy: "all" that planners would have to do is duplicate the past. Even that task would not be all that easy in an absolute sense, since, as stressed before, there would be much that is not known to planners about what consumers are actually consuming.[4] The world in which we live, however, is a highly dynamic one. A major complaint of industrial policy advocates is that the world is changing too rapidly. Planners are not likely to do a very good job in such a world because the information requirements are multiplied. Furthermore, planners must rely on computerized, mathematical, econometric models of the economy founded on "regularities" observed in the past that, by definition of "change," no longer exist or will not exist for very long. Rather than being an argument for planning, a changing world is an argument against planning, for changes have a nasty habit of making plans irrelevant.

---

[4]On the other hand, the case for planning, which is often predicated upon market failures, would also be weaker in a static world. This is because there would be fewer market mistakes, since in a static world it would be easier for markets to satisfy the needs of consumers.

Fifth, the task of the planners is greatly complicated by the fact that even "resources" (which planners must allocate) cannot be known outside a market process. A person with computer skills is useless unless people want the services of computers, just as flint is just another rock outside a society that relies on arrows for weapons. The demand for resources cannot be directly observed or measured. Such demands are derived from the demand for the final product and are dependent upon available (changing) technologies and resources that are available as substitutes and complements in production. Because they are not involved directly in production, planners will necessarily know little about these matters.

In addition, "resources" represent what people consider *valuable* in production and what people are willing to do with things. "Resources" are as grounded in people's subjective evaluations as goods and services, and such evaluations are not knowable to outside observers (planners) without some means by which people can reveal their preferences. For example, to surmise that the country has "so much" labor, as represented by a given number of working-age people, is a total misconstruction of labor as a resource. "Effort" and "time" are just as important as "size of the labor force" in getting things produced, but we really know little about how much "effort" people are willing to expend at given tasks until the tasks are specified and until the workers have to confront the particulars of employment, namely, the wage and fringe benefits, working conditions, and competition for the jobs. The amount of time and effort expended on a job varies with hundreds of largely subjective factors, most of which will not be known by planners or subject to quantification and computerization.

Sixth, it may appear that the information problem could be largely solved through surveys of consumer wants. But, as noted, people often do not determine very accurately what they want unless pressured by the costs of making errors and failing to seize upon the opportunities at hand. Just what they want is greatly influenced by the costs of the goods they buy, which may not be very well understood or appreciated at the time the surveys are taken. Finally, people's expressed preferences, when assessed in a survey, are just that: expressions of tastes that must ultimately be reconciled with the competing tastes of others. If the unreconciled expressions of preferences of people were simply summed by planners, the aggregates would very often make no sense. Social philosopher and opponent of central planning Michael Polanyi stressed this particular information problem faced by planners with a chess analogy. Attempts by planners to aggregate consumer preferences at any point in time are

> as if the manager of a team of chess players were to go find out from each individual player what his next move was going to be and would then sum up the result by saying: "The plan of my team is to advance 45 pawns by one place, move 20 bishops by an average of three places, 15 castles by an average of four places, etc." He could pretend to have a plan for his team, but actually he would be only announcing a nonsensical summary of an aggregate of plans.[5]

After obtaining the aggregates on what people want, the planner would still know very little of people's private plans, for he would not know how people planned to react to the planning strategies of others.

Seventh, the planning problem is further complicated by the fact that the supply and demand envisioned by economists as lines on a graph don't really exist outside a competitive market process. Demand curves may be drawn with considerable care and precision in graphs; however, it should be understood that such curves are methodological devices, not descriptions of the real world as it might exist given specific central plans. The demand curve in Figure 5.2 represents the *maximum* prices (not just any set of prices) consumers are willing to pay for *given* quantities of a *given* good during a *particular* time in the market.[6] Consumers are not likely to pay these maximum prices unless they are forced by competition to do so. If they are really "maximizing consumers," they will pay as little as the competition will allow. Similarly, the supply curve represents the *minimum* prices producers will charge for a product before offering various quantities of it for sale, but few producers will turn away prices that are higher than their minimum.[7] They will accept the minimum prices only if they are required, by com-

[5]Michael Polanyi, *The Logic of Liberty* (Chicago: University of Chicago Press, 1951), p.134.

[6]The demand curve is actually a *boundary*, not a curve as such, between the price-quantity combinations acceptable (those below the demand curve) and unacceptable (those above the demand curve) to consumers.

[7]The supply curve is also a *boundary*, not a curve as such, between the price-quantity combinations acceptable (those above the supply curve) and unacceptable (those below the supply curve) to producers.

petitive forces, to do so.[8] If central planners wait and allow the markets to reveal what supply and demand are, the function of the planners will have been largely usurped. But planners trying to anticipate market supply and demand do not have access to the information they need to devise their plans, which are necessarily anticipations. Competition in the market process is necessary to get consumers and producers to move to their limits (i.e., to operate on their respective curves).

The moral of the story is very simple: contrary to the hopes and desires of planning proponents, planning cannot supplant the function of the market if, in fact, planning is designed to satisfy the needs and wants of the general public, as opposed to the planners. George Mason University economist Don Lavoie sums up the impossibility of effective central national planning by extending Polanyi's chess analogy:

> The possible moves available to a chess player in any particular context are finite and could be listed by anyone who knows the rules. The possible choices of an economic decisionmaker, by contrast, are unbounded. His inability to list all his options is due not only to their sheer number but also to the fact that complete surprises are possible. Even given an infinite amount of time, some possibilities might never occur to him. Under such conditions of radical uncertainty, the decisionmaker is forced all the more to rely on habitual modes of behavior established by a process of evolutionary selection in a profit and loss environment. His choices are not straightforward calculations. They are of necessity based on tacit hunches. Such hunches do play an important role in chess as well, but it is at least conceivable that chess could be played by examining every possible contingency and computing the best move. This possibility is not even remote in the case of economic decision-making.
>
> A more significant difference between decision-making in a chess team and in an economy is the fact that chess team players

[8]Economics instructors will typically explain the operation of the market by first drawing supply and demand curves and then explaining the logic by which market participants grope toward the intersection (or "equilibrium") price and quantity. It may be more accurate to teach, however, that portions of the supply and demand curves will be traced (or revealed) as the price moves toward equilibrium. The entirety of the curves will never be known, only those portions that extend from the initial price to the equilibrium price. The remaining parts of the curves are never revealed because consumers and producers are never faced with the prospect of operating in those price ranges.

are only rivals of single opposing players and need not coordinate their activities with one another. Each game can be viewed in isolation, and thus the combined intelligence of all the players on one team is only a function of their average intelligence. But in the case of economies the overall intelligence of the system is greatly enhanced by the process of mutual interaction—the method of adjustment of each participant to the signals supplied by his fellows. In other words, whereas for the chess team captain to plan his teammates' moves he need only know all of their strategies in each of the specific games, for the economic planner to direct the economy would require that he know all the individual decisionmakers' strategies and also that he know something none of them know: how their competitive pulling and tugging will affect one another's choices.[9]

Managed Capitalism (or Partial Planning)

Proponents of national industrial policies lament the association of their proposals with grand designs at national economic planning. To the claim that their proposals amount to central planning, proponents are likely to contend that they do not seek control of the entire economy. Indeed, "all" they advocate is strategic government intervention organized to accomplish two objectives. First, they want to minimize the adverse economic consequences of so-called market failures, distortions in the allocation of resources emanating primarily from monopolies and externalities. Government is perceived as the only potentially effective economic force capable of "countervailing" against the restrictive production practices of powerful monopolistic, multinational corporations. And government is needed to reduce environmental destruction caused by industrial polluters and to decrease the social damage that is wreaked when economic adjustments (plant closings and openings) occur in response to changes in consumer tastes, production technologies, and market competition.

Second, proponents want to "rationalize" and "coordinate" government industrial policies that are already on the books or will likely be put on the books in an ad hoc manner. Advocates of industrial policies stress that upwards of $100 billion worth of government benefits currently go annually to businesses through direct government loans and loan guarantees, grants, import protection,

[9]Don Lavoie, "National Industrial Policy: Son of Central Planning," Heritage Foundation Backgrounder (Washington, December 27, 1983), pp. 6–7.

and domestic market controls (for example, acreage allotments in agriculture and restrictions on entry into banking and insurance).[10] Businesses are constantly proposing new laws and tax rules that would affect the future competitiveness of U.S. industry. What we need, industrial policy proponents contend, is some means of making sense of the profusion of policies that are administered by a variety of government agencies and that are coordinated by no one or no central federal office. They suggest that, as opposed to proposing to plan the entire economy, they seek to "manage capitalism."

While appealing, the arguments for "managed capitalism" are seriously flawed. Proponents do not wish merely to plan a stable and general tax and policy climate within which businesses would be allowed to search out their own economic destinies. Rather, they intend for the federal government to intervene at the industry level, to "target" particular industries (iron and steel, automobiles, and textiles) for government aid, to help some industries emerge ("high-tech" is currently in vogue), and to ease the pain of failure encountered by other industries. Although they do not intend to plan the entire economy, they do intend to plan a sizable portion of it, possibly the basic industries, the sunset industries, and/or the sunrise industries. The information problem they would confront is, admittedly, not nearly as threatening under "managed capitalism" as it would be under a totally planned economy; still, the information that capitalism's managers would likely require to do their job effectively would be immense. The basic industries alone cover thousands of intermediate and final products on the markets and many more that do not now exist but will be developed in the future. These industries necessarily interact with other industries that may be deemed "less basic" and less in need of government guidance, and capitalism's managers cannot ignore the consequences their policies would have for all of the industries outside the realm of their initial policy charge. To adequately control and guide the targeted industries, capitalism's managers would necessarily have to consider planning much of the rest of the economy, which is a way of saying that the initial controls directed at targeted industries would spawn additional controls for other sectors of the economy, or that "managed capitalism" would be expected to give way gradually to progressively more inclusive planning.

---

[10]Congressional Budget Office, *Federal Support of U.S. Business* (Washington, 1984).

In fact, this control scenario, which is little more than a very brief recounting of a theme in Hayek's *Road to Serfdom*[11] written prophetically over four decades ago, is at the heart of industrial policy programs. Advocates have effectively argued, "We have many government controls; they are a mishmash, leading to unintended consequences; what is needed is more controls (in the form of production and investment subsidies and market restrictions) over more (industrial) sectors of the economy and more centralized control over the controls already in existence and those that will be legislated."

The automobile industry may be in trouble today, industrial policy advocates may contend, in part because of the growing competitiveness of the world automobile market. Auto executives, however, have sought protection from imports on the grounds that auto producers in other countries, in particular Japan, have a sizable cost advantage (up to $2,000 per car). One prominent reason they have a cost advantage is U.S. import restrictions on steel. These hike the cost of steel to domestic auto firms (because they either have to pay the tariffs on imported steel or pay for the more costly domestically produced steel, made even more expensive because of union wage demands) and lower the cost of steel to foreign auto firms (because the supply of steel to foreign auto manufacturers from low-cost foreign steel producers is greater than it would be in the absence of U.S. import controls on steel). Auto executives have, in effect, appealed for controls in the auto market because of controls in the steel market (as well as the textile and rubber markets).

The Politicization of the Industrial Policy Process

Industrial policy advocates seem to believe that national industrial goals and plans and specific industrial policies would be devised and administered in a politically neutral democratic environment. Of course, if they do acknowledge that politics would play a role in program formulation, advocates seem to believe that political factions would be neutralized and/or led to seek the public interest (which understandably would tend to coincide with the industrial policy agenda of the person making the argument).[12]

[11]F. A. Hayek, *The Road to Serfdom* (Chicago: University of Chicago Press, 1944).

[12]Few industrial policy advocates seem willing to imagine that the political process they propose to use to a greater extent would go off "half-cocked" and would orchestrate an industrial policy agenda at considerable odds with their recommended agenda.

118

The proposed government planning council, sometimes called the "Council of Industrial Competitiveness" or the "Council for Economic Development," would likely be nothing but political. Such a council would be composed of a relatively small number of people, perhaps 12, 15, or 20 men and women representing 3 very broad groups: business, labor, and government. As in the case of the RFC discussed in the preceding chapter, several of the "tripartite council" members could be administration appointees—for example, the secretary of the treasury, the secretary of commerce, the chairman of the Council of Economic Advisers, or the director of the Office of Management and Budget—but the others would come from the private sector and would likely reflect the political and economic power structure. The council would have considerable economic and political power, and those already holding substantial economic or political power would want to use their influence to make certain of appointment or election to the council. They would want to be members if for no other reason than to defend themselves against others who might, in their absence, take their place and use their position to further their own interests or the interests of their political constituencies. We might, therefore, expect the remaining council seats to go to the heads of the AFL-CIO, the U.S. Chamber of Commerce, the National Association of Manufacturers, and, possibly, the Consumers Union or the Audubon Society. Few proposals for tripartite councils make provisions for appointing ordinary citizens (non-leaders) or people who are not identified with any interest group. Ardent opponents of industrial policy would surely be excluded from membership, a fact that should cast doubts on the true *democratic* intentions of tripartite councils.

The important point to remember is that the appointed council representatives would have their own narrow interests, which they would think just as important, if not more so, than the causes promoted by others. Furthermore, we could expect all of them to hold and promote their positions with conviction and with limited capacity and desire to comprehend the special interests of others. Because the council would have to be relatively small for it to be workable, not all interest groups would be represented on it. This suggests that most groups would want to be represented in order to use their position to redistribute the nation's resources not to further the country's welfare, but to advance their own. One must wonder if the advocates of industrial policy agendas would be in favor of such necessarily discriminatory (or partial) planning if they found out beforehand that their particular interests would not be represented on the planning councils and that they would be the ones whose economic interests were sacrificed by council decrees promoting the economic interests of others. We must doubt that Chrysler's Lee Iacocca or AFL-CIO president Lane Kirkland would be in favor of industrial planning if they believed that such a policy would not lend political and financial support to "basic industries," defined to include the automobile industry.

Industrial policy proponents contend that the limited planning they envision would be contained by democratic rules and procedures, presumed to introduce an element of fairness into economic decisions, since everyone would have a vote. But that cannot be the case when the planning council is restricted to a few people who are incapable, because of their limited intelligence if not private interests, of understanding the interests of everyone else. It is also unlikely that the council would fully represent all political interests because democracy cannot very well represent all political interests, especially those of future generations not now existing and not having a vote. Planning council members might indeed, within bounds, take account of future economic effects of industrial policies adopted currently, but surely the interest groups of the future would have a more direct interest in the welfare of future generations. Emerging industries of the future would not likely be represented on the council simply because no one now knows what those emerging industries will be. We cannot know exactly what technological advances the future will hold or how consumer tastes will change or how workers will change their skills or locations, and we certainly know little of how people of the future will react to one another as all of the possible economic variables change over time.

In short, we simply have very little knowledge of what industries will achieve *comparative* (not absolute) cost advantages and will therefore become successes in the competitive process. Of course, many industrial policy advocates seek nothing less than to supplant the competitive market process with a political process. Such a position seems self-serving, a call for ensuring that their own economic and political interests are promoted by and through government.

Industrial policy advocates maintain that the country already has an industrial policy, one that is fragmented across a host of government agencies and that, as a result, leads to inconsistent and contradictory results. The Department of Agriculture seeks to protect and promote efficiency in the tobacco industry while the Surgeon General's office seeks to discourage smoking and production of cigarettes. The tax code attempts to encourage savings at the same time the Environmental Protection Agency and the Occupational Safety and Health Administration promulgate rules and regulations that increase the cost of doing business and reduce the rate of return on investment. Federal subsidies are provided to industries that, because of their limited capital requirements, have limited depreciation allowances and pay corporate income taxes at abnormally high rates. Surely, it is reasonable for government to improve the efficiency of its own operations by reconciling conflicting policies and eliminating federal rules and regulations that do little more than impose unnecessary costs on American industry. What seems equally unreasonable is that government policies have remained uncoordinated and unrationalized—though it would appear that such rationalization and coordination could be pursued without a federal industrial policy.

The point of the matter is that the distribution of government programs across agencies probably reflects political realities to a significant degree, that is, it already embodies the type of system sought by the various politically influential interest groups. There is no reason to believe that a Council of Industrial Competitiveness would accomplish anything more than could be accomplished in its absence, unless, of course, we allowed the council to supplant Congress, which would mean that we would have a new set of interests and representatives guiding public policies.

We should also be concerned that "rationalization" and "coordination" are nothing more than buzz words for more fundamental objectives, namely, more centralized federal control of the economy that translates into greater political and economic power for those interests represented on the council. In the absence of more evidence to the contrary, we cannot be sure that "rationalized" and "coordinated" government policies would necessarily lead to a welfare improvement, especially if the objective is one of expanded government intervention in the economy and is appended to policy programs designed to rationalize and coordinate government policies. The maze of government policies may not only become more "rationalized" and "coordinated," but also more complicated and more costly and ineffective through the creation of another council.

Concluding Comments

Proponents of "managed capitalism" appeal for reasonableness in the development of government policies. They tell us that the relevant policy choice facing our political leaders is not one of extremes—a totally planned economy vs. a completely free market. Harvard professor Robert Reich tells us that "this choice is falsely posed. In advanced industrial nations like the United States, drawing such sharp distinctions between government and the market has long ceased to exist."[13] While such a position is hardly contestable, it is clearly not correct to then infer that we should move to some middle ground of "managed capitalism" involving more government intervention in the economy. Few free market advocates have earnestly suggested that government be dispensed with, and the arguments presented here are not marshaled as an attempt to ensure that the federal government withdraw from the economy altogether. The government will always retain a judicial responsibility for the enforcement of contracts, the prevention of fraud, and the abatement of pollution (and of other problems relating to spillover costs and benefits). Rather, the arguments in this chapter seek only to show why a move toward "managed capitalism," with its appendage of tripartite planning councils, would likely be counterproductive as far as the nation's general welfare is concerned. Such a move, however, might very well serve the interests of the groups that would have a strategic role in managing the economy.

The critical point overlooked by advocates of industrial policy in the case for limited government is this: economic powers that are entrusted to government, advocated and adopted in the interest of pursuing national objectives, will tend to be usurped by politically powerful interest groups that would prefer to earn their living through the exercise of government's coercive powers than through the stresses of competitive markets. The case for limiting the powers of government is a case for limiting the economic powers of interest groups.

---

[13]Reich continues, "Government creates the market by defining the terms and boundaries of business activity, guided by public perceptions of governmental responsibility for the overall health of the economy. Business, meanwhile, is taking on tasks that once were the exclusive province of government. Robert Reich, *The Next American Frontier* (New York: Times Books, 1983), p. 5.

VI. Worker Rights to Their Jobs

Job security is at the core of the industrial policy debate. All of the discussion about capital mobility due to technological change or to the changing competitiveness of world markets and about the need to create new jobs by way of helping the emergence of sunrise (high-tech) industries or "easing the pain" of sunset (smokestack) industries is founded on the concern of workers and policymakers to enhance job security. Lester Thurow had job security in mind when he testified that "interest in industrial policy springs from a simple four-letter word—fear,"[1] and Robert Reich spoke to the concern of workers over job security when he suggested that what we need is a renewed economic system based on "equity, security, and participation," not on "greed and fear."[2]

In the interest of increasing the job security of workers, a number of bills have been proposed (several of which have been passed) that effectively restrict the right of employers to terminate their workers. Proposed plant closing laws, which incorporate requirements for prenotification of pending plant closings and mandate extensive severance pay, are innovative means of reducing the incentives, or increasing the disincentives, of firms to close their plants and terminate the jobs of their workers.[3] Many other proposed national industrial policies, ranging from added protection from imports to federal bailouts of firms, are modern means of reducing the fears of workers that their jobs will be pulled from underneath them. Through the creation of an "industrial (or economic) democracy" in which workers would have a say in management decisions, industrial policy advocates see a means of

---

[1]Lester C. Thurow, testimony prepared for the House Subcommittee on Economic Stabilization, June 14, 1983, p. 1.

[2]Robert Reich, *The Next American Frontier* (New York: Times Books, 1983), p. 14.

[3]For extended discussion of the types of plant closing restrictions proponents have in mind and their economic consequences, see Richard B. McKenzie, ed., *Plant Closings: Public or Private Choices?* rev. ed. (Washington: Cato Institute, 1984) and idem, *Fugitive Industry: The Economics and Politics of Deindustrialization* (San Francisco: Pacific Institute for Public Policy Research, 1984).

retarding capital mobility by tempering the controlling influence of the profit motive over firm owners. All these policies are means of providing workers with job security through the recognition of "job rights."[4]

Perspectives on Job Rights

Two closely related perspectives on worker job rights can be identified in industrial policy discussions. A first perspective is descriptive of what is presumed to be the state of the law, that is, the *actual* division of "rights" in employment between employers and workers. According to this view, workers actually *have*, by the fact of their employment, intrinsic "rights" to their "jobs." By continuing to work for a company, workers help create their jobs. Workers "invest" in their work and, accordingly, have "rights" to the fruits of their investment of labor, just as capitalists have "rights" to the returns on their investment of money in firms. In short, they "own," albeit in a restricted sense, their "jobs."

Industrial policy arguments suggest that these purported property rights are being abridged by the growing mobility of capital, as well as by a number of other economic and political forces such as the willful firing of employees and the reckless pursuit of profits by large corporations. The misalignment of economic strength between workers and employers is due largely to the relatively greater ability of capital over people to move across regional and national boundaries.[5] Government must assert its authority, argue job rights advocates, and protect the property rights of workers as vigorously as it protects investors' rights in firms' "assets," which include, among other things, physical and financial capital *and* a stock of jobs that yield benefits to workers, owners, and members of the broader community (if not the nation). This position on worker rights was aggressively expounded by the National Labor Relations Board in a decision on a firm's duty to bargain with its workers' union over the closing of a plant, a decision, incidentally, never appealed in the courts:

> With all respect to the Court of Appeals for the Third and Eighth Circuit, we do not believe that the question whether a particular

---

[4]The added firing costs implied in laws prohibiting racial, sexual, and age discrimination reflect, in part, the interest of legislators in raising worker security by reducing the incidence of firings and increasing, at least on average, the job tenure of workers. Such laws, however, are not the central concern of this chapter.

[5]See Reich.

124

management decision must be bargained about should turn on whether the decision involves the commitment of investment capital or on whether it may be characterized as involving [a] "major" or "basic" change in the nature of the employer's business. True it is that decisions of this nature are, by definition, of significance for the employer. It is equally true, however, and ought not to be lost sight of, that an employer's decisions to make a "major" change in the nature of his business, such as the termination of a portion thereof, is also of significance for those employees whose jobs will be lost by the termination. *For, just as the employer has invested capital in the business, so the employee has invested years of his working life, accumulating seniority, accruing pension rights, and developing skills that may or may not be salable to another employer. And, just as the employer's interest in the protection of his capital investment is entitled to consideration in our interpretation of the Act, so too is the employee's interest in the protection of his livelihood* [emphasis added].[6]

While the Supreme Court, as well as circuit courts, has shown a reluctance to adopt the NLRB's concept of job rights,[7] the NLRB's position is still widely accepted in public policy debates. The appeal industrial policy advocates make to the "justice" of restricting capital mobility is inspired, in part, by the belief that workers have justly acquired some forms of job security—some rights to their jobs that are legally similar, if not identical, to "property rights."

A second perspective on job rights is prescriptive, an assertion of the "rights" workers *should* have, if they do not already, de jure, have them. Proponents of this view may concede that our past economic system, presumably founded to a substantial degree on the goal of economic efficiency with little regard to the goals of equity and security, may have been highly desirable in the sense that it expanded the economic pie. However, they now are tempted to reason that the country has developed to the point that such goals as equity and security not only should, but can, take greater prominence in directing public policy. The authors of *Beyond the Waste Land: A Democratic Alternative to Economic Decline* contend, for example, that sustained economic recovery from the country's current economic malaise requires "new institutions, new laws, and

---

[6]*Ozark Trailers, Inc.*, 161 NLRB 561, 63 LRRM at 1267 (1966).
[7]See *First National Maintenance Corp.* v. *NLRB*, 452 U.S. 666, 107 LRRM 2705 (1981).

new ways of organizing the economy."[8] Such a new economic system must be founded on an "economic bill of rights" that, among other things, includes "rights to a decent job."[9] Greater job security mandates greater equality in the workplace, which necessitates a shifting of managerial rights to workers. Without such a shift of rights, workers and communities will remain vulnerable to the whims of managers who, because of their concern for profits, do not always have the workers' (or society's) interests at stake or at heart. Besides, contrary to what may be normally presumed by economists and policymakers, "democratic economists"—those economists who distinguish themselves from the "neoliberals," as well as from "supply siders" and "Keynesians," by their dedication to the application of democratic principles in the workplace and to policy councils[10]—contend that there is no necessary tradeoff between goals of efficiency (or production) and equity: "More democracy [in the workplace] does not have to mean more inefficiency and waste."[11] Stated somewhat differently, job rights *should* be assigned (or transferred) to workers simply because such an assignment can promote an expansion of the "social product." Job security, advanced by

[8]Samuel Bowles, David M. Gordon, and Thomas E. Weisskopf, *Beyond the Waste Land: A Democratic Alternative to Economic Decline* (Garden City, N.Y.: Doubleday, Anchor Press, 1983), p. 263.

[9]Ibid., p. 270. Although the word may have had a different meaning to him than to modern job rights advocates, Franklin Roosevelt used job rights phraseology in his 1944 State of the Union address: "We have come to a clear realization of the fact that true individual freedom cannot exist without economic security. . . . We have accepted, so to speak, a second bill of rights under which a new basis of security and prosperity can be established for all, regardless of station, race, or creed. Among these are: . . . The right to a useful and remunerative job in the industries or shops or farms or mines of the nation." Quoted in Martin Carnoy, Derek Shearer, and Russell Rumberger, *A New Social Contract: The Economy and Government After Reagan* (New York: Harper and Row, 1983), p. 228. The authors of this book adopt the philosophy of "economic democracy" and advocate "a right to a decent job for all those willing to work." Ibid., p. 231.

[10]"Democratic economists" are prone to dissociate their views from those of "neoliberals" because neoliberals are "fundamentally elitists": "They believe that in this technologically oriented world, 'experts' should make decisions for the mass of nonexperts. It is no accident that Gary Hart—product of the JFK era—should embrace the neoliberal technocracy. The early 1960s were the zenith of belief in technical solutions to social problems. . . . But experts have a way of making serious errors because of their distance from the political and economic consequences of their acts." Ibid., p. 155.

[11]Ibid., p. 264.

126

participation in workplace decisions and a sense of fairness in rewards from work, contributes to worker productivity and, thereby, to the "social product." To these policy reformers, job rights proposals should be considered in the same way that land reform proposals are supposedly assessed, namely, in terms of the extent to which they simultaneously support equity and efficiency goals.

Obviously, job rights advocates raise important social issues, not the least of which are the following: What exactly is meant by "job (property) rights"? Can the assignment or transfer of "job rights" to workers accomplish the objectives of their advocates? An understanding of these thorny issues is crucial to comprehending the industrial policy debate.

Jobs as Property

Although the phrase "job rights" is widely used, its meaning is not always clear, perhaps purposely so since ambiguity is not an unrecognized virtue in the politics of social policy.[12] Several interpretations of "job rights" have become entangled in policy discussions. On the one hand, "job rights" is meant to suggest the image of property and ownership of "jobs," just as "investment rights" suggests the image of ownership of physical capital. When it is said that a worker has a "right to his job," the phrase may mean that he in fact "owns" his job (a position that implicitly presumes a "job" actually can be "owned").

Such a conception of job rights reflects some confusion over the nature of a "job." Job rights advocates appear to believe that a "job" is something no less tangible than, say, a stock option and no less capable of being possessed from a legal standpoint than, say, a drill press. After all, people are hired into "positions"; workers "fill" positions, which are presumed to exist independently of the workers who are in them. The "position descriptions" that fill the files of corporate personnel offices suggest that a "job" can be given legal meaning in the same sense that a deed gives legal meaning to a lot that may be "owned." Certainly, professional football and basketball teams have clearly defined "jobs," and many of the players who hold such positions are treated on the teams' tax returns very much the same as the clubhouse: both the players and

---

[12]Factions within political coalitions may interpret "job rights" differently while assuming that their interpretation is shared by all other factions, a semblance of agreement that can break down when actual policies must be formulated and adopted.

127

the clubhouse (when "owned") are depreciated according to their estimated "useful" life.

However, there are clear conceptual distinctions between a "job" and a drill press. A drill press exists independently of what is done with it. A job is something that is always in the process of being done. A drill press can be owned without anything being done with it. It can, but doesn't have to, be employed. A job is, by definition, a state of employment. The rights of ownership in the drill press can be "owned" and protected without imposing obligations on its owner to use it or on any potential employer to actually provide employment, a job, for it. To own the drill press is not to "own" a right to a job for the drill press. "Ownership" of a job for the drill press either abridges the rights of a potential employer or, if the press owner and the press employer are the same person, abridges ownership rights, one of which is the right to use or not to use the drill press.

Similarly, to say that a worker has an ownership right in a job is the same as saying that the employer must supply the job in question: the employer has no choice in supplying identified jobs to identified "employee-owners" of the jobs. In short, the employee–job owner is given rights in use of assets by denying such rights to the employer–job supplier. The issue at stake is not altogether one of whether employees *should*, from some fairness perspective, be given job rights, although that issue is certainly important; rather, the issue involves also a fundamental principle of law, namely, the equal application of the law, which presumably assumes that everyone, regardless of his economic status as employee or employer, should be treated the same under the law.

The concept of job ownership is necessarily a discriminatory legal principle, one given to one class of workers, "employees," and, at the same time, denied to another class of workers, "employers," who also work, albeit at the task of employing other people.[13]

The points raised here are not, of course, intended to imply that job rights advocates would object to granting workers special privileges at the expense of their employers; however, the discriminatory implications of proposed job rights should certainly rob them

---

[13]This point was first made clear to me by Morgan O. Reynolds in "How Job Security Laws Destroy Jobs," Heritage Foundation Backgrounder (Washington, 1983), p. 4.

of much of their claim to being a clear-cut welfare improvement, one that helps one group without, at the same time, harming another.

Ownership of a "thing"—again, for example, a drill press—is conceptually different from ownership of a job. Usually, a "thing" is not, under our legal system, given the same status as people;[14] it does not have legal rights on par with the person who owns it; hence, ownership does not rob a "thing" of rights previously held. A "thing" does not have standing in court. A job, on the other hand, requires the participation of both an employee and employer, both of whom are equal legal entities. Requiring an employer to supply a worker with a job amounts to requiring another worker to supply someone else with a drill press or a building or a television *without agreement*. "Job ownership," in other words, has many of the attributes of slavery, and can be opposed for that reason alone, as well as for its internal inconsistency as a legal principle. The oddity in this case is that the employer is made the slave of the employee, who can make the employer do as the employee wants in providing work and payment.

Job rights advocates may object to this argument on the grounds that employers are capitalists, controlling resources that are vital to productive employment opportunities. Again, we must insist on legal consistency in policy proposals. Productive resources, capital, or even land, do not just "exist," but rather are brought together by capitalists who are necessarily workers in much the same sense that production employees are. In offering themselves for work, employees bring together a wide variety of skills incorporated in human and physical capital. And in order to acquire the skills in their possession, such employees may have had to employ a variety of educational resources, including other people who performed functions that were not terribly dissimilar to those performed by their capitalist employers. Again, it's very hard to understand how job ownership rights can be asserted for employees without violating the same rights for employers.

Even if we could agree that it is entirely possible, from a conceptual perspective, for workers to "own" their jobs, it is hard to imagine that workers would have job resale rights, that is, the legal authority to sell their "jobs" to someone else. The employer is

---

[14]The point is qualified with "usually" because some people seriously insist that "rocks do (or should) have rights" and "trees do (or should) have standing" in our legal system. For the time being, however, these points are largely of academic interest.

typically interested in having his or her jobs filled by *particular* people with *particular* talents, attitudes, and productivity levels. Indeed, the employer is probably an employer in part because he or she has a comparative advantage in supervising people and in obtaining from them a given quantity and quality of goods. If the employer's employees could sell their jobs, the employer would not then be taking advantage of his or her comparative advantage, and the employee, who presumably does not have a comparative advantage in supervision, would then become in effect an employer. If the employee were as effective at supervision as the employer, we would not expect the employee to remain an employee; we would expect him or her to become an employer in his or her own right through the creation of a productive enterprise (not through legislated job ownership rights).

Now, of course, firms in a sense sell "jobs" all the time. They subcontract their work. However, because the firm loses a great deal of control over workers hired in this way, the subcontract is usually specified in terms of so much product of a given quality and type. The subcontractors then become "employers," responsible for seeing that the jobs are filled. In a free society workers always have the option of becoming subcontractors, but in assuming that role they become residual claimants, not employees in the strict sense of the term. That is, they accept all the risks associated with supervising workers and meeting production schedules in exchange for the profits left after all expenses have been deducted from the negotiated sale price.

Jobs as Bundles of Exchanged Rights

A "job" may be best understood as the intersection of the interests of the employee (who seeks money income for output) and the employer (who seeks output for money income). The employment relationship is mutual, that is, the employee employs the employer at the same time the employer employs the employee.[15] The "job"

[15]This point was made by Armen Alchian: "The relationship of each team member to the *owner* of the firm (i.e., the party common to all input contracts *and* the residual claimant) is simply a 'quid pro quo' contract. Each makes a purchase and a sale. The employee 'orders' the owner of the team to pay him money in the same sense that the employer directs the team member to perform certain acts. The employee can terminate the contract as readily as can the employer, and the long-term contracts, therefore, are not an essential attribute of the firm. Nor are 'authoritarian,' 'dictatorial,' or 'fiat' attributes relevant to the conception of the firm or its efficiency." *Economic Forces at Work* (Indianapolis: Liberty Press, 1977), p. 85.

represents the mutually agreed-upon terms of the mutually beneficial employment relationship. The "job" is a contractual relationship, a specification of the things that each party will (and must) do for the other in order for the employment relationship to continue. The job is, insofar as it is legally binding, a specification of *exchanged rights*. Seen this way, the claim that a worker has rights to a job means that a worker has rights to the rights that are specified, explicitly or implicitly, in the employment contract. Few can object to such an interpretation. If workers do not have rights to receive what they have contracted for, then the employment contract is meaningless, and workers can become victims of what amounts to business theft. Such thefts cannot be condoned any more than the theft of a common mugger, and for essentially the same reasons. This interpretation of a "job" permits an equal application of the law, for the employee rights in the contract can be upheld without violating the rights of the employers.

Perhaps job rights advocates mean that there are certain rights that must be a part of every employment contract. Rights to tenure, to a specified notification of a plant closing, and to severance pay in the event a plant closes may be considered so important that they must be a part of every employment contract. This view of job rights raises an important but hidden concern. A job is actually a "bundle" of perhaps hundreds of rights—including such frequently cited categories of rights as current and future wages, fringe benefits, and work conditions, as well as severance pay and notification of plant closings. Assuming that workers seek the maximum "bundle" they can get at all times, the inclusion of one specified set of rights by legislation—say, severance pay and prenotification—must mean excluding or modifying other rights, for example, wages or fringe benefits.[16]

There is no reason to believe that the welfare of all workers would

[16]If severance pay and prenotification did not come at a cost to employers, we would expect such benefits to be offered workers by their employers. After all, such rights are presumed to benefit employees. Because of the costs imposed on employers by legislated rights, we would expect the demand for workers to fall. This is because the maximum amount employers would then be willing to pay workers would be reduced by the costs incurred in providing severance pay and prenotification benefits. Furthermore, to the extent that severance pay and prenotification were beneficial to workers, we would expect the supply of workers covered by job rights to increase. Both these market changes—the decrease in the demand for labor and the increase in the supply of labor—would suppress the wages or fringe benefits received by labor.

be improved by a mandated change in the bundle of rights. Whether or not worker welfare is improved would depend on the relative value of the governmentally mandated rights and of the rights that would be "pushed out" of the contract. Established government industrial policies may ensure that workers get severance pay in the event their jobs are terminated, but the cost of the severance pay would be imposed on workers in the form of lower wages or fringe benefits or something else that workers value. Workers in competitive markets will always tend to get competitive contracts in one form or another. There does not appear to be anything in job rights proposals per se that would change the overall competitiveness of labor markets.[17] Just because competition is thwarted by legislation with respect to one set of rights does not mean that competition has been fully suppressed.[18]

The Tradeoffs in Job Rights

Understanding the inevitable tradeoffs between legislated job rights and other job rights is important for three main reasons.

First, not all workers are the same or want the same things out of their work. Some workers may prefer severance pay to higher wages, but others will not. Legislated job rights can be opposed simply because they standardize the employment contract for all and, as a consequence, reduce both the flexibility in the terms of the contract and the opportunity of workers and employers to come up with innovative employment arrangements. Also, standardization of employment contracts reduces the ability of employers and employees to tailor their contracts to the particular desires and circumstances of individual worker groups.

Job rights advocates assume a sobering arrogance to think that they can speak intelligently on the issue of what should (and should not) be included in the employment contract for millions of workers whose employment circumstances they can hardly understand. Because of their ignorance of various employment circumstances, job rights advocates must rely on the only information at their

---

[17]It is interesting that job rights advocates usually combine job rights proposals with advocacy of greater unionization of labor markets.

[18]Job rights advocates fail to see the similarities between gas in a balloon and competition in labor markets. If a balloon is pinched, the pressure of the gas causes the balloon to expand elsewhere. If competition is suppressed in one dimension of the contract, it will be expressed in other dimensions.

disposal: what they themselves, not others, want. We should not be surprised to learn that the job rights advocated are often an expression of the private interests of their advocates.

Second, legislating job rights poses a threat of growing restrictions on employment contracts. When the specification of a given set of rights results in a reduction in other benefits, job rights advocates will likely believe that the solution is greater control of the employment contract, meaning more restrictions on what employees and employers can agree on, a process likely to spawn additional controls. Competition could eventually be suppressed with controls, and much individual worker freedom would be lost in the process.

Third, employment contracts can include many so-called job rights without government intervention. Employers can give workers the "right" to extensive prenotification of a pending plant closing and can provide for several years of severance pay as part of the labor contract, as long as workers are willing to pay the attendant costs in terms of reductions in the value of other rights such as wages and retirement benefits. If workers are willing to make the sacrifice necessary to cover the cost of notification and severance benefits, there is no reason why "profit-hungry capitalists" should be hesitant to make the trade.

The Market for Job Rights

A variety of "job rights" have in fact been obtained by labor through contract negotiation. According to one sample survey of union contracts, 36 percent of union contracts settled between 1980 and 1981 contained provisions that restricted plant movements.[19] Also, unions have begun to negotiate minimum employment guarantees to reduce the risk of worker layoffs and income disruptions; in exchange, however, they have had to give up work rules that have in the past reduced the flexibility of management to shift workers between various production assignments.[20] At a Ford plant in Rawsonville, Michigan, over 2,500 workers were guaranteed a minimum of 32 hours of work per week through September 1987.

[19]B. R. Skelton, "Plant Closings and Labor Law" (Clemson, S.C.: Clemson University Economics Department, 1982), ms.

[20]For a brief review of recent efforts of workers to obtain job security through contract means, see "Unions' Latest Goal: A Job for Life," *U.S. News and World Report*, May 21, 1984, pp. 74–75.

At a GM plant in Warren, Ohio, more than 6,700 workers are on the "protected list," meaning that they cannot be laid off for more than six weeks during the term of their contracts. Presumably, both parties to these agreements gained: the workers gained income security, and management achieved greater ability to respond to changes in product market forces.

Not all workers, however, have accepted employment protection proposals. Ford workers in Chicago turned down job protection because they did not want to give up work rules that restrict management from shifting plant workers from one job to another. The fact that few employers ("fewer than 100 of the nation's major employers")[21] have "strategies to stabilize employment" reflects, in part, the newness of job security as a top priority of labor. But it also supports the contention that not all workers want the same bundle of rights and that for many worker groups the costs to employers of greater job security, which must be covered ultimately by workers, are at times greater than the value workers attribute to specified job rights.

The point here is not that workers do not place a value on job rights; the attention workers and their unions have given the subject over the past several years does indeed indicate that workers may place a significant value on such rights. It is to say, however, that when attainable plant closing rights (or any other job rights) are not secured voluntarily, legislated job rights effectively require labor to accept a "bad" bargain, meaning a contract that forces workers to give up rights to wages and other job benefits that they themselves might view as more valuable than the prescribed closing (or any other job) rights. Such government intervention in labor negotiations would be on par with the government requiring consumers to buy cars they had considered but rejected as not worth the price. In effect, government would be saying to workers, "We know you prefer higher wages or more medical insurance to job security, but you are wrong; we will force you to buy what we know is best."

Job rights proponents may counter by stressing that such job rights as closing rights apply to all workers and that individual (especially nonunion) workers do not have the necessary bargaining power and incentive to negotiate for job rights that benefit all workers. The contention is, in economists' jargon, that closing rights are a "public good," the benefits of which must necessarily

[21]Ibid., p. 74.

134

be shared by all workers regardless of whether they work to secure them. Because each worker may benefit in only a minor way but some may have to incur significant personal costs to campaign for closing rights, all workers may "free ride," that is, do nothing to obtain them. Hence, even though closing rights may be valued collectively by workers at more than the required costs, they will still not be provided (or they will be obtained at inadequate levels).

Those who use this argument fail to realize that employers have provided many work-related benefits, from air conditioning to health policies, that simultaneously apply to all workers and that employers do have a market incentive to provide closing benefits *if their workers' collective valuation of closing rights is greater than their valuation of the costs.* An employer can simply change the bundle of employment rights to include closing rights. If workers truly value those rights at more than their costs, more workers will seek work with that employer, and the closing benefits will be self-financing through downward adjustments in the market wage (or other benefits). The employer who makes the terms of employment more favorable to labor and who ensures that any included closing rights are self-financed will face lower overall production costs (even though workers would be getting, on balance, more benefits from their employment). Firms with lower costs should be able to underprice their competition in the product market, a result that should induce other employers to change the bundle of rights in their own labor contracts.

Our purpose here is not to contend that government has no role in protecting workers. On the contrary, we have stressed that government must play a central role in the protection of contracts of all kinds. The problem of plant closings can include the absence of sufficient information on, for example, a company's closing policy; in other words, workers may have an unclear or incomplete understanding of what their contract really is—what their rights actually are—with respect to plant closings. In addition, one can imagine that workers are often misled by their employers on the company's closing policy. A company may suggest that it will provide prenotification of plant closings of, say, six months, and because of this implied commitment, workers may accept lower wages. If nothing is written out, however, the "contract" may not be legally binding and the firm may move away or close without compensating workers for wages forgone in anticipation of a prenotification period. One solution to the information problem (both for the courts and for workers) would be to legislate a standardized prenotification period, which has been proposed by former vice president Walter Mondale, consumer advocate Ralph Nader, and Michigan congressman William Ford.[22] Another solution would simply be to say that the workaday world is tough and that workers should have realized that and gotten a legally binding commitment on the company's plant closing policy.[23]

Alternately, those who argue that workers lack information on their firms' closing policies should, through their own private channels (which they have used extensively in the debate over closing restrictions), alert workers to the current state of the law, which is that unless a firm has explicitly or implicitly stated its policy to the contrary, it has the right to close plants more or less on a moment's notice.[24] Workers could then adjust their wage demands accordingly, forcing firms to compensate employees for the risk of losing their jobs to the closing judgments of management. The high wage bills that firms might have to incur would be an economic incentive for them to announce closing policies that were in accord with worker preferences, that is, with the wage and fringe benefit concessions workers might be willing to make.

Assuming that workers actually benefit from prenotification, we would expect prenotification periods to be paid off through lower wages. Indeed, we would not expect firms to announce closing policies that do not pay for themselves. Rather, we would expect them to extend the prenotification period (or severance pay, or any other right) up to the point that the additional cost of extending it was no longer lower than the wage concessions workers were willing to make for an extension. Again, we return to the simple point that workers bear costs for the rights they obtain and that such costs are precisely what must ultimately constrain worker demands and force an appropriate (efficient) allocation of worker talents.

Those who object to the competitive labor market process because

[22]For a review of plant closing restrictions, see McKenzie, *Fugitive Industry.*

[23]One might reasonably argue that since the plant closing policy was not spelled out in legally binding terms, the workers assessed the probability that their firm would not live up to its unwritten commitment and built into their wages a risk premium. However, such an argument sidesteps the premise that workers were misled and that misinformation or disinformation can distort the allocation of resources.

[24]This proposal is explained in greater detail in Richard B. McKenzie, *National Industrial Policies: Commentaries in Dissent* (Dallas: Fisher Institute, 1984), pp. 31–34.

labor has to bear the cost of achieving more favorable labor contracts are imbued with the delusion that the fabled "free lunch" actually does exist and can be had, if only government would mandate it. If only the world would operate on the "free lunch" principle, we could and would boost social welfare by government decree, which may be what is actually being attempted in the campaign for job rights.

Opponents and proponents of industrial policies share the important social goal of expanding job opportunities for workers. They differ, however, over the expected consequences of proposed policies. The most fundamental objection to legislated job rights is that they would likely decrease employment opportunities, an outcome that would make both employers and employees less well off. As long as legislated job rights have to be imposed on labor market participants, we must presume, as explained above, that the costs of such rights exceed the benefits, as laborers evaluate the costs and benefits. The excess of costs over benefits would likely be shared by employers *and* employees.[25] The extra costs imposed on the employer would reduce incentives to produce the types of jobs workers want; similarly, the extra costs imposed on workers would reduce workers' incentives to offer themselves for employment. Both employers and employees would be forced to accept second-best uses of their time, which means that there would be fewer jobs covered by the legislated job rights.[26]

Labor Markets and Worker Skills

The lesson of the foregoing sections is not that workers do not have rights in their jobs. Indeed, employment constitutes an exchange of rights: workers agree to perform certain services or tasks in exchange for various forms of compensation and other work-related benefits. Employment is a contract, and the rights that are exchanged should be as enforceable as the rights in any other contract. If a worker performs the required services and his employer balks at providing compensation, the worker has the "right" to seek a remedy through the courts for nonpayment of compensation and for

---

[25]How the excess costs would be split is not important here; all that is important is recognition of the excess costs and the likely splitting of them.

[26]How many such jobs would be destroyed depends, of course, on the job rights that were mandated, on the degree that their costs exceeded their benefits, and on exactly how responsive the supply of jobs was.

the legal expenses incurred. If a worker "invests" in his job by spending personal funds to upgrade his skills because his employer has agreed to pay higher wages in return, but the additional compensation is not forthcoming, the worker again, under normal contract law, has rights to a remedy. If an employer announces a plant closing policy, setting out the severance pay and prenotification benefits, and workers accept lower wages and fringe benefits in return, contract law again dictates that the worker has a legal right to redress in the event that his employer fails to provide the stated severance pay or to give the necessary prenotification of the plant closing.

Granted, rights established through contracts are never absolute. Many contracts are unenforceable because they are unclear, unwritten, or lack specificity as to what rights have actually been exchanged. A party to a labor contract can never be certain that the other party will not claim rights that have not been clearly included in the contract. There is, for example, some probability that the courts would accept the argument that an employer has by his actions and statements committed him or herself to a plant closing prenotification policy that was never spelled out in the labor contract or in the personnel policy manuals of the company. Labor contracts may also remain unenforced because of the legal expense involved (and the limited benefits to be gained by legal action) and because one party is incapable of meeting the terms of the contract. A firm that goes bankrupt with little in the way of cash reserves and salable assets in excess of its debts may not be in a position to meet the established severance pay and prenotification requirements of its labor contract. Like creditors, workers must accept the inescapable risk inherent in their contracts. Nevertheless, just as we would expect a creditor to scale the interest return required on a loan to the risk of a firm's failure, we would expect workers to be compensated for the risks inherent in their contracts. The more risks the employee must assume, with everything else constant, the greater the wage compensation should be. If an employer fails to compensate workers for necessary risks, then we can expect those workers to move elsewhere in a competitive labor market.

It needs to be stressed here that labor market risks are not, because of risk compensation, always intentionally avoided by workers. Workers may willingly accept risky jobs, in terms of both job tenure and exposure to hazards, simply because of the wage premium for doing so. To eliminate all risks could, as a consequence, make some workers worse off because they would then have to give up the risk premium in their wages.

In passing, note that the employer must also accept the risk that the employee will not live up to his or her end of the labor contract. The employee might not provide the requisite amount and quality of work and might quit without giving the required notification of his or her resignation. The labor contract is, to a large extent, an exchange of risks as well as rights.

Worker Protection

Contrary to what may be presumed by many industrial policy advocates, markets do afford workers opportunities for protection from employers who default on their contracts. As mentioned, the wages paid can include a risk premium to account for unreliable employment records. If a worker invests in skills that are useful to many firms and is then terminated by one employer, he is protected in that he can still be compensated for his investment by securing a comparable competitive wage in other firms. The worker's investment, in other words, should be self-financing through higher wage rates. Indeed, generally speaking, we would not expect a worker to undertake investment in his skills unless he achieved some degree of self-satisfaction from having greater skills and/or unless that investment were self-financing.

Skill requirements for a particular job in a particular firm are often unique to the job and the firm. Workers who invest their own money and time in acquiring such skills assume a substantial risk that their employers might renege on any contractual agreement to compensate them, through higher wages, for their investment. Employees who make such an investment and whose employers do renege have no opportunity to use those skills and are unable, therefore, to secure compensation for them. But workers should still be able to protect themselves in two ways. First, they could simply refuse to take jobs requiring further training unless their employers agreed to finance the job-related investment, a typical solution. Second, workers should be able to prove in court that their skills were unique to their employment and that they would not have undertaken the necessary investment unless there had been a commitment, albeit implied, by the employer to finance it over time through higher wages. Those who lament that such protections are imperfect are simply acknowledging the nature of the economic world in which we live.

Market Uncertainty and Rights

"Job rights" is an appealing concept. Most of us are workers, and we all would like to have "rights" that give protection from disruptions in our employment and incomes. However, economic protections come at a cost, sometimes a very high cost, because we live in a risky and uncertain world where we can only very imperfectly predict the future. We have only a primitive understanding of what other people want, of how their wants will change, and of how others will respond to changes in people's wants. Our problem not knowing the future is further complicated for most of us, who have only a primitive knowledge of how existing inventions, such as the integrated circuit, will be applied to products already on the market, much less to products still on the drawing board. We know even less about what new inventions might emerge in the future. Both risk, which can be evaluated in probabilistic terms and insured against, and uncertainty, which cannot be calculated and cannot be insured against, spell miscalculations of future events and necessarily translate into economic losses. (Otherwise we would be able to accurately calculate future events and there would be, by definition, no risk or uncertainty.) It would be very nice to wish away the economic losses that stem from risk and uncertainty, but that is not possible. UCLA economist Armen Alchian reminds us that

> the search for "protection from welfare losses" in an uncertain world is like the search for perpetual motion or the fountain of youth. Uncertainty, by definition, reduces welfare compared to what it would be with less uncertainty. No one can escape that. The pertinent issue is "who is to bear the welfare losses I suffer because of uncertainty, not all of which need have been so great, nor as significant, had I in anticipation altered my investments so as to be less affected by the uncertain materializations?"[27]

"Job rights" is a seductively simple means of absolving workers of losses that stem from an uncertain world. Alchian raises a complication that should not be ignored. In effect, he asks, "If it could be achieved by way of legislated job rights, would we want to completely or even partially protect workers in an uncertain world?" If the economic losses caused by uncertainty were a given, meaning

---

[27]Armen Alchian, "Comments on Eirik Furubotn's 'Rights to Jobs,' " paper presented at a symposium sponsored by the Liberty Fund (Washington: March 15–17, 1984), p. 6.

unchangeable and unchanged by worker decisions, then no inefficiency would result from legislated job rights. Welfare losses due to miscalculations and misjudgments would be the same regardless of what workers did. However, welfare losses are to a degree, at least, a consequence of the amount of information and insurance that people, workers included, acquire. If we simply absolved workers of any loss that stemmed from a failure to acquire information and insurance, then we could be confident that they would acquire little of either. Why pay for information if no costs are to be borne for failing to buy it? The net effect of such a rights structure would be for welfare losses to expand. On balance, workers could be worse off through legislated protection than they would be if required to negotiate the protection they might want. In the final analysis, workers cannot be fully protected from welfare losses, even if they are given "secure job rights"; they would lose through contraction in the economic pie, net of welfare losses and freedom dilution.

Concluding Comments

Proponents of job rights may not be swayed by a number of the arguments marshaled here. They may see nothing wrong with affording legal rights to one largely arbitrary group of people, "workers," and at the same time denying those rights to another largely arbitrary group of people, "employers" (or "owners"). After all, job rights proponents do not always speak kindly about "employers," who are viewed as the agents of "capitalists." Job rights advocates may not care about the consequences of a discriminatory application of rights. Consistency in the application of the law and equality before the law may likewise be of little interest to them. However, they should be disturbed by another consideration: legislated job rights can reduce job opportunities and the effective welfare of workers, the people whom job rights advocates seek to protect.

VII. Capital Taxation and Industrial Policy

The national industrial policy debate has focused public policy discussion on the growing mobility of capital, the obverse of which is the growing inability of unions to extract wages and of governments, especially local governments, to tax capital. Barry Bluestone and Bennett Harrison pose the emerging dilemma faced by the threat of growing capital mobility:

> Management found [in the 1970s] that it could no longer afford the social contract and maintain its accustomed level of profit. Instead of accepting the new realities of the world marketplace, one firm after another began to contemplate fresh ways to circumvent union rules and to hold the line on wages. Of course, labor was not initially ready to concede its hard-won victories; therefore, to accomplish its goal of reasserting its authority, management had to find some mechanism for disarming organized labor of its standard weapons: the grievance process, various job actions, and work stoppages. The solution was capital mobility. . . .
>
> The capital mobility strategy is not merely aimed at organized labor. The newly enhanced ability to move capital between regions within the same country provides corporate management with the necessary economic and political clout to insist upon reductions in local taxation, and therefore cuts in community services and the social safety net.[1]

An important purpose of this chapter is to explain why and how many industrial policy proposals—such as protectionism, plant closing restrictions, and so-called unitary tax systems—would slow down the mobility of capital and lead to higher tax rates. Of course, this is very likely what is intended. The net effect of such policies, if ever enacted as a part of an industrial policy agenda, would be a tendency for government to "exploit" the capital base, which means

---

[1]Barry Bluestone and Bennett Harrison, *The Deindustrialization of America: Plant Closings, Community Abandonment, and the Dismantling of Basic Industries* (New York: Basic Books, 1982), pp. 17, 18.

charging tax rates that are "too high" to maximize *long-run* tax revenues as well as the long-run growth rate of the economy.

The central lesson of this chapter is that capital taxation offers government (and its constituencies) the opportunity to increase current consumption by draining the capital base of its income-generating potential (without making provision for renewal) and, accordingly, shifting the tax burden to future generations through reduced capital stock and income flows. Many proposed industrial policies can thus be seen as disguised methods of capital taxation. In order to see these points, however, we must first review elemental points on the proclivity of government to "over-tax" the capital base.

The Tendency toward Excessive Capital Taxation

A common presumption in discussions of tax policies is that government is intent upon acquiring only so much revenue, perhaps only enough to finance a given set of public goods and services. This is a presumption, in other words, that government does not act to extract all the revenue it can. In such a case, government could be expected to choose the tax base that minimized the extent to which tax rates distorted the allocation of resources, and we would not want to restrict its tax base. Indeed, we would want to give the government total flexibility in choosing its tax base, for the definition of the tax base would not, by assumption, affect the amount of taxes collected; flexibility in defining the tax base could only reduce inefficiency in the taxes collected.

Suppose, however, that government were viewed as a revenue maximizer, a "Leviathan," Thomas Hobbes's characterization of government in a model now being reconsidered by public finance theorists. That is to say, what if government tried to collect all the taxes it could? Indeed, such a revenue-maximizing government, constitutionally unconstrained in its revenue sources aside from restrictions imposed by the rules of democracy, could be expected to seek capital as an important source of taxation.

This point has been developed in detail and with considerable precision by public choice economists James Buchanan and Dwight Lee.[2] The key to their argument is the distinction between long- and short-run desires for income (as opposed to leisure or other

[2]James M. Buchanan and Dwight R. Lee, "Politics, Time, and the Laffer Curve," *Journal of Political Economy* 90, no. 4 (1982): 816–19.

commodities). The short-run demand for income is more inelastic (i.e., unresponsive) with respect to tax rates than are long-run demands. This is because the human or physical capital stock held by taxpayers cannot be immediately altered when tax rates are either raised or reduced. It takes time to increase the capital stock in response to a tax rate reduction, and there is no necessary reason for the capital stock to be reduced at a rate faster than its natural depreciation rate in response to a tax rate increase. Workers who are paid for the "sweat of their brow" can, however, alter the number of hours worked with relative ease if taxes on labor income are increased.

This distinction between the long- and short-run demands for income by taxpayers is important because of the institutional constraints of competitive politics that force politicians to devise tax policies in the short run with an eye to being elected or reelected in the short run, say, in two, four, or at most six years. Current tax rate increases may lower the capital stock and the revenue received by government; similarly, current tax rate reductions may lead to an increase in the capital stock, along with an increase in government revenues. However, it needs to be stressed that the effects of capital taxation on the capital stock, national income, and tax revenues are realized in the long run; and many politicians can understandably reason that many of these effects will not be realized until some time after their tenure in office.

For that matter, voting for policy courses directed toward maximizing future income and future tax revenues can shorten a politician's political career. Politicians who vote for tax rate reductions, argue Buchanan and Lee, might be charged with fiscal irresponsibility, as were supporters of Reagan's 1981 three-year tax cut package, since tax rate reductions translate in the short run to lower tax revenues and higher budget deficits. They might also be caricatured as lacking a social conscience for their focus on the long-run, rather than short-run, health of the economy. Such politicians might, for instance, oppose current tax rate increases that could generate tax revenues needed to finance current welfare programs.

In other words, politicians interested in maximizing government benefits going to their constituencies will choose tax rates that may maximize short-run tax revenues but hold long-run tax revenues below the maximum level possible. This is, again, because taxpayers' short-run demand for income is more inelastic than their long-run demand. The capital stock, which is responsible for a growing

145

portion of people's incomes in industrial societies, cannot be changed very readily in the short-run in response to tax rate changes.

These points can be explained more carefully with the use of examples and graphs. The revenue received by the government is necessarily related to the tax rate and the amount of income earned. However, because the income earned is inversely dependent on the tax rate, total tax collections can rise or fall, depending upon the relative magnitudes of the tax rate and income changes. For example, a 10 percent tax rate applied to an income base of $10 billion yields total tax revenue of $1 billion (.10 × $10 billion); if the tax rate is raised to 20 percent and the income earned falls to $8 billion (which describes the inverse relationship between tax rates and collections pictured in the downward-sloping demand curve in Figure 7.1), total tax revenues rise to $1.6 billion (.20 × $8 billion). However, total tax revenues would fall if the income earned fell to $4 billion when the tax rate was increased to 20 percent. Again, total tax collections may rise or fall, given the same tax rate change; it all depends upon the extent to which people respond to that change.

For example, consider the income demand curve in Figure 7.1,

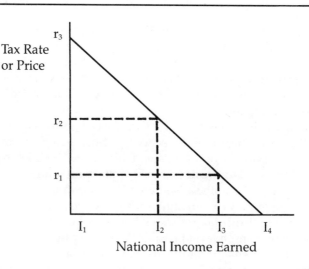

Figure 7.1

INCOME DEMAND CURVE

which relates the amount of income earned (demanded) to the tax-price, stated as a percentage. Such a downward-sloping curve is based on the intuitively plausible and empirically supported assumption that a lower tax rate will induce people to work harder and save and invest more to obtain more earned income. After all, the after-tax reward is greater as the tax rate falls. At a tax rate of zero in Figure 7.1, taxpayers may earn a lot of income (I_4), but the government gets no revenue ($0 \times I_4 = 0$). However, if the tax rate is raised to r_1, income may fall, but a tax rate of r_1 times the income level of I_3 yields total tax collections above zero. If the tax rate is raised above r_1, the total tax collections of government may, for a while, rise. At some point, on the other hand, we know that total tax collections must fall. This is because at a tax rate of r_3 (the point at which the income demand curve intersects the vertical axis of Figure 7.1), total tax collections again fall to zero ($r_3 \times 0 = 0$).

In short, a plotting of all tax revenue levels against all tax rates will yield a curve that looks like the one in Figure 7.2, a curve that is popularly known as the "Laffer curve." All this curve does is describe the normal, expected relationship between tax rates and tax collections deduced from the highly plausible proposition that taxpayers will earn more income at low tax rates than at high ones.

Figure 7.2

LAFFER CURVE

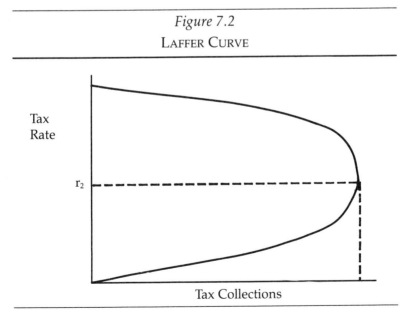

Tax Rate

r_2

Tax Collections

The peak of the Laffer curve in Figure 7.2 occurs at a tax rate of r_2, which is the tax rate in the middle of the income demand curve in Figure 7.1.[3]

Because it is derived from demand curve analysis, few economists dispute the *general* shape of the Laffer curve. What has caused a great deal of controversy, however, is the argument made by "supply-side" economists that a reduction in tax rates will necessarily lead to more (not less or the same level of) tax revenues. In other words, supply-siders claim that government is on the upper half of the Laffer curve. The credibility of supply-side theory became suspect when supply-siders were unable initially to explain why this would necessarily be true for the economies of California and Massachusetts, where the first supply-side tax battles were fought, much less for the whole United States.

On the surface, it appears silly for government to be on the upper half of the Laffer curve. At such "high" tax rates, taxpayers earn less income and enjoy life less than at lower rates. Politicians, who must vote on tax rates, must suffer the consequences of a dissatisfied electorate, and the government has less money than it could have to spend on its constituencies. Fortunately, Buchanan and Lee have devised a theory of politics that may explain why the political process results in tax rates that are "too high," meaning above the point where the Laffer curve starts to bend backward. Their theory is founded on the distinction between the long-run and short-run demands for income.

To understand their explanation consider Figure 7.3, in which the representative taxpayer's *long-run* demand curve for income with respect to tax rates is the more elastic (or flatter) curve labeled D_{lr}.[4] That curve indicates that if tax rates are adjusted downward, taxpayers will demand more future income through greater investment. In the long run investors have enough time to reduce their capital stock in response to a tax increase, and vice versa. Given the long-run demand curve D_{lr} in Figure 7.3, long-run revenue is maximized at a tax rate of r_1 (which, because the curves are linear

[3]Why the Laffer curve starts bending backward at the midpoint of the straight-line income demand curve requires a mathematical digression that would unnecessarily complicate our discussion. See Buchanan and Lee.

[4]Following Buchanan and Lee, I assume, for expository reasons, that the optimum tax level is unaffected by the cost of government goods and services. Such an assumption does not disturb the central conclusion of their analysis, which is that governments will tend to "overtax."

148

Figure 7.3
LONG-RUN DEMAND CURVE

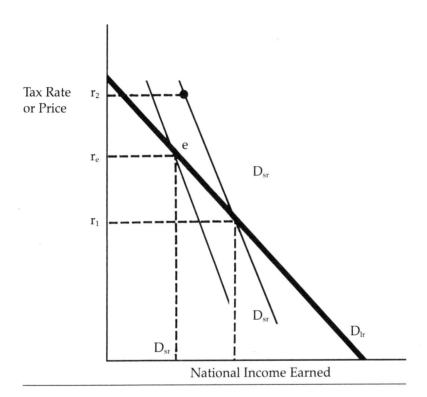

for purposes of illustation, is necessarily the midpoint of D_{lr}). However, if the short-run demand curve is more inelastic, because of the taxpayer's inability to readily adjust his capital stock, then there is a short-run demand curve (D_{sr}) that cuts the long-run demand curve (D_{lr}) at its midpoint. The midpoint of this short-run demand curve is up and to the left of the midpoint of the long-run curve. Short-run tax collections are maximized at the midpoint of the short-run demand curve, at a tax rate of r_2, not r_1.

Over the long run, however, tax revenues will not remain at the maximum at a rate of r_2. This is because a tax rate of r_2 will discourage saving and investment in the long run. The capital stock will, therefore, contract in response to r_2, reducing the ability of future

149

generations to earn income. The short-run income demand curve in the future will, as a consequence, shift inward, reflecting the reduced capital stock. Politicians with a short-run political perspective will still, however, attempt to maximize short-run government revenues and will move the tax rate to the midpoint of the then short-run income demand curve, a move that should lower tax rates since the midpoint of a demand curve closer to the origin is at a lower tax rate.

Ultimately, the tax rate will be adjusted (and the capital stock will adjust to the tax rate) until the midpoint of the short-run income demand curve lies on the long-run income demand curve. At that tax rate the capital stock will be stable. Accordingly, the income level will be stable. This stable or "equilibrium" tax rate occurs at r_e in Figure 7.3. It is at the turning point of the short-run Laffer curve (since it is at the midpoint of the short-run income demand curve), but it is at a point above the turning point of the long-run Laffer curve. (Notice that r_e is above the midpoint of the long-run income demand curve, which is where the turning point of the long-run Laffer curve occurs. The midpoint of the short-run, more inelastic income demand curve will necessarily lie up and to the left of the long-run, more elastic income demand curve.)

The central point of the Buchanan/Lee model of a shortsighted political process is that politicians have a tendency to vote for tax rates that tend to be on the upper half of the long-run Laffer curve— that tend to hold tax collections below the long-run maximum that could be achieved.

Buchanan/Lee's argument is developed in terms of income taxation and the residual effects of such taxation on the capital stock. Their argument would appear to be all the stronger if, or when, government has the authority to tax capital directly. Shortsighted politicians would then have an incentive to exploit the immobility of capital and drain away future income.

Embedded in the mechanics of the Buchanan/Lee analysis is a case for restricting, by constitutional means, the ability of government to tax capital, which is to say that the institutional framework within which capital taxation is permitted should be made congruent with the productive life of capital assets. Such congruency between political time horizons and the productive life of capital assets may dictate a prohibition of capital taxation. Barring such a stringent restriction, congruency may mean that capital taxation should be permitted only by local governments constrained by the forces of other, competing local governments in the tax rates that can be imposed. Clearly, the Buchanan/Lee perspective suggests that the case for constitutional restrictions on capital taxation is stronger than that for such restrictions on income taxation.

Capital taxation, either directly or indirectly, inevitably poses a problem for policymakers. Unless the tax revenues are used for equally productive public capital projects, capital taxation transfers the burden of current government programs from the present to future generations. Greater consumption in the current time period is made possible by a diversion of resources away from capital formation and by the consequent reduction in income flow in future time periods.

Because of the cumulative effects of capital taxation on the size of the capital stock available in future time periods, a tax rate reduction on capital will at some point necessarily increase future income sufficiently to increase future tax revenues. However, the inherent political problem is that of ensuring that the political process will allow capital tax rates to be set so that long-run revenues may be maximized.

Constitutional restrictions on capital taxation, or social norms that restrict the appetite of political leaders to impose capital taxes, may be necessary, but such restrictions could be expected to weaken with the passage of time. This is because as the capital stock grows over time in response to zero or constitutionally restricted tax rates, the temptation to tax capital can grow. With growth in the capital stock there is simply more for the voting population to extort from future generations. Even Marx praised capitalism, an economy with little government intervention, for its ability to build a capital stock that would become so huge at some point that the communist state, where people would be taxed according to their abilities and subsidized according to their needs, would be feasible.

Interest in capital taxation has been partially a product of social attitudes not present in the past, attitudes that seek greater goods and services produced by government. Recent attitudes can be linked to shifts in taxpayer tastes, increases in consumer income, and expansions in the population, all of which have led to an increase in demand for publicly delivered goods and services. However, such factors are not the whole story. There is more capital now than in the past; the temptation to tax capital has simply been greater of late. In addition, past generations of citizens were simply prohibited by constitutional means and social norms from expanding government intervention in the economy.[5] The breakdown of constitutional barriers to expanded government has effectively given recent generations of voters greater freedom to tax the capital stock—and to force future generations to share the cost of their consumption. Greater reliance on a democratic process unconstrained by fiscal restrictions is apt to reduce the growth of the capital stock.

The Democratic Bias against Capital

Advocates of expanded taxation often contend that decisions regarding taxes should be left to the democratic policy process. After all, democracy is a "fair" political game in the sense that everyone—through the power of the vote—is given equal standing in the political process. Therefore, to the extent that the political setting in which such decisions are made is "fair," tax rates higher than the turning point of the long-run Laffer curve may be deemed "just."

On the surface this philosophical position may appear to be supported, at least to a limited degree, by the work of Harvard philosopher John Rawls, who contends that behind the "veil of ignorance," a methodological device that effectively cuts people off from information on their absolute and relative social and economic status, people would choose to give everyone an equal vote on such social policies as taxation.[6] As Richard Wagner, a Florida State University economist, has stressed, however, real-world democracies do not meet the stringent fairness tests set forth by Rawls.[7] People in the real world, out from behind the veil of ignorance, know their positions in life (they know, for example, that they exist in the current generation) and will vote their interests, a fact that robs democracy of much of its ethical claim, especially with regard to transfer policies, which tend to dampen incentives to save and invest.

Unrestrained democracy is "unfair" for another, more funda-

[5]See Terry Anderson and Peter J. Hill, *The Birth of a Transfer Society* (Stanford: Hoover Institution Press, 1980), for a discussion of the breakdown in constitutional restrictions on taxation. See James M. Buchanan and Richard E. Wagner, *Democracy in Deficit: The Destructive Legacy of Lord Keynes* (New York: Academic Press, 1977), for an account of the breakdown in the "balanced budget norm," which permitted an expansion of government activities.

[6]John Rawls, *A Theory of Justice* (Cambridge: Harvard University Press, 1971).

[7]Richard E. Wagner, "Politics, Bureaucracy, and Budgetary Choice: The Brookings Budget for 1971," *Journal of Money, Credit and Banking* (August 1974): 367–83.

mental reason: democracy typically restricts votes to the current generation. Future generations cannot vote, for the simple fact that most of them do not now exist. Granted, the current generation of voters may have an interest, on account of their children, in the welfare of future generations. But there is no reason to believe (and every reason to assume the contrary) that current voters will not be as concerned about the welfare of future generations, especially ones far removed, as will the future generations themselves.

A basic problem of democracy has been the tendency of political interest groups to use their political clout to redistribute income from others to themselves. That tendency is reflected in such transfer programs as import protection, support prices for agricultural goods, and Social Security. Such a redistributive tendency should be just as frequently, if not more so, observed in the willingness of the current generation to redistribute income from future generations—which are precluded from voting—to themselves, the people with all the votes. The essential means of making such a transfer is through a taxation of capital that has income consequences that do not become manifest until the very long run.[8] Taxes that discourage current capital formation free up resources for the production of a greater quantity of currently consumed consumer goods and increase the welfare of current consumers, many of whom would not live to benefit from the capital forgone. In short, because of who is allowed to vote, democracies have a built-in bias against capital formation, especially capital with a long pay-out period.[9]

Seen from this perspective, studies showing that Social Security, for example, has reduced the nation's capital stock and the income stream of future generations reveal that the program has, perhaps, had the desired consequence: a redistribution of consumption from future to current generations. To the extent that deficits crowd out private investment, deficit spending is a means of taxing future generations for the benefit of the current generation, which has the votes. To the extent that capital, especially physical capital, becomes

[8]One may reasonably surmise that the current generation will be tempted to tax capital according to how far in the future the benefits are received.

[9]Markets have built-in means of handling, albeit imperfectly, the demands of future generations: they are interest rates and prices. Interest rates and prices rise to reflect the anticipated demands of future generations. But when economic decisions are moved from markets to politics, the demands of future generations are discounted simply because the intent of the shift is largely to override the dictates of market-determined interest rates and prices.

a progressively more important source of people's income, as must be the case in developing economies, we should anticipate that current voters will progressively attempt to tax capital as a means of redistributing income from future to current generations. This inference leads to the conclusion that to the extent that deficit spending actually affects capital, it will tend, over time, to become a more prominent means of financing government expenditures.

Capital Mobility and Centralization of Taxing Authority

The theory of competitive government teaches that tax rates among local governments will tend to be lower than tax rates among states; and state tax rates will tend to be lower than the tax rates imposed by the federal government, assuming everything else is held constant. This is because the elasticity of demand for living in any given local government jurisdiction, by virtue of the narrowness of the jurisdiction, will tend to be higher than that for living in any given state; and the elasticity of demand for living in any given state will tend to be higher than that for living within the federal tax jurisdiction, the entire country. The number of alternative places in which to live and escape taxation is greater at the local level than at the state level, and greater at the state level than at the federal level. As is to be expected in markets for private goods, the greater the number of alternatives, the greater the competition and the closer that tax rates will move toward the marginal costs of the goods and services provided.

The ability of people to escape increases in tax rates is dependent upon the costs of moving out from under those tax rates, and moving costs are a function of the distance that must be traveled and the cost of physical movement, i.e., the transportation costs. The lower the cost of movement, generally speaking, the more difficult it is for a governmental unit to charge monopoly tax rates. Therefore, it stands to reason that reductions in transportation costs (or any other charge that increases capital mobility) will tend, all else being equal, to enhance competition among governments and lower tax rates from what they otherwise would be.[10]

It follows that beneficiaries of government transfer programs will seek to maintain their benefits in times of growing capital mobility

[10]Reductions in mobility costs are likely to affect the revenue-raising capacity of states more than that of local governments, since a local government's tax rates are more likely to be closer to the competitive tax rates.

by working for the centralization of taxing authority, first in state governments and then in the federal government. Tax rates imposed by a more inclusive government will be imposed across a broader jurisdiction, resulting, in turn, in an increase in the transportation costs that must be incurred to escape higher taxation.

Centralization of taxation can, from this perspective, be seen as a governmental-institutional device for overriding the tax rate consequences of the growing mobility of capital.[11] Increasingly, in a developed economy such as the United States this mobility is embodied in people (in the form of human capital) and is due to improvements in transportation and communications systems. Protectionism may be seen as a device for offsetting the advantages of moving capital abroad (and importing goods back to the United States). Proponents of plant closing restrictions, which would increase the cost of shutting down plants, argue that the growing mobility of capital enables firms to pit communities (and countries) against one another in the struggle for the jobs and tax bases at stake. They effectively argue that plant closing restrictions are a means of holding firms hostage and, thereby, keeping tax rates (as well as wages) up.[12]

In the perspective of the foregoing discussion, the growing hostility of government officials to the emergence and proliferation of multinational corporations becomes more understandable. Multinationals are a form of business organization that reduces mobility costs and therefore reduces the ability of government at all levels to extract monopoly rents through capital taxation. Multinationals can more readily move work from plant to plant across more tax jurisdictions in response to tax rate changes than can firms bound to a given area. As a consequence, the multinational can achieve tax and benefit concessions that cannot be acquired by companies bound by the taxing authority of given countries or communities. To this extent, the capital tax burden imposed at jurisdictional levels

[11]Of course, growth in capital mobility may, on the margin, be inspired by growth in government tax rates.

[12]For a presentation of the case for plant closing restrictions, see Bluestone and Harrison. For a critique of Bluestone and Harrison's arguments for plant closing laws, see Richard B. McKenzie, *Fugitive Industry: The Economics and Politics of Deindustrialization* (San Francisco: Pacific Institute for Public Policy Research, 1984); idem, ed., *Plant Closings: Public or Private Choices?* rev. ed. (Washington: Cato Institute, 1984).

below the national level can be disproportionally borne by firms that do not have the capacity to shift work among tax jurisdictions.

The lesson here is that capital taxation can alter the rational structure of business; it can induce firms to spread out among tax districts to a much greater extent than they would in the absence of capital taxation and, perhaps, induce them to maintain a higher degree of excess capacity than could otherwise be justified. The cost of the excess capacity and the added flexibility would be financed by way of capital tax concessions obtained through movement or, perhaps more importantly, the threat of movement.

Similarly, elements of proposed national industrial policy agendas may be interpreted as concessions that must, or should, be made by governments in response to the growing mobility of capital. Clearly, the growing mobility of capital is a frequent complaint of industrial policy proponents concerned over the growing economic power of business. Industrial policy proponents want to establish national boards and banks that would have the authority to allocate capital by way of grants, interest subsidies, and loan guarantees across industries and regions, principally to save so-called basic industries. Translated into the terms of this chapter, such government programs would be a means of granting concessions to capital in face of growing capital mobility and the threat of plant closures. Protectionist measures can be seen as devices for increasing the profits of domestic firms, profits that can then be divided up among their workers (through higher wages), the governmental units that support and provide the protection (through higher tax rates), and the owners (through higher retained earnings.

In short, protectionism may be as much a means of *increasing* capital taxation, in terms of both tax base and tax rates, as it is a means of raising the prices, payrolls, and profits of the protected industry. Clearly, protectionism can, by diverting resources away from a country's comparative advantages, reduce the country's future capital stock and tax revenues in favor of current generations, whether intentionally or unintentionally. Furthermore, protectionism can redistribute the capital stock, enabling well-identified local governments to increase their tax revenues by way of an increase in *their* capital stock and tax rates. In an unrestrained democracy, the state of Pennsylvania can fully support its steel workers union in its drive for protection against steel imports on the grounds that such restrictions would permit greater investment in steel capacity in Pennsylvania and, as a consequence, higher tax rates on industrial capital across the board in that state. Similarly, the state of South Carolina can support textile protectionism on the grounds that its taxing capacity would be enhanced. If all states engage in a competitive struggle for protection of their industries, all can lose, even in the short run. However, as long as states are not constitutionally prevented from seeking protection, then all can reason that they each had better seek protection or else become even worse losers in the competitive protectionist game (if all other states obtain protection for their industries and they do not).

Finally, the points presented here may explain the growing interest of states in "unitary taxation," meaning the taxation of the worldwide income of corporations that have plants inside and outside a state's geographical jurisdiction. Unitary taxation may be viewed as a means of reducing the effective mobility of national and multinational companies. Such taxing authority would not only allow states to increase their tax bases but to raise their tax rates (to the extent that all states adopt such taxing methods). Without question, states that permit unitary taxation will, because of competition from non-unitary tax states, be interested in having federal tax laws requiring unitary taxation in all states.

Concluding Comments

The subject of capital taxation has tended to be considered by economists in technical terms—how capital taxation affects the capital stock and how capital taxes are distributed among owners, workers, and consumers. Little has been written on the interdependence of capital taxation and the political decision-making process. A recurrent theme of this chapter is that capital taxation provides voters with an opportunity to extort the income of people who have saved, or refrained from consumption, in anticipation of future income. Because of the disincentive effects of taxes on capital formation, capital taxation offers current generations of voters the opportunity to transfer consumption goods, via reductions in income growth, from future generations to themselves. Voters in future generations are simply not around to defend themselves politically. Many proposed industrial policies can be seen as hidden means of increasing current tax rates on capital and transferring income from future to current generations.

Economists have also spent much energy considering how political operatives attempt to use their command over votes to redistribute income from others to themselves. The focus of these studies has implicitly been on redistributive schemes within the current voting population. The lesson of this chapter is that more attention should be given to how the current generations of voters can—under, for example, the guise of national industrial policy—use their political clout to redistribute income to themselves from future generations. More attention should be devoted to understanding how the political process can be effectively constrained to restrict the ability of current generations to exploit their favored political positions. One reason industrial policy advocates should be feared is that they propose to do what they say they want to do: reduce the mobility of capital so that capital can be more heavily taxed by government at all levels and so that capital can be more easily exploited by worker groups.

VIII. The Holy Grail of Protectionism

> To expect that the freedom of trade should ever be entirely restored in Great Britain, is as absurd as to expect that an Oceana or Utopia should ever be established in it. Not only the prejudices of the public, but what is more unconquerable, the private interests of many individuals, irresistibly oppose it. . . .
>
> The member of parliament who supports every proposal for strengthening this monopoly [through import protection or any other market entry restriction] is sure to acquire not only the reputation of understanding trade, but great popularity and influence with an order of men whose numbers and wealth render them of great importance. If he opposes them, on the contrary, and still more if he has the authority enough to be able to thwart them, neither the most acknowledged probity, nor the highest rank, nor the greatest public services, can protect him from the most infamous abuse and detraction, from personal insults, nor sometimes real danger, arising from the insolent outrage of furious and disappointed monopolists.
>
> —Adam Smith

The industrial policy debate is never more heated than over the subject of foreign imports, especially imports of such basic products as steel, machine tools, textiles, automobiles, and motorcycles. Proponents of protectionism almost without exception point to the economic and social destruction imports wreak. Former vice president Walter Mondale observed:

> to allow current trends [in imports] to continue unabated is to condemn many industries, communities, and workers to hardship. It means large write-offs of the public and private capital already sunk in factories, roads, and water systems, and even larger expenditures to recreate these facilities elsewhere. It means huge sums for unemployment benefits, welfare, and retraining. This is why my proposals [of import protection] are less costly than a do-nothing laissez-faire policy.[1]

---

[1]Walter F. Mondale, "Trade Tiff," *New Republic,* December 13, 1982, p. 2.

159

Bethlehem Steel vice president Eugene Kline, in a public letter, recounted his company's efforts to pass the Fair Trade in Steel Act of 1982[2] (which would limit foreign imports to 15 percent of the U.S. markets) and noted that

> despite all those efforts steel imports continue to flood into this country. . . . It's clear that, in face of dumped steel and subsidies by foreign governments, the American steel industry cannot survive without decisive action by the federal government. The accelerated liquidation of our domestic steel industry threatens America's role as a world leader. And it threatens the economic and social health of many communities.[3]

Anthony Harrigan, president of the U.S. Business and Industrial Council, sounded a similar alarm when he wrote,

> Key U.S. industries have been targeted by foreign governments so lucrative markets can be more easily captured. The result: the U.S. national security is vulnerable as basic industries die and America's unemployed worker figures for these industries increase dramatically.[4]

A common theme in the various arguments for import protection is that the premises underlying laissez-faire theory are no longer descriptive of the contemporary international economy. "The classical theory of free trade," writes Bob Kuttner,

> was based on what economists call "factor endowment"—a nation's natural advantages in climate, minerals, arable land, or plentiful labor. The theory doesn't fit a world of learning curves, economies of scale, and floating exchange rates. And it certainly doesn't deal with the fact that much "comparative advantage" today is created not by markets but by government action.[5]

Protection, in other words, is warranted not only because cheap labor gives many countries an immense cost advantage in the production of many goods, but also because the prices of many imports

[2]The House and Senate versions are, respectively, H.R. 5081 and S. 2380.

[3]Eugene R. Kline, letter, March 23, 1984.

[4]Anthony Harrigan, United States Business and Industrial Council, public letter, April 9, 1984.

[5]Bob Kuttner, "The Free Trade Fallacy," *New Republic,* March 28, 1983, p. 16.

do not always reflect their true production costs.[6] *All* that many protectionists seek is "fair trade," which seems to mean the opportunity for domestic industries to compete on an equal footing (in terms of labor costs and government subsidies) with foreign firms. What could be more reasonable? As this chapter will show, there is only one problem with the proposed solution, import protection: it will not work. Trade restrictions for some industries would make the country as a whole poorer and would not solve the presumed problems created by imports, i.e., lost jobs and the need to protect American industries from "cheap" foreign imports. Our purpose in this chapter is to explain this ironic conclusion. We start with the issue that is at the core of the case for protection, cheap foreign labor. Later, the issue of the subsidization of foreign industries will be considered.

Low Wages and Comparative Costs

One of the most pervasive and mistaken economic notions perpetrated by industrial protectionists is that low wages in foreign countries make it impossible for U.S. industries to compete with imports. The image of "coolie" labor working in turn-of-the-century sweatshops while American workers stand in long unemployment lines is evident in the remarks of Mondale, Kline, Harrigan, and Kuttner reported above. However, Wolfgang Hager, a visiting professor at Georgetown University, captured the full power of the low-wage argument when he wrote in "praise" of protectionism in the *Washington Post,*

> The problem with free trade is simple: The world has an endless supply of subsistence-wage labor, and we have learned how to make both basic and sophisticated goods in poor, developing countries. Without trade barriers, rich countries are bound to suck in cheap imports from low-wage countries, destroying the domestic industries that used to make those products.[7]

[6]The protectionist's position, as articulated by Kuttner and others, is actually contradictory. One can't argue that the principle of comparative advantage doesn't operate in the modern world economy and, at the same time, fault low wages based on the abundance of subsistence laborers available to foreign producers for U.S. trade problems. Subsidies given to foreign producers are a means of distorting relative international prices, but such price distortions do not invalidate the principle of comparative advantage. Indeed, they confirm that trade patterns are established according to relative prices, which happen to be warped by subsidies.

[7]Wolfgang Hager, "Let Us Now Praise Trade Protectionism," *Washington Post,* May 15, 1983, p. B-1.

Professor Hager went on to stress that developed countries could not count on high-tech industries to replace the jobs lost in "traditional" industries and that "unrestricted trade would eventually destroy the economies of all high-wage, developed countries."[8]

Cheap labor is presumed to be a major cause of, if not fully responsible for, the eroding market shares of American firms in automobiles, steel, textiles, shipbuilding, televisions, robotics, and a host of other industries. Protection in the form of tariffs, quotas, and quality controls imposed on U.S. imports and in the form of "voluntary" restraint programs followed by exporting countries is a presumed solution for reestablishing "fair international trade" and giving back to American companies *their* American markets.

Industrial protectionists ask prophetically, how can U.S. firms hope to compete with foreigners who pay their workers 17 cents an hour? The answer, of course, is that we do compete in many industrial and agricultural areas, as suggested by the fact that we pay high American wages and still export a variety of goods to cheap-labor countries such as Korea, Hong Kong, Japan, and Italy. This feat is accomplished in cases where American wages reflect relatively higher levels of productivity and where American industries have comparative cost advantages.[9]

While low wages may be endemic in the production of almost all imports, low wages in and of themselves fail to explain the composition of our imports—and which industries in the country must compete with imports. What is important in explaining imports and exports, or the directional flow of goods and services across national boundaries, are the *comparative* costs of production of various goods in the United States and other countries with which we trade. A low wage rate is only one factor among many that may explain differences in countries' comparative costs of production. And by comparative costs we mean not the absolute level of wages, but rather what must be forgone to produce products for export.

A country like Mexico that has low wages and has to give up, for example, four tons of steel in order to produce an additional ton of wheat will have a higher cost in the production of wheat than the United States if the United States has to give up only three (or

[8]Ibid.

[9]Indeed, high American wages generally mirror levels of productivity not observed in other countries. If American wages were not in line with productivity, then those wages could not be maintained in face of international competition.

anything less than four) tons of steel to produce an additional ton of wheat. The United States can, in absolute terms, be far more productive in the production of steel than Mexico, but it will still have a comparative cost advantage in the production of wheat—and a comparative cost *dis*advantage in the production of steel (since the United States will have to forgo a third of a ton of wheat to produce a ton of steel, whereas Mexico will have to forgo only a fourth of a ton of wheat to obtain the additional steel).

Regardless of the absolute dollar and peso prices of steel and wheat in their respective countries, the United States will tend to trade its wheat for Mexican steel. This is because more steel (as much as four tons) can be obtained from Mexico for a ton of wheat than can be produced in the United States (three tons) if a ton of wheat is not produced and the resources are transferred to steel production. Similarly, Mexico will trade its steel for wheat because it can get more wheat (one-third of a ton) from the United States for a ton of steel than it could produce if it reduced its production of steel by a ton and used the resources to produce wheat (which would only amount to one-fourth of a ton of wheat).[10]

Admittedly, because costs must be compared across goods *and* across countries, the principle of comparative (cost) advantage is elusive. However, the underlying points are relatively straightfor-

---

[10]To see these points in light of real dollar and peso prices, consider the following reconstruction of the problem. If three tons of steel have to be given up in the United States to produce a ton of wheat, the dollar price of a ton of steel will be one-third the price of a ton of wheat, for example, $1 per ton of steel versus $3 per ton of wheat. On the other hand, if four tons of steel have to be given up in Mexico to produce a ton of wheat, the peso price of steel will be one-fourth the price of a ton of wheat, for example, 1 peso per ton of steel versus 4 pesos per ton of wheat. A U.S. importer could agree to buy pesos at an exchange rate of, say, $1 for 1.25 pesos. With a dollar, the U.S. importer could buy 1.25 pesos and then buy 1.25 tons of steel in Mexico. The U.S. importer gains in the process, since he gets from Mexico more steel (25 percent more in our illustration) with a dollar than he could have gotten in the United States. Similarly, at an exchange rate of $1 for 1.25 pesos, a Mexican importer can sell 4 pesos for $3.20 and buy 1.07 tons of wheat, which is more wheat than he could have purchased in Mexico with 4 pesos. We could double or quadruple the dollar and/or peso prices of steel and wheat in the two countries to reflect changes in the absolute level of wages of workers, and we would still come to the same conclusion: the relative costs of steel and wheat in the two countries will determine the directional flow of trade. The directional flow of trade could be reversed if the cost of producing a ton of wheat in the United States were five times the cost of producing a ton of American steel and if the cost of producing a ton of wheat in Mexico remained at four times the cost of producing a ton of Mexican steel.

ward. Perhaps the principle can be more easily understood by simply acknowledging (1) that international trade must ultimately be bilateral (in two directions) and (2) that wages are typically low across industries in low-wage countries. Trade is necessarily bilateral because no country will long persist in using its scarce resources to produce goods that are shipped abroad without getting anything in return. If a country like Japan exports "low wage" products, it typically will—to make trade bilateral, meaning worthwhile—import "high wage" products; otherwise, trade would do nothing more than drain the low-wage country of its resources. To repeat an important theme, if low wages "explain" trade, we must wonder how the United States could ever export anything, since our wages across the industrial board are generally higher than industrial wages elsewhere in the world.

Of course, protection advocates such as Professor Hager argue that unless protection is provided to U.S. industries, all U.S. industries will be at the mercy of foreign low-wage producers—an absurd conclusion if we recognize that a foreign country's ultimate motivation for engaging in exports is its demand for imports, including imports from the United States and other high-wage countries. To suggest, in the words of political scientist Chalmers Johnson that "the United States is in danger of ending the 20th century as the leading producer of ICBMs and soybeans, while the Japanese monopolize everything else" is tantamount to saying that the Japanese are so stupid that they will, through their exports, sell off practically everything they have without getting anything concrete in return just to achieve "monopolies," a contradiction of immense proportions. How could a country smart enough to monopolize world markets be stupid enough never to demand payment in something real and tangible—that is, goods and services from abroad—not just in dollars, which are just so much paper (or blips on a bank's computer tape) if they are never spent?

International trade actually emerges for many reasons other than just cost. It may occur because people in one country find foreign goods to be higher in quality, prettier, more durable, and/or more dependable. It may also occur because foreign producers are more convenient sources of supply or provide better credit terms. In any case, if American importers do find foreign goods such as Japanese textiles more attractive, there are two reasons for believing that American demand for Japanese textiles will lead to U.S. exports.

First, Americans will need yen to buy Japanese textiles, and they will have to buy yen with dollars. The Japanese who part with their yen must want dollars for some reason, such as buying American goods.

Second, the international exchange rate between the yen and the dollar will adjust to ensure that trade is bidirectional—that the Japanese will want dollars in order to buy American goods. The demand for yen from Americans who want to buy Japanese textiles will drive the dollar price of yen up (or, which is the same thing, the yen price of dollars down) until the Japanese find at least some American goods a bargain.[11] This exchange-rate adjustment upward will occur even when the American goods in question are produced with high-priced labor. Furthermore, Mr. Kuttner's commentary on comparative costs notwithstanding, the exchange-rate adjustment will occur in response to differences in production costs, regardless of whether those cost differences are founded on differences in "factor endowments" or learning curves and economies of scale.[12] Learning curves and economies of scale will simply work themselves into relative cost differences, which will influence the market clearing prices in foreign exchange markets.

Trade and Industrial Survival

Industrial policy alarmists frequently contend, as Hager most definitely has, that the U.S. economy will decay into total ruin unless protection is forthcoming. The principle of comparative costs speaks to the absurdity of that conclusion. Again, the principle of comparative costs insists that regardless of the absolute level of wages in a country, if the Japanese have a comparative cost advantage in the production of a product like textiles, then the United

[11]To illustrate, suppose the dollar/yen exchange rate goes from $0.25/yen to $0.50/yen due to American demand for Japanese textiles. The change will result in the price of a $50 U.S. good falling from 200 yen to 100 yen.

[12]Earlier writers in international economics actually concentrated their analytical focus on "factor endowments" not so much because they were unaware of learning curves and economies of scale, but because they were intent upon making the simple point that production conditions do differ among countries and that these differences could be based on factor differences, among other things. The differences in conditions of production would lead to cost differences, which would, in turn, affect the directional flow of trade.

States must have a comparative cost advantage in something else, like soybeans or computers.[13]

Contrary to what is normally preached in industrial policy debates, the theory of comparative costs does not even imply necessarily that domestic industries encountering foreign competition would be eliminated in toto from the U.S. industrial scene. To see why, suppose that when trade between Japan and the United States is initially contemplated, Japan has a comparative advantage in the production of cars. Japan's initial comparative advantage may mean that Japanese firms sell cars in the United States, but it does not necessarily follow that U.S. car manufacturers cannot coexist along with imports, even in the absence of protection. Comparative costs in the two countries will change as the production of cars expands in Japan and contracts in the United States. As a consequence of the opening up of international trade, the *relative* cost of Japanese cars will tend to increase. As car production expands in Japan, resources to produce additional cars will have to be drawn from progressively more valuable and profitable alternative production processes, and drawn away at increasing prices. The reverse will happen in the United States. All in all, the comparative cost of expanded car production will, on the margin, rise in Japan, and in the process the cost increase will negate the comparative cost advantage for further expansion of Japanese car sales in the United States.

An understanding of changing comparative costs under conditions of international trade leads to the conclusion that some American firms will survive the international competitive threat, not that American industries will be eliminated wholesale. How many and which ones depends greatly on how firms are able to control their costs (relative to other industries) and on how productive they become in response to the international competitive challenge. We can surmise, however, that those auto firms and plants that are *relatively* less efficient at producing cars will be taken out of production. Those auto firms that are relatively more efficient will survive, perhaps taking a larger share of the domestic market (which

[13]Our insistence on comparative costs as the basis for *two-way* trade emerges directly from what is meant by "comparative cost." If Japan has a comparative cost advantage in one or more products, it must also have a comparative cost *dis*advantage in one or more other products, since "comparative" implies gradations of costs for products. Conversely, Japan's comparative cost disadvantages would translate into a comparative cost advantage for the production of one or more products in the United States.

will expand because of lower prices). In the process, as the relatively less costly foreign cars are substituted in consumer purchases for the relatively more costly domestic cars, the real income of the country is raised.

This increase in the nation's real aggregate income may hardly be seen by the car (or steel or textile) industry as a blessing, since its workers, owners, and suppliers will suffer due to the competitive pressure on prices and the contraction of domestic firms' share of the domestic market. However, their suffering at the hands of foreign competition does not necessarily mean that they and their workers are worse off as a consequence of an open and unrestricted competitive market system. Auto workers benefit from competition in a host of other domestic and international markets where competition has induced greater output and lower prices for the products auto workers (and owners) buy—that is, they benefit from competition elsewhere in the economy that has raised the real incomes of auto workers.

A case for restrictions on market activities can always be made with considerable emotional appeal when the analytical focus is narrowed to individual markets, small groups of workers, and highly confined market periods. Changes in specific markets, whether from technological innovation or emerging international competition, will always result in winners and losers. Auto workers unemployed due to the influx of foreign autos are clearly losers—in the narrow context of car imports—but their loss in that narrow context does not, by itself, justify a protectionist program that effectively transfers income from others in the economy to the auto industry. Before we engage in such a transfer program, we should at least consider three important questions directly related to the social ethics of protection for a particular industry like automobiles.

First, are auto workers consistent losers over the course of time and through a series of domestic and international market events, some of which benefit auto workers directly, some of which harm auto workers directly? To the extent that auto workers have for decades earned above-average wages, income transfers through protectionist programs are hard to justify. Protection would mean that people who have earned less than auto workers (and gained less on balance from the economic system) would be forced to pay for subsidizing auto worker wages and job security.

Second, is the protection of the auto industry an unmitigated gain for the country? The answer is emphatically no. Auto workers would gain at the expense of consumers who would have to pay higher prices for the goods they buy.

Third and most importantly, if all industries were accorded the same protection from competition, both domestic and international (since worker groups are harmed by both), that protectionists propose for auto workers (and other industry groups), would auto workers (or the protected workers in general) be better off? Indeed, we might ask a more revealing question: would auto workers (and owners) agree to a system of protection under which *everyone* was granted the protection from the forces of market competition that auto workers want for themselves? Auto workers would, under such a system, have their own jobs and incomes protected, with the cost of that protection imposed on others through higher prices; but they would also have to pay, through higher prices on the goods they buy, their share of the costs of protection given to all other similarly situated industries.

Of course, industrial policy advocates often do not propose that all worker groups be accorded equal protection under the law; they want discriminatory treatment for identified industries, fully aware that discriminatory protection is the only certain way that the "targeted" groups' welfares can be, on balance, improved. We must worry about arguments for public policies that cannot be readily generalized and applied equally to the rest of the population. Such discriminatory power is available only to the politically powerful, which means that the politically powerless will be made consistent losers from deliberate transfer schemes.

Jobs and Protection

Proponents of protectionism maintain that import protection is indeed in the public interest because through it, jobs are saved. Although we might agree that import protection can save jobs in protected industries, we cannot conclude (as protectionists incorrectly do) that imports force a contraction of the country's total employment opportunities. We must not forget that such countries as Japan want to be paid for their exports with something we produce. As a result, imports, which surely destroy jobs in the import sector, give rise to exports, which just as surely create jobs. Furthermore, this country's (and other countries') greater real income that arises from open international trade should add to the demand for U.S. goods and services simply because greater real income translates into greater purchasing power for all trading partners.

The principle of comparative costs tells us that import protection for the steel industry, for example, will only shift, not increase, employment demand within the country—and will actually reduce, on balance, the nation's employment opportunities. Why, you ask? First, the reduction in U.S. imports will lead to a reduction in U.S. exports. (This point should now be boring to those who recognize that trade is ultimately in two directions.) The Japanese will simply not be able to buy as many U.S. goods if they are unable to sell as many goods in the United States.

Second, a tariff on, say, steel will raise the relative price of steel. This change will mean that the United States then has a comparative cost *dis*advantage in something else that will, as a result, be subjected to new and more intense competition from abroad. In other words, the relative price change means that the tariff has shifted the cost disadvantage to something else—away from steel to other industries.[14] In their attempt to sell us goods in order to pay for the American goods and services they want, the Japanese will invade other American markets.

Furthermore, shifts in the dollar/yen exchange rate will ensure that the Japanese will be able to export other goods. A tariff on steel will mean that Americans will demand fewer yen to buy Japanese steel, but the reduced demand for yen will cause the dollar price of yen to fall, say, from $0.25 per yen to $0.24 per yen. The lower dollar price of yen will mean that Japanese goods other than steel will then become relatively less expensive to Americans, giving rise to U.S. importation of them. Steel protection, therefore, translates into an inducement for the Japanese to run other, more cost-competitive U.S. firms out of business. Restrictions on steel imports, far from being a political device for promoting the public interest, will thus tend to protect the jobs of steelworkers while jeopardizing the jobs of workers in other U.S. export industries and in other domestic industries that are, because of import restrictions on steel, subjected to competition from abroad. The reduction in the nation's real income arising from the contraction of international trade will, of course, further reduce employment opportunities for Americans.

---

[14]The overall level of international trade will fall in spite of the tariff-induced shift of imports from steel to other products. This contraction of trade will reduce the country's income, making Americans less capable of buying goods from abroad. The reduced volume of imports will mean that foreign countries will also be less able to buy American goods.

The critical lesson to be learned from the principle of comparative advantage is quite clear: if we as a country are really serious about protecting U.S. industries from "lower-priced foreign imports" (and are intent upon treating all industries the same under the law), protection afforded one industry will expose one or more other U.S. industries to foreign competition. These exposed industries will then need protection, which, if protection is granted, will expose other industries to foreign competition—and so on ad nauseam. The protectionist movement could, consistently applying the low-cost argument of the protectionists, lead to an isolation of virtually all U.S. markets from foreign competition, meaning the virtual elimination of international trade. The rate of contraction of Americans' real income would, naturally, escalate with the contraction of America's involvement in world trade.[15]

Competition for the Country's Comparative Cost Advantage

Proponents of protectionism appear to labor under the delusion that foreign firms are the most important, if not the only, source of the competitive troubles of U.S. industries. Their problem, they say in effect, is with foreigners, not Americans. Clearly, foreign steel firms place considerable pressure on American steel makers to control their costs and prices, improve their quality, and more accurately tailor their products to the needs of American consumers. However, there are steel firms in this country that are just as efficient as firms in foreign countries. They contribute to the domestic supply of steel and they also contribute to the downward pressure on prices that makes competitive life difficult for a number of less efficient U.S. firms. That this role of efficient U.S. firms is seldom recognized probably has a political basis: they have votes, while foreign firms do not.

Furthermore, it cannot be emphasized enough that the principle of comparative costs teaches a simple point: *comparative,* not absolute, costs matter in international trade, and the relevant comparison is among the costs of industries within the United States as well as within Japan. This means that all industries in the United States are, in effect, competing for this country's comparative advantage—or the capacity to be this country's low-cost, compar-

---

[15]The cost of protectionism to the United States for just a few trade restrictions was estimated at $71 billion in 1983. Murray Weidenbaum and Michael Munger, "Protection at Any Price?" *Regulation* (July/August 1983): 17.

170

atively speaking, producers. The computer industry, for example, is constantly attempting to keep its costs down so that it can be the one to export its products without having to face the threat of foreign competition. Similarly, the agricultural industry is constantly attempting to control its costs so that it, not the computer or textile or steel industries, has the comparative advantage. In an important respect, *the principle of comparative advantage tells us that the steel industry has to face stiff competition from foreign steel producers in part because other industries in the United States have been more successful than steel in controlling costs or improving productivity.* To protect the steel industry is to protect an industry that has, relatively speaking, been less competitive than other U.S. industries. This is not to say that the steel industry may not have done its best to control its costs; it may have worked just as hard as other industries. The principle simply means that the conditions for producing steel (or whatever else is considered for protection) are not, on the margin, as favorable in this country as they are in other countries.

Unfortunately, the steel industry's troubles are, at least in part, very much the result of its own making. Between 1972 and 1977 (a period in which steel was a highly protected industry), the real hourly wages of steel production workers rose by nearly 60 percent while their productivity (in terms of output per man-hour) increased by only 5 percent. This greatly raised the relative cost of producing steel in this country and widened the gap between the price of steel produced in the United States and in other major industrial countries.[16] To the extent that the competitive troubles of the steel industry have been the fault of the industry, protection encourages further troubles. An industry protected from competition after it has become noncompetitive can hardly be expected to control its costs, which, through the guise of protection, are spread to the larger community.

Proponents of industrial policy believe that they have a rational means of dealing with the inherent disincentives of protection: they

[16]Kent Jones, "Saving the Steel Industry," Heritage Foundation Backgrounder (Washington, May 21, 1984), p. 5. The employment cost per ton of shipped steel in 1978 was $114.10 in the United States, $107.35 in West Germany, $96.21 in the United Kingdom, and $71.46 in Japan. The cost differential between the United States and Japan in 1978 largely reflected the difference in the employment cost per man-hour in the two countries ($14.73 per man-hour in the United States and $9.86 per man-hour in Japan). The productivity of labor in Japan in 1978 was only 5 percent higher than the productivity of labor in the United States.

171

propose to give "temporary" protection only when an industry agrees to restructure itself to become more competitive. There are several problems with the argument.

First, even if the protected industry becomes more cost-competitive, there is no reason to believe that its political clout, which is responsible for the protection in the first place, will have waned when the protection is scheduled to end; there is no reason to believe that the industry will not be able to retain its protection more or less permanently. The protection itself will increase resources available to the protected domestic industry that can be used to gain political favors from Congress. After all, the major industries at the center of the protectionist battle and currently seeking "temporary protection"—automobiles, steel, and textiles—have had protection in one form or another for decades.

Second, protection ultimately reduces a firm's incentive to maintain its ability to compete. Protection accorded industries that have allowed themselves to become noncompetitive will be seen by other industries as an incentive to allow themselves to become marginally less competitive in the expectation that they, too, can obtain protection.

Third, the protection of one set of industries will, in effect, impose a tax on other industries, making other industries less competitive. These other affected industries will then have an argument that they, too, should be protected in order to restructure themselves to become more competitive.

Finally, we must question why firms actually need protection to modernize and become more competitive. The firms that seek (additional) protection contend, in effect, that modernization, which would make them more profitable as well as more productive, can come only through greater investment, which requires larger profits. If it were indeed true that, say, the steel industry could become more profitable through modernization, then protection, and the income transfer implied in it, would be unnecessary. Steel firms in need of modernization could go to the private capital markets for the needed investment funds. Private investors will gladly invest in profitable ventures, even if their return must be delayed for a period of years until the new equipment is in place and the firms are well down on their "learning curves."

But currently the steel industry is resisting investing in itself. Industrial policy protectionists lament the steel firms' use of their retained earnings on non-steel investments. Rather than being socially undesirable, however, such investments are an admission by the steel industry that other investments have a higher return than steel and that an import protection program, accompanied by investment restrictions, would not be socially productive. Through import and reinvestment restrictions the country might get more domestic steel produced, but it would also lose production of other, more valuable goods and services.

Foreign Subsidies

Domestic industries seeking protection lament in particular the subsidies that foreign governments supply foreign industries. As noted, Bob Kuttner was careful to stress that comparative advantage today is guided as much by government industrial aid programs as it is by differences in "factor endowments."[17] The steel, textile, machine tool, and automobile industries, as well as just about all other industries that seek protection, point to government subsidies in foreign countries as a major source of their competitive difficulties. They tell us that all they want is "fair trade," or a "level playing field," one that is not tilted by government aid in favor of foreign firms. They also point out that such subsidies distort relative prices and misallocate resources internationally, contributing to economic inefficiency on a worldwide basis.

While foreign industrial subsidies may cause the contraction of several U.S. industries, it does not follow that American employment opportunities are, on balance, destroyed. Again, trade is a two-way street. If Americans buy subsidized foreign products, then more American products will be purchased by foreigners who will have dollars obtained from their subsidized exports. The increased demand for, say, yen spawned by the greater demand for Japanese steel that, in turn, is induced by Japanese government subsidies will lead to an increase in the dollar price of yen. This is another way of saying that the Japanese can then buy more dollars with each yen and can buy more American goods per yen earned. The depreciation of the dollar caused by Japanese industrial subsidies, in short, lowers the prices of American goods to the Japanese.

Through foreign subsidies on exports, some U.S. industries are harmed, but others are helped. The net effect of the subsidies is an increase in the real aggregate income of the United States (and a reduction in the real aggregate income of Japan and any other

[17]Kuttner, p. 16.

country that provides industrial subsidies). As opposed to discouraging the subsidization of foreign industries, the United States should look upon such subsidies as an opportunity to improve the welfare of Americans. The subsidization of foreign exports enables Americans to tap into the income bases of foreign countries and impose a tax on foreigners every time a subsidized product is imported into this country. Communist China, for example, would never consider allowing the U.S. government to tax its one billion citizens directly; nevertheless, that is what China permits indirectly through the subsidies it gives its exporting industries, for example, textiles. The tax is realized in terms of higher prices and lower real incomes in China and lower prices and higher real incomes in the United States.

Granted, foreign subsidies impose risks on the United States. They can weaken the economies (and defense capabilities) of the countries that provide them, including those of our allies. In addition, such subsidies may be unstable: given today, they may be withdrawn tomorrow, resulting in unnecessary adjustment costs to the U.S. economy as American firms withdraw from industries that have to compete with subsidized foreign products only to return when the subsidies are removed. Granted, it is never a good idea for the country to allow itself to become dependent upon a sole source of supply, especially if it is foreign and especially if the foreign government is hostile to the national security goals of the United States. Having said that, however, there is no necessary reason that even a major share of the domestic market should be supplied by domestic producers. This is especially true if subsidized imports originate in a variety of countries. As long as the political climate in which the subsidies emerge is stable and no country obtains a monopolistic hold on the U.S. economy, it would appear that the inclination of other countries to subsidize their industries should be viewed by the United States in the same way that favorable weather for growing crops in other parts of the world is perceived, as an advantage to be fully exploited through trade.

Trade Deficits

Former Texas governor John Connally remarked during his 1980 presidential bid:

> It's time we said to Japan: "If we can't come into your markets with equal openness and fairness as you come into ours, you had

better be prepared to sit on the docks of Yokohama in your little Datsuns and your little Toyotas while you stare at your own little television sets and eat your mandarin oranges, because we've had all we're going to take!"[18]

Walter Mondale has also complained:

> Now I'm not a protectionist but I'm not a sucker. And I believe our country and its leaders and its negotiators simply must get tougher in negotiations and say something like this: "From now on it's going to be fair. If you want to close yourself off from our markets then we're going to take steps to make certain our markets are not going to be available to you."[19]

Proponents of protection point to the growing U.S. balance of trade deficit with Japan, which in 1984 was approaching $37 billion, as evidence that the principle of comparative advantage is intellectually bankrupt. "Look at the record," proponents in effect suggest, "and you will see that trade is not bilateral. We buy goods from the Japanese, but they do not buy what we produce in return. Open, unrestricted trade on balance destroys American jobs." Because Japan does restrict imports, our trading relations with that country should be of considerable concern to policymakers. But such import restrictions can be denounced independently of the U.S. trade deficit with Japan: they reduce the welfare of both countries because they reduce both Japan's imports from us and its ability to sell goods to us.

However, this country's trade deficit with Japan is a grand example of how a social problem can be imagined when the analytical focus is narrowed to two trading partners. If we consider Japan's worldwide trading relations, it is not at all clear that our trade deficit with Japan, on balance, destroys jobs in the United States. Japan may sell us goods, accepting dollars in return; but those dollars represent purchasing power that can be used by Japan to buy goods from the United States or from other countries (since people in other countries will accept dollars in anticipation of using those dollars to buy goods from the United States). If Japan did not anticipate using dollars not spent directly on U.S. imports, we

---

[18]Martin Schram, " 'Big Fritz': Tough Talk And a Flag," *Washington Post*, October 7, 1982, p. A-12.

[19]Ibid.

175

would have to wonder about the intelligence of its industrial policy. Japan would be exporting real goods and services in exchange for paper (or blips on a bank's computer tape), not a very wise arrangement since paper is generally much cheaper to produce than exports.

As a matter of fact, Japan has had a balance of trade surplus with the United States but a balance of trade deficit with other countries; the United States has had a balance of trade surplus with Western Europe. In fact, Figures 8.1A and 8.1B reveal that our trade deficit with Japan tended in the 1973–82 period to be offset by trade surpluses with Western Europe. Between 1979 and 1982, the accumulated surplus with Western Europe exceeded the accumulated deficit with Japan by over $7 billion.

Our surplus with Western Europe was surely inspired partially by our deficits with Japan: the Japanese bought goods and services from Western Europe with the dollars they earned on exports to the United States, and the Europeans were able to run a deficit with the United States because of the dollars accumulated on surpluses with Japan.[20] Of course, trading relations are actually more complicated than what is suggested here, for there are over a hundred countries in the world. Our sales to any one of them may have provided the means for the United States to run a trade deficit with Japan.

Still, the U.S. merchandise trade deficit on a worldwide scale was running at an annual rate of more than $120 billion in 1984. Doesn't this prove that trade, on balance, destroys jobs? If we import more than we export, are not more jobs destroyed than created through trade? Actually, no—not as a general tendency over time. The balance of payments, which includes both trade in goods and services and international flows of capital, necessarily balances—simply because of the double-entry bookkeeping methods used (or, to put it another way, because every transaction must have a means of payment). The merchandise trade deficit must be offset exactly by a surplus in services or in capital flows.

As many industrial policy proponents argue, the trade deficit could have been caused in part by capital inflows induced by rela-

---

[20]Changing the perspective, it might be instructive to note that our deficit with Japan was probably caused in part by our surplus with Europe. Because of that surplus, people in the United States may have had a supply of marks, pounds, and lira that could be used to buy yen on the international exchange market. The yen were then used to buy goods from Japan.

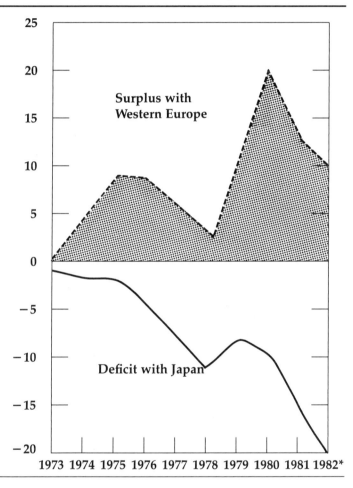

Figure 8.1A

U.S. Trade Balance with Western Europe
and Japan, 1973–82
(Imports minus Exports)

Surplus with
Western Europe

Deficit with Japan

1973 1974 1975 1976 1977 1978 1979 1980 1981 1982*

tively high interest rates in the United States. These capital inflows have, so it is argued, increased the demand for dollars, which has pushed up the value of the dollar on international exchange markets. The appreciation of the dollar has made American goods less competitive in world markets. At a time when the federal govern-

Figure 8.1B
NET U.S. TRADE BALANCE WITH WESTERN EUROPE AND JAPAN, 1973–82
(IMPORTS MINUS EXPORTS)

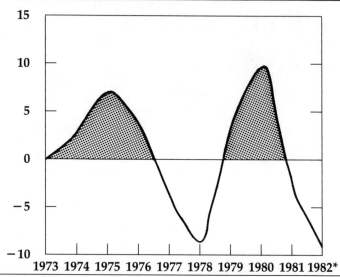

SOURCE: Murray L. Weidenbaum with Michael C. Munger and Ronald J. Penoyer, *Toward a More Open Trade Policy* (St Louis: Center for the Study of American Business, Washington University, 1983), p. 14.
*Estimated annualized basis.

ment is running $200-plus billion budget deficits, the concern over capital inflow is legitimate, and the country does have a problem in controlling its federal expenditures and budget deficits. Aside from that caveat, however, which speaks more to the misallocation of resources between the public and private sectors in the United States, the surplus in the international capital account is not as destructive to U.S. jobs and the future of the country as may be first supposed. The capital account surplus can be interpreted to mean that American suppliers of financial assets have been providing foreigners with better deals than have American suppliers of such goods and services as steel, textiles, and automobiles.

The inflow of investment funds into the United States from Europe or Japan or Africa will end up as the purchase of real goods and

178

services, which will give rise to jobs in the same way that exports do. Indeed, the investment inflow (and the resulting trade deficit) may mean that the country has undertaken a major public and private redevelopment program, which should lead to greater growth—more income and jobs—in the future. If we protect basic industries because of the balance of trade deficit, we can reduce the capital inflow, which can retard investment and reduce the stock of jobs in the investment goods industry—and impair the country's productivity growth.

If the federal budget deficit were the culprit causing unwarranted distortions in the international value of the dollar, protectionist measures would be on par with using band-aids to cure smallpox; the protection remedy would not accomplish the desired objective. Import restrictions may save jobs in protected industries, but to the extent that they restrict capital inflows from abroad (by denying foreign investors an increased flow of funds from imports), they can cause the federal deficit to soak up a larger share of domestic savings and to reduce domestic investment and jobs that would have been created in the investment goods industry.

Quotas vs. Tariffs

Professor Gottfried Haberler has denounced quotas as the "worst possible method [of restricting imports], much worse than an import tariff."[21] He suggests that if the country pursues protectionism, which he clearly believes is wrong, then tariffs should be preferred to quotas. At first glance, it would appear that substituting tariffs for quotas would be a sensible course, for although international trade might be restricted by them, the damage would be reduced. Unfortunately, Professor Haberler's well-intended advice may lead to more stringent trade restrictions.[22] In other words, when the politics of trade policies are considered, free trade advocates should prefer quotas, in terms of import quantities, to tariffs. Let me explain.

Economists have long noted that, in the words of Professor Haberler, "any restriction on imports drives a wedge between the

[21]Gottfried Haberler, "Should Quotas Be Alien to Imports?" *Wall Street Journal*, July 7, 1984, p. 15.

[22]At the very least, we can argue here that this conclusion, often drawn by economists and policymakers interested in improving the efficiency of the U.S. economy, is not necessarily correct. Quotas may not be more restrictive or inefficient than tariffs.

price inside and outside the protected area," distorting the allocation of domestic and international resources. But quotas are thought
to be more pernicious than tariffs for three reasons.

First, quotas typically do not allow imports to expand with domestic
sales; they are simply more restrictive.[23]

Second, as Haberler notes, "under a tariff the U.S. terms of trade
improve [because the tariff pushes the import price down]; under
the quota system they deteriorate [because foreign exporters can
raise their prices]."

Third, and perhaps most important, a quota funnels American
income to foreigners, whereas the tariff revenue "goes ultimately
to the U.S. taxpayers."

Brookings Institution senior fellow Robert Crandall supported
the substitution of a tariff for the 1981–85 "voluntary" restraint
program, which amounted to a 1.85 million-car quota on Japanese
car imports, on the grounds that the program diverted $2 billion a
year in income from American consumers to Japanese producers:
"From the standpoint of American taxpayers, a tariff clearly would
have been a better policy choice than the voluntary restraint."[24]

Also, because of the potential income transfer under quotas,
Federal Trade Commission staff economists recently told the International Trade Commission that if quotas are imposed on steel, the
quotas should be auctioned.[25] In this way at least the U.S. Treasury,
not foreigners with export licenses, would garner a part of the
income given up by American citizens.

A major problem with conventional comparative analysis of quotas and tariffs is that the comparison is made strictly on the presumption that quotas and tariffs are equally restrictive. Conven-

[23]Protectionists have dulled the impact of this objection to quotas by proposals to
limit imports to a set maximum percentage of the domestic market. Therefore, when
the domestic market expands, imports can too.

[24]Robert W. Crandall, "Import Quotas and the Automobile Industry: The Costs
of Protectionism," *Brookings Review* (Summer 1984): 8–16. As quoted in Stuart Auerbach, "Report Says Auto Limits Boosted Japan's Profits," *Washington Post*, June 22,
1984. Crandall also found, in contrast to the benefits of the voluntary restraint
program, that the U.S. firms benefited only to the tune of $1.2 billion a year.

[25]Federal Trade Commission, *Prehearing Brief on Remedy, before the International
Trade Commission, on the case of Carbon and Certain Alloy Steel Products*, Investigation
no. TA-201-51, June 1984. See also Stuart Auerbach, "FTC Proposes Auction for the
Right to Sell Foreign Steel in U.S.," *Washington Post*, June 22, 1984, p. D-7. In selling
quotas, foreign and domestic firms would, at the limit, bid prices equal to the
economic profits that could be had from the trade restriction.

tional analysis assumes, more or less implicitly, that the political incentives of quotas and tariffs are the same, or that they can be made to be the same. But the political problem involved in replacing quotas with tariffs is that tariffs would ease the pain of protectionism—and hence make the economic damage caused by protection less visible—to American voters, making the adoption of tariffs more likely. And we cannot suppose, as Haberler, Crandall, and the FTC staff economists apparently do, that quota and tariff systems are, as adopted, equally restrictive. We would, in fact, expect any tariff to be more restrictive than a quota—precisely because of an advantage attributed to it, i.e., the tariff revenue.

Because of the lower taxes or the greater government-financed benefits that tariff revenue could allow, fewer voters would oppose protectionist proposals. Supporters of import protection should therefore be able to muscle through Congress a marginally more restrictive trade policy with tariffs than with quotas. The FTC's proposed auction system should, for these same reasons, lead to more stringent U.S. quotas.

Because of fewer imports, we would expect the domestic price of protected products to be higher under a tariff system than under a quota system. The greater domestic profits from the more stringent tariff restrictions could also be expected to translate into more diligent efforts on the part of a greater number of industry and worker groups to obtain protection. After all, the expected return on their political investment would be greater.

In concrete terms, a policy move on the part of the Reagan administration to replace the voluntary restraint program with a tariff or to auction off the quota would likely have meant that fewer than 1.85 million Japanese cars would have been allowed into the country each year. Accordingly, American car companies would have been able to raise their prices by more than they already did. Auto workers would naturally be able to soak up additional monopoly "rents" from protectionism. And of course, the resources wasted by interest groups in lobbying for a portion of the tariff revenues and/or additional protection should be added to the overall inefficiency of the tariff.

Finally, foreign countries are much more likely to retaliate, with trade restrictions of their own, against tariffs than against quotas. This is because they are harmed to a greater degree by the more restrictive tariffs. The substitution of tariffs for quotas should, as a result, escalate international trade tensions; and the greater cost of the more restrictive trade policies of other countries must be included in any comparative calculation of the inefficiency of U.S. tariffs and quotas.

The moral of the argument presented here is straightforward: we should always remember, to quote Lindley Clark, that "the purpose of trade, in international markets or at the corner grocery, is to get the best possible products at the lowest possible prices."[26] Although quotas are another bad idea whose time may have come, they can still be preferred to their more restrictive alternative, tariffs.

Market Ownership

Proponents of protectionism often contend that tariffs, quotas, and other import restrictions are warranted because imports represent an invasion of American markets that should rightfully be left, to a substantial degree if not totally, to American producers. Protectionists fail to see that any restriction of foreign imports to a certain percentage of domestic sales inevitably translates into a grant of ownership of American markets to American producers, often a handful of producers, and that such assignment of market ownership rights increases the monopoly power of American firms, which may use their newly acquired market power to exploit consumers. Such an ownership assignment also amounts to a denial of market rights to American consumers, who have an equal claim to American markets. Through import restrictions, consumers are denied the right to buy what they want—higher quality products at lower prices. Consumers are in effect told that their individual freedom should be decreased and their income reduced so that the freedom of others from the constraints of competition can be increased.

Such a transfer of individual freedom and personal income might be justified if the assignment of market ownership rights to producers could be justified. However, in order for viable markets to exist, both consumers and producers are required; both consumers and producers are, in varying degrees, jointly responsible for the creation of markets. There is no particular reason to assume a priori that producers are any more responsible for the creation of American markets than are consumers. Any argument for free markets is an explicit denial of market ownership rights to producers *and*

[26]Lindley Clark, "The Case for Free Trade Still Hasn't Been Made," *Wall Street Journal*, June 26, 1984, p. 35.

consumers, and an argument for the assignment of market access rights to everyone, regardless of where they happen to live. Market access rights are assigned because they can give rise to open competition that can enhance the welfare of *both* producers and consumers.

Concluding Comments

Regardless of the power of free trade arguments, trade restrictions are likely to remain with us. As Adam Smith recognized more than two hundred years ago (in the quote heading this chapter), the creation of free international trade is no more likely than the establishment of an Oceana or a Utopia. The real problem is not one of compelling logic. Free traders have always tended to win arguments; but they have also tended to lose the votes mainly because, to echo Smith again, of public prejudices and the private interests that support protectionism at public expense. Industrial protectionists have always had the upper hand in the political arena. The benefits they receive from import protection are sufficiently concentrated to make political activity in support of protection a paying proposition, whereas the costs of protection are so thinly spread over the general public that the average citizen has little incentive to politically counter the private interests of protectionists.

One of the more hopeful signs of the shifting political balance against protectionism is that more and more export industries have begun to realize that their ability to export to other countries is dependent upon the ability of other countries to penetrate American markets free of trade restrictions. Accordingly, because the U.S. soybean industry sells a sizable amount of its crop to the Chinese, it opposed the Reagan administration's attempts to impose textile import quotas in 1983. Boeing Aircraft also took the lead in the political battle against those restrictions on Chinese textile imports on the grounds that its aircraft sales might be dependent upon Chinese textile sales in the United States. The computer industry has begun to recognize that its foreign computer sales can be advanced by loosening U.S import restrictions and has, accordingly, made freer trade one of the industry's primary political objectives. Midwestern farmers have begun to recognize that the restriction of Japanese car imports into the United States unnecessarily increases their costs of production and reduces their ability to compete effectively in world markets. General Motors has begun to realize that car parts can be made in many areas of the world and that its ability to compete in domestic and international markets is dependent upon its ability to import parts from abroad. In general, the public has begun to wise up and to understand that the claim made by protectionists that they seek only to "save jobs" is merely a smoke screen. The enormous bonuses (ranging up to the millions of dollars) given auto executives in 1984, at a time when Japanese cars were being "voluntarily" withheld from American markets, revealed the full extent to which protectionism represents another corporate welfare program.

IX. Rent-Seeking Industrialists

It is always a temptation to an armed and agile nation
  To call upon a neighbor and to say:—
"We invaded you last night—we are quite prepared to fight,
  Unless you pay us cash to go away." . . .

It is always a temptation to a rich and lazy nation,
  To puff and look important and to say:—
"Though we know we should defeat you, we have not the time
    to meet you.
We will therefore pay you cash to go away."
                        —Rudyard Kipling[1]

As our study to this point reveals, the national industrial policy movement is founded on two premises: First, industrial markets unfettered by government planning controls are inefficient, at least on the margin and in their ability to serve commonly acknowledged collective or *national* industrial goals. Second, government *should* develop a "grand design" for the industrial structure of the U.S. economy and *should* then create profitable opportunities (which would not otherwise exist) for industries to restructure themselves in line with the collective design for the economy. Proposals to protect industries from imports and to subsidize and/or guarantee corporate investments, for example, smack of using market incentives to alter and direct corporate investment and employment strategies.

Proponents of these industrial strategies argue that once the economic profits or "rents" are created through government, resources will move in the desired direction and the economy will work more efficiently. The income transfers embodied in the governmentally created economic rents can be justified in terms of greater economic efficiency as well as enhanced equity. The targeted industries, in other words, may get more income due to import

---

[1]Rudyard Kipling, "Dane-Geld," in *Rudyard Kipling's Verse* (Garden City, N.Y.: Doubleday and Co., 1940), pp. 716–17.

185

protection or investment subsidies, but, it is argued, the general public would also benefit from industrial policies through a more efficient economy—one that produces more "social goods," supports the "social wage," smooths out economic adjustments, and increases "economic security."

This is their case in a nutshell. Proponents fail, however, to recognize that the process by which "rents" were created through government would, in itself, affect the allocation of resources. National industrial policy proponents may not like market results based largely, but not exclusively, on the profit motive; but the creation of a national industrial policy would not destroy the profit motive and/or the competitive drive that goes with it. A national industrial policy would merely shift the arena within which the profit motive would be felt. Private entrepreneurs will be just as eager to seek government-created rents as they are to seek the rents that emerge more or less naturally in markets due to shifts in market forces. As we will argue in this chapter, "rent seeking" in the political arena can negate most, if not all, of the efficiency benefits envisioned through industrial policies.

Rent Seeking

The theory of rent seeking attempts to correct a flaw in conventional economic theory. Economic theory of industrial structure has to a significant extent been founded on what is termed "static analysis." That is, economists have evaluated the relative efficiency of competitive and monopoly markets by assuming *given* market structures, by which is meant given degrees of "competitiveness." The central concern has been the extent to which monopoly power, which is the antithesis of competitiveness, distorts the allocation of scarce and valuable resources. The allocation of the country's resources is viewed as "distorted" or "inefficient" if resources are left unemployed or, if employed, could be employed more productively elsewhere. Generally, this market structure analysis has led economists to the conclusion that monopolies generate inefficiency. A monopolist interested in profits will, using its market power, take the attitude of "the public be damned" and cut back on production for the purpose of boosting market prices and firm profits.

The inefficiency of monopoly power emerges precisely from the fact that consumers would gladly buy more of the monopolist's product at a price that exceeds the monopolist's production costs. However, the monopolist will not supply the extra quantity simply because it would have to lower its price on *all* units produced just to sell a few additional units, with profits falling as a result.[2]

The "inefficiency" of monopoly is conventionally viewed as the result of lost production. It does not, conventionally, include the "rents" received by the monopolist. This is because the rents, or monopoly profits, represent a transfer from consumers to producers. Of course, consumers would prefer to have a lower price for the monopolist's product so as not to give up the income received by the monopolist as rents; but this preference is irrelevant to the central point, which is that the rents are a *transfer* of purchasing power from one group (consumers) to another group (owners and employees of the monopoly). The transfer is assumed to be costless, meaning that no resources are used in instituting or in making it. While we can argue with conviction that the restricted supply of the monopolized product means that the community is "worse off" because of the income transfer, the welfare of one group has gone down, *but* the welfare of another group has gone up. And when dealing in economic theory, nothing much is resolved by declaring that one group's welfare is more important than another's. Assessments of the welfare of different groups vary, and we can all disagree on what constitutes a welfare improvement when income transfer, not income creation, is the issue.

The foregoing analysis may not be considered very useful by national industrial policy advocates. They may reason that in the practical world of everyday politics, assessments are made all the time as to the relative merits of the welfare of various groups after income transfers. In fact, an industrial policy to impose a quota on steel imports is implicitly, if not explicitly, a political assessment that in that instance the welfare of steelworkers and steel companies is more important or meritorious than the welfare of consumers. Proponents of industrial policies might contend, as they do, that the "equity benefits," measured by the transfers, of an "improved" income distribution more than offset the "inefficiency" of policies that are purposefully designed to distort the allocation of resources.

Unfortunately, however, advocates of industrial policy mistak-

---

[2]The economic purist may detect that the possibility of monopolistic price discrimination has been sidestepped, which it has been in order to present the general thrust of the rent-seeking counterarguments and to ease the presentation. The avoidance of price discrimination does not affect the power of the conclusions drawn later in the chapter.

enly make the conventional assumption that monopoly power, and the rents that go with it, exists costlessly and is independent of the political process. Hence they mistakenly conclude, as do many economists, that in any transfer program the income gained by the targeted group, for example, steelworkers and company owners, equals (or comes very close) to the income lost by others, for example, consumers of steel products. In short, they adopt the conventional perspective on monopoly rents and presume that resources are not used up or "wasted" in the process of creating such rents or in making rent transfers—which is not likely to be the case.

If the government has the authority to create "rents," through either subsidies or the protection of monopoly power, we should expect people to actively compete to exploit government's transfer authority and to seek the rents created. In short, we should expect people to engage in "rent seeking," which means using real and valuable resources to persuade or coax government (i.e., elected representatives and their appointed bureaucrats) to create rents for them (or transfer income from everyone else to themselves).

A government that has the authority to create rents in any form will, unfortunately, be viewed by entrepreneurs as a potential investment outlet, one that may yield a higher rate of return than other market investment alternatives. And profit-motivated private investors should be willing to extend their investment in resources to sway the rent-seeking policies of government in their favor, as long as the profits or rents from doing so are greater than those that could be obtained by investing the same amount in their own production facilities (or best alternative investment outlet). After all, as we noted at the start, firms are interested in making profits, and rent-creating government policies do not destroy or even temper the profit motive. The prospects of rent creation, in other words, will distort the allocation of the country's resources just as surely as the monopolist's production cutbacks do. The lawyers and business executives who spend their time in Washington attempting to get the government to impose a tariff or approve a subsidy could have been doing something else, and the production forgone in their quest for government-contrived rents is largely, if not totally, a "waste" because income is not created.

"The implications of the economic wastefulness of rent-seeking activity are," writes George Mason University economist Robert Tollison in his survey of the burgeoning rent-seeking literature, difficult to escape once an artificial scarcity has been created [by government that results in contrived rents]. At one level the king can allow individuals to compete for the playing card monopoly and waste resources through such activities as bribery. Such outright venality is perhaps the simplest and most readily understood level of rent seeking. At a second level the state could sell the monopoly right to the highest bidder and put the proceeds at the disposal of government officials. In this case the monopoly rents will most likely show up in the wages of state officials, and to capture rents at this level individuals will compete to become civil servants. This competition might be thought of in terms of excess returns to bureaucratic agents where these returns are competed away by excessive expenditures on education to prepare for civil service examination. At still another level should the monopoly right be sold to the highest bidder and the resources dispersed through the state budget in terms of expenditure increases and/or tax reductions, rent-seeking costs will be incurred as individuals seek to become members of the group favored by the tax–expenditure program.[3]

The lesson that should be drawn from our discussion is that if government has the capacity to create rents, then entrepreneurs, especially those with a comparative advantage in "politicking," will seek to create and obtain those rents.

Each rent-seeking competitor should also be willing, at the limit, to invest resources in rent seeking up to the value of the rents to be acquired. For example, if the government offers to create and sell a monopoly franchise for a television station in a given area with expected future profits worth $1 million in today's terms,[4] entrepreneurs should be willing to pay the government up to $1 million for the franchise. If the television monopoly is awarded on the basis of political favoritism, then people should be willing to invest up to $1 million in bribes, campaign contributions, and lobbying expenses in order to be selected for the franchise.

The same could be said of rents created by way of industrial policies, for example, import protection and government subsidies: industrialists should be willing to invest resources in searching out

[3]Robert D. Tollison, "Rent Seeking: A Survey," *Kyklos* 35 (1982): 578–79.

[4]All future profits, for this example, have been appropriately discounted. This means that the owner of the television monopoly would be willing to trade his franchise and the future profits that go with it for $1 million and remain equally well off.

industrial policies that create rents for them, and this is evidently what many industrialists have been doing. Chrysler chairman Lee Iacocca and Bethlehem Steel chairman Donald Trautlein (to name just two among a horde of corporate executives who spend a great deal of time in the halls of government) have been avid and prominent Washington rent seekers over the past several years.

The overwhelming problem is that in a "rent-seeking society," which will emerge whenever the government has the capacity to affect income transfers by way of market intervention, a lot of resources will be wasted by both successful *and* unsuccessful rent seekers trying to alter government policies to their benefit.[5] The very valuable resources they use will be diverted away from largely productive (product creation) investments in the market arena to largely unproductive rent-seeking (transfer creation) investments in the political arena. As noted, this diversion of resources creates market inefficiency in the same sense that monopolist production cutbacks do; as a consequence, the nation's income-generating capacity is impaired.

Furthermore, proponents of rent-creating industrial policies should understand that because of rent seeking, the beneficiaries of government transfer programs might not be, to the degree imagined, the targeted industries. The beneficiaries will likely include the politicians who supply the rent-producing industrial policies, the bureaucrats who administer the programs, and the lobbyists who ply the streets of Washington and make their living by channeling and rechanneling government-contrived rents.

The question, should we have a national industrial policy? is critically important because stopping the resource waste involved in industrial-policy rent seeking is difficult once it starts. If rents can be garnered from changes in industrial policies, executives will be pressured to devote a growing share of their firms' resources to rent seeking for two reasons.

First, the executives' bosses, i.e., their firms' owners, who are

---

[5]Gordon Tullock has shown that the extent to which rents are fully dissipated by rent seeking is dependent upon the number of rent seekers and the costs of expanding rent-seeking efforts. He has also shown that the sum of resources wasted by all successful and unsuccessful rent seekers can actually, under the right conditions, result in resource waste that is greater than the rents. "Efficient Rent Seeking," in *Towards a Theory of the Rent Seeking Society*, ed. James M. Buchanan, Robert D. Tollison, and Gordon Tullock (College Station, Tex.: Texas A&M University Press, 1980), pp. 3–15.

interested in making money wherever it can be found, will push executives to seek government-created rents. Executives who resist will tend to be replaced. Steel industry executives understood in 1984 that they had to seek import protection; otherwise, their jobs would have been on the line. They understood that they could easily be replaced by people who would seek government-contrived rents through lobbying the International Trade Commission, the Office of the U.S. Trade Representative, and the White House.

Second, executives understand that if they do not engage in rent seeking, others will, and their firms will be saddled with the rent-seeking costs imposed on American consumers and businesses by others, with no offsetting rents of their own.

In summary, opening up government to vast new rent-seeking opportunities, promoted under the guise of industrial policy, would be a rent seeker's dream. The dream may, however, be a counter-productive nightmare for the country as a whole, with virtually every interest group banging on government doors in an attempt to acquire industrial rents and protection from all the other rent seekers. Charles Schultze has crystallized the seductive politics of the industrial policy debate:

> One does not have to be a cynic to forecast that the surest way to multiply unwarranted subsidies and protectionist measures is to legitimize their existence under the rubric of industrial policy. The likely outcome of an industrial policy that encompassed some elements of both "protecting the losers" and "picking the win-ners" is that the losers would back subsidies for the winners in return for the latter's support on issues of trade protection.[6]

An unheralded advantage of having government adopt, to the fullest extent possible, a "hands-off industrial policy" would be to force industrialists to do what they do best: to seek profits through cost reductions and product development, not through contrived market scarcities or government subsidies. In an important respect, a hands-off industrial policy is a means of protecting people, indus-trialists included, from themselves.

---

[6]Charles L. Schultze, "Industrial Policy: A Dissent," *Brookings Review* (Fall 1983): 11. Reprinted in *Plant Closings: Public or Private Choices?* ed. Richard B. McKenzie, rev. ed. (Washington: Cato Institute, 1984).

Tax/Compensation Proposals

Our analysis up to this point in the chapter has assumed that we do not, for all intents and purposes, have an industrial policy. However, we have noted in earlier chapters the extensive import protection and subsidies that industries in the country do have. If these government policies, which are the source of economic rents, are inefficient, then how do we get rid of them? Economists have long advocated what have been called "tax/compensation (or buy-out) policies" as a means of achieving general agreement on the elimination of tariffs, quotas, and other forms of restrictive and efficiency-reducing forms of regulation. Conventional economic theory clearly reveals that tariffs, for example, result in a dead-weight loss to the economy. Hence, a policy shift that eliminates a tariff and the market inefficiency that goes with it will result in benefits to the "gainers" (consumers) that exceed the losses to the "losers" (producers). By taxing the gainers sufficiently to more than compensate the losers for their losses from the policy shift, the protective control of markets can be dissolved, or so it is argued. An appropriately constructed tax and compensation schedule should leave everyone "better off" and, thereby, in perfect accord over the policy change. The tax/compensation scheme is therefore advocated as a political solution to the policy stalemate over what to do about government-created rents and inefficiency.

Again, however, the conclusion often drawn that "policy buy-outs" will lead to less protection and less market inefficiency is mistaken, if the prospects of rent seeking in an unconstrained political environment are considered. Several critically important but seriously flawed assumptions undergird this standard tax/compensation analysis.

The analysis presumes that a tax/compensation scheme will install new incentives to rescind protective regulation, which it may do temporarily in the narrow context of any given buyout. However, the conventional analysis fails to recognize that a "buyout" of a protected industry, by definition, amounts to an increase in the rewards expected to come from protection, or else the protected industry would not consent to being bought out. To the extent that rent seeking is a function of government-provided benefits, which is assumed to be the case in the rent-seeking literature, such buyouts should inspire greater rent seeking—that is, more resources being tied up and "wasted" in lobbying government for protection. To the extent that rent-seeking activities are effective, a tax/compensation scheme will increase, not decrease, the degree of protection and, consequently, the deadweight loss from protection. This is especially true if the buyout contract does not prevent the once-protected industry from petitioning government again for protection after it has been bought out. And it is difficult to see how the bought-out industry could be so prevented, short of a constitutional prohibition against protective regulation.[7]

Because of the buyout, the bought-out industry will not only have a greater incentive to seek protection again, since the return on its political investment will have been raised, but it will have greater wealth, i.e., the funds from the buyout, with which to seek the rents it once had. Other industries will, of course, attempt to follow the example of the bought-out industry and acquire protection with the intent of seeking compensation for a buyout.[8] In addition to seeking government protection in order to acquire the added rents, many of these industries will be coaxed, as noted above, into competing for those rents just to protect themselves from being part of the segment of the business population that must, on balance, bear the costs of protective regulation.

Proponents of tax/compensation schemes assume that their proposals should achieve unanimous consent within the community, since everyone is presumed to gain from the policy change. These policy proponents must be left to wonder why such schemes are so rarely taken seriously in the political process. Indeed, tax/compensation schemes are generally dismissed almost without a second thought even by protected industries (which on balance should, by the standards of the cost-benefit calculus on which the proposals are founded, gain from them).

The rent-seeking perspective developed in this chapter suggests that in the absence of constitutional constraints preventing or containing the amount of rent seeking induced by tax/compensation policies (and such constraints are not usually considered in the context of tax/compensation proposals), the tax/compensation pol-

[7]If a specific set of companies is bought out and, at the same time, is prevented from seeking protective tariffs again, then it would appear that the companies could be dissolved only to reemerge with new legal identities but with the capital of the owners of the previously bought-out firms.

[8]There is an unavoidable similarity between arguments for tax/compensation schemes and proposals to "buy off" muggers. Such proposed buyoffs can only make mugging more profitable and more common.

icy route would create a world of rampant rent seeking because the rewards from securing protection repeatedly would be substantial.[9] Our rent-seeking perspective suggests that tax/compensation proposals are likely to be largely ignored for one major reason: in a world without prohibitions or limitations on rent seeking, the presumed "gainers," meaning the general public, of any particular buyout are likely to be net "losers." This is especially the case when the industry that is initially protected represents a relatively small part of the import-competing industries and when the threat of additional rent seeking is taken into account.

The very fact that tax/compensation schemes are being considered is evidence that the necessary prohibition against future rent seeking is not in place. Indeed tax/compensation proposals may be evidence of rent seeking by a protected industry, since the compensation may be construed as just another form of rent. If protected industries can obtain rents by way of tariffs and higher prices, then they should be able to obtain rents by way of government buyouts whose costs are spread thinly over the taxpaying citizenry.[10]

[9]Of course, the compensation paid in a buyout would be adjusted downward in response to repeated rent seeking. To make a buyout mutually beneficial to both losers and gainers in the policy shift, the compensation would vary directly with the expected time period during which the buyout would actually reduce protective regulation. The compensation paid in any given buyout would also vary inversely with the additional rent seeking inspired among other industries. This is because in order to make a buyout efficient, the public that is paying for the compensation must be left better off after it takes place. If the public must incur higher rent-seeking costs from sources that are not parties to the buyout, then it would have less in the way of efficiency gains to pay. In situations where rent seeking was perfectly responsive to increases in rent-seeking rewards, the potential compensation would fade to zero. The required compensation could, of course, become negative, which means that a buyout could not occur.

[10]Our last point enables us to note that tax/compensation schemes assume that a protected industry has achieved maximum profits from restrictions on its market. The escalating costs of rent seeking, especially those costs relating to industry efforts to work unitedly for protection, are likely to lead in many, if not most, instances of protection to situations in which the protected industry does not maximize industry profits. Protection is restricted to some optimum level, circumscribed by the costs incurred by rent seekers and by the costs the losing public will allow. The argument that tax/compensation schemes will be adopted in the face of the additional rent seeking that the tax/compensation will inspire and the consequent additional costs that the losing public will have to absorb suggests two internally inconsistent lines of thought. First, tax/compensation schemes propose to introduce a new rent-seeking technology that changes the political equilibrium in favor of more rent seeking. A

Generally speaking, tax/compensation proposals are tendered on the assumption that the tax will be more or less evenly distributed among the citizenry—or, at the very least, that people will readily consent to paying their "fair share" of the compensation burden, which may be loosely tied to the benefits they may receive from the elimination of protective regulation. There is no particular reason to expect that to be the case. Indeed, the rent-seeking perspective would suggest that such interest groups as exporters, who through the impact of expanded imports or exports may be prime beneficiaries of the elimination of protective tariffs, will seek a tax schedule that in no way reflects their relative benefits. They may offer a tax/compensation scheme as part and parcel of their own rent-seeking designs. The substitution of one rent-seeking equilibrium for another, both of which are beset with inefficiencies, would hardly represent an efficient move. Further, the rent seeking that may emerge in the development of a buyout may do nothing more than simply add to the social waste generated by the initial instance in which government powers were used to suppress competition.

Concluding Comments

The central message of this chapter was probably best captured by Rudyard Kipling when he wrote of the Dane's conquest of his country more than a thousand years ago. He added to the quote heading this chapter:

> And that is called paying the Dane-geld;
> But we've proved it again and again,

---

hidden assumption in this argument is that the public, which limits the amount of protection in the first place, will be seduced into accepting additional costs that would not have been accepted through greater market restrictions for protected industries. And second, the schemes assume that protected industries did not initially exhaust their potential for gaining protection. If additional costs can be imposed on the public through tax/compensation devices and the rent-seeking activities they induce, then it stands to reason that protected industries could have imposed more costs on the offended public through more protection. It might reasonably be argued that the amount of transfers an interest group can obtain is inversely dependent upon how "obvious," or easy to monitor, the transfer is. One might hypothesize that transfers from buyouts are far more obvious to the polity than transfers from restrictions on market supplies. To the extent that this is the case, the public will be resistant to helping the protected industries through tax/compensation schemes. Additionally, buyouts might, so to speak, "blow the transfer cover" of protected industries, shifting the political equilibrium toward less protection (and toward less in the way of reward from any proposed buyout).

That if once you have paid the Dane-geld
  You never get rid of the Dane.

It is wrong to put temptation in the path of any nation,
  For fear they should succumb and go astray;
So when you are requested to pay up or be molested,
  You will find it better policy to say:—

"We never pay *any*-one Dane-geld,
  No matter how trifling the cost;
For the end of that game is oppression and shame,
  And the nation that plays it is lost!"[11]

An equally important auxiliary message of the rent-seeking literature, also suggested by Kipling's poem, is that constitutional checks
on government economic powers are necessary in order to prevent
"wasteful" attempts by competitors to use the unchecked redistributive powers of government. Without such constitutional checks,
the presumed industrial policy solution, buyouts, may come to be
part of the problem.

Economists have implicitly assumed that their ideas do not count
in political calculations. But to the extent that tax/compensation
schemes have been promoted as an efficient policy, such schemes
have probably encouraged rent seeking and protection. Regret-
tably, the possibility of tax/compensation schemes has reduced the
expected costs of protection, since they would provide a potential
means of eliminating protection. They should, as a consequence,
marginally reduce public opposition to protective regulation. Because
they have also increased the expected rewards of protection, they
should, on this account as well, marginally encourage rent seeking
and the wastes associated with it.

[11]Kipling, p. 717.

X. An Alternative Vision of Our Economic Future

A major business publication recently acknowledged that "the industrial policy bandwagon is under attack,"[1] and for good reason. As detailed in foregoing chapters, proponents of a national industrial policy have argued that the country is deindustrializing, in spite of much evidence to the contrary. They have, as a consequence, argued in a variety of policy forums that the economic difficulties faced by the United States can be cured only by greater reliance on the federal government, that is, by greater federal expenditures, more federal restrictions on domestic and international trade, and more centralized decision making in Washington—in short, more government subsidies, bailouts, and regulation of American businesses and workers. They seek to manage the industrial economy as if it were one big firm.

These industrial policy advocates offer the problem as the solution. They tell us that all they seek is more "rational federal policies," but suggest more of the same policies that have been tried repeatedly with results industrial policy advocates now seek to remedy.

Economic growth in terms of jobs, productivity, income, and wealth is a common goal of people on all parts of the political spectrum. Most Americans fully acknowledge that the U.S. economy has failed to achieve the desired level of economic growth. Most recognize that the country could have done much better, if only the appropriate mix of economic policies had been followed. Most worry, however, that a continuation of many current policies—which include high and expanding federal expenditures, taxes, and deficits; rapid and unstable monetary growth; and federal regulatory intrusions in markets, hampering the domestic and international competitiveness of U.S. industries—will mean that our economic future can be no more hopeful than our immediate past.

---

[1]"The Attack on Industrial Policy," *Fortune*, October 3, 1983, p. 56.

Americans of all political persuasions agree on the simple proposition that we can do better—that our past need not be the blueprint for our economic future, that we can reclaim the American dream of economic improvement for ourselves and our children. Americans understand that a growing economy inspires its own continued success and facilitates the attainment of other, noneconomic national objectives, namely, growing freedom of opportunity, especially for the disadvantaged among us, and the maintenance of national security and peace. They recognize that the revitalization of America's industrial and business competitiveness requires a long-term strategy for economic development. We as a country must rethink America's industrial future with an eye toward redirecting discussions of public policies away from attempts to have government relieve the multitude of social ills the nation confronts on a daily basis, which few can deny exist, and toward resolution of problems of governmental-institutional design. We need a new vision of what is possible for the American economy—founded, as it must be in a free society, on private, individual initiative.

The critical challenge facing policymakers is one of seeking useful alternatives to a government process that appears to be out of control and that results in many policies that, over the long run, have done more harm than good. Few question the laudable objectives that motivated and activated many current policies; but a casual perusal of the results leads most to doubt the wisdom of a variety of policies followed and advocated in the name of a "national industrial policy." Many past policies, which have relied on bigger government, simply have not worked.

While there is considerable unity over broad national goals, there is substantial debate over how government policies should be altered. In the name of revitalizing the economy, many industrial policy advocates, we have noted, recommend a smorgasbord of changes that translate into more government expenditures and greater government intrusions in markets. The overriding conclusion of the foregoing analysis is that such an industrial policy course—leading to higher tax rates, lower real incomes for consumers, slower economic growth, more freedom for government, and less freedom for individuals—would be highly counterproductive.

A Different Policy Course

Still, opponents of past national industrial policy proposals, like this author, generally hold the view that economic revitalization of the American economy is a practical political objective, provided that the policies adopted encourage—that is, do not restrict—market processes. They generally subscribe to the view that inefficiencies in government policies frequently offer an opportunity for constructing policy changes that are beneficial to most competing political interests. They sincerely believe that policy changes that encourage market processes are far more likely to benefit the relatively poor and disadvantaged than are policies designed to centralize economic decision making in the hands of government. The art of political economy involves the search for policy changes that allow the competing parties to share the economic benefits that must emerge when inefficient policies are removed or altered. Accordingly, in the midst of the industrial policy debate, I set out to develop, with the aid of my academic colleagues from across the country and under the sponsorship of the Heritage Foundation, a program for economic revitalization predicated upon two simple selection requirements:[2]

- The policy change must not result in increases in budget totals, namely, federal expenditures and taxes. Wherever possible, taxes and expenditures should be reduced to eliminate the deadweight loss that comes with the disincentive effects of higher federal tax rates and the crowding-out effects on work and investment of higher federal expenditures and deficits. Serious discussions of controlling federal expenditures must begin and end with curtailing significantly the projected growth of the federal budget.

- The policy change should promote greater reliance on markets to allocate the nation's growing stock of scarce resources. Control of markets by federal pricing, taxing, and purchasing policies has been the chief source of the country's economic malaise, mainly because federal market intrusions have diverted private initiatives away from the essentially productive activity associated with saving, working, and investing and toward the essentially counterproduc-

[2]Richard B. McKenzie, ed., *Blueprint for Jobs and Industrial Growth* (Washington: Heritage Foundation, 1984). The policy proposals mentioned in the remainder of this chapter are discussed in some detail in this publication, which also includes references to much longer supporting studies.

tive activity associated with lobbying the government for
subsidies and protection from competition.

The policy course that was developed is founded upon 10 underlying premises:

First, growth in the nation's income and wealth will emerge,
primarily, as a consequence of the private actions of individuals
who understand their own interests and who are encouraged, through
open markets, to compete for the dollars of consumers.

Second, all resources, including environmental resources, have
competing uses. A means must be found for allocating these resources
to their highest-valued uses. Environmental resources are particularly troublesome to allocate, mainly because their use affects so
many people. Nevertheless, they must be allocated, and ways exist
for allocating environmental resources via market mechanisms.
Market-oriented policy options exist to achieve the laudable objective of improving environmental quality at lower cost.

International competition mandates that we employ every means
available to achieve all environmental regulatory goals in the most
cost-effective way. This means we should expand the use of the
"bubble concept" in pollution control, providing industry with
greater flexibility as to how established pollution standards can be
met and a more creative method for reducing air pollution. It also
means we should give firms greater flexibility in selling their "emis-
sion standards," a market process that would permit enhanced
environmental quality at lower firm cost. Finally, it implies that the
emerging water crisis must be averted in part by the assignment of
property rights to water, a policy that would result in greater water
conservation, a reallocation of the country's water supplies to higher-
valued uses, and greater national output at lower cost in money
and water terms.

Third, governments at all levels need to ensure that many services
are provided. However, such a position does not imply that the
governments themselves must provide the services. Through the
privatization of public services, many services can be provided at
lower cost through the competitive bidding process. The federal
government may need to ensure that national defense is provided,
but it can obtain many of its services and hardware from private
contractors under competitive bids and should make as much use
of the bidding process as possible. The same argument can be
applied to the delivery of education and many local services, from

garbage collection to fire protection. The result of efforts to privatize public services can lower the cost of government and, to that extent, reduce the disincentive effects of taxation.

Fourth, international trade is growing in importance to the U.S. economy. Because of the mutual benefits to the countries involved, free international trade should be encouraged. Protectionism reduces the competitive drive facing American producers, hurts American consumers, invites foreign retaliation, and reduces exports. Protectionist measures may "save" or "create" jobs in the protected industries, but they will destroy or jeopardize jobs in other export sectors. As explained earlier, the ability of foreign countries to buy from American firms is dependent upon their ability to sell to us. Protectionism tends to be a counterproductive industrial strategy. Job creation in export industries can be encouraged by reducing barriers to imports.

Fifth, regulation should be undertaken only in the presence of clear market failures, should be cost-effective, and should not unnecessarily discriminate against domestic firms. Regulation should be used only very sparingly to alter the demands of reasonably informed citizens. Regulation is too often used to promote the private interests of firms that want to monopolize their markets under the guise of achieving some other noble social objective. Such protective regulation has no place in a free competitive economy.

Social and environmental regulations must be reevaluated to ensure that undue costs are not being imposed on American producers. Specifically, cost-benefit analysis must figure more prominently in regulatory decisions, especially in the development of performance standards. Furthermore, performance standards should be more widely used, replacing engineering standards. Current wasteful conflicts among regulatory policies in government agencies must be reconciled by a coordinating agency, preferably the Office of Management and Budget. The deregulation of the transportation industry should be completed with the elimination of all remaining government-inspired entry and pricing restrictions.

Sixth, maintenance of competitive markets is a fundamental objective of the federal government. However, competitive markets are ultimately dependent upon their "openness," that is, the ability to enter and leave them, not on the number of existing firms or on the absolute sizes of existing firms. *Potential* competition can be as important to achievement of competitive prices and output levels as *actual* competition. Antitrust policy should be directed toward the elimination of artificial (mainly legally contrived) barriers to entry and exit, that is, barriers that are not associated with a firm's efforts to reduce production costs and prices and to offer more attractive products. Too often antitrust laws have been used to thwart essentially competitive, cost-saving business practices under the incorrect claim that such activities constitute monopolistic practices.

Antitrust policies must not continue to be "anticompetitive" policies. Hence, the focus of enforcement policy must be shifted away from firm size and industry concentration, which are often the consequence of highly competitive market processes and present no threat to competition. The "rule of reason," which effectively abolishes the automatic trebling of damages in antitrust cases (except in overt cases of monopoly practices) must be institutionalized to reduce attempts by businesses to obstruct competition through nuisance suits—the central purpose of which is often to force firms to agree to lucrative out-of-court settlements rather than spending years of valuable time and millions of dollars defending themselves in court. State- and municipally organized and condoned monopolies should be no more exempt from antitrust law than privately inspired cartels. All monopolies should be subject to the same legal constraints.

Seventh, to the extent possible, taxes should be neutral in their impact on the allocation of individual and business purchases. Tax laws that discriminate unnecessarily against people's incentives to work, save, and invest thwart economic development.

Tax policies must be altered to encourage saving and capital formation. This requires lowering the double taxation of savings and capital by exempting a larger proportion of personal and business savings from taxation, lowering the corporate income tax, and reducing immediately (and eventually removing) capital gains taxation (bringing our tax system more in line with the Japanese system). It means also that we recognize that depreciation schedules for capital assets discriminate arbitrarily against fast-growing, especially high-tech, industries in which capital obsolescence is accelerating. We must move toward "immediate expensing" of all capital purchases.

Eighth, labor is a particularly important resource in production. To the extent possible, legal impediments to freely negotiate contracts between labor and management should be eliminated. Restrictions on labor markets tend to reduce employment opportunities. The right of workers to belong to unions of their own choosing should be affirmed as part and parcel of the basic right of free association. However, the right of free association includes the right not to belong. Federal law should, to the extent possible, be neutral in its effect on union membership.

Labor policies must be revamped to ensure that government is not creating and prolonging unemployment. This objective can be partially met by replacing the federal supplemental unemployment compensation program (which induces extended unemployment) with a program of unemployment loans; by adjusting unemployment insurance rates to more accurately reflect the unemployment experience of firms (thereby reducing the subsidy going to firms responsible for the unemployment problem); by freezing the minimum wage for adults and setting a sub-minimum wage for teenagers; and by repealing or modifying such laws as the Davis-Bacon Act, which reduce employment opportunities by artificially hiking the costs of federal projects. In addition, more cooperative labor-management working environments can be encouraged by once again allowing "company unions" to compete in union elections supervised by the National Labor Relations Board. And competitive labor markets can be encouraged by amending the Hobbs Act to ensure that labor violence that obstructs interstate commerce is, once and for all, made a federal crime.

Ninth, to a significant extent, economic growth will be the product of improvements in human skills. To improve the skills of the American labor force, education dollars must be used more effectively. The institutional setting of education must be altered to allow for more competition for rewards among teachers and among schools. Opportunities for education should be expanded not by increasing per-pupil funding for public schools (especially at the federal level), but rather by giving parents greater say over where and under what educational circumstances their educational dollars will be spent.

Tenth, a reinvigorated growth-oriented economy requires that savings be allocated to their highest-valued uses. This can be accomplished in part by amending the Glass-Steagall Act to once again allow banks to act as investment bankers and by amending the McFadden Act to speed up the emergence of interstate branch banking. We must also replace the Federal Deposit Insurance Corporation with a system of private deposit insurance that will encourage rational, price-constrained risk taking on the part of banks. The deregulation of the services provided by U.S. financial institutions must be completed to enhance the returns to savers, which will foster greater saving. Such a program seeks to "unmanage" capitalism.

"Winners" and "Losers"

The concept of a national industrial policy presents many members of Congress with a political dilemma. They favor government doing what it can to expand the industrial base, but are afraid of voting for anything that carries the threat of creeping socialism and government planning. They want, in other words, to support industrial policy as a concept without approving the substance of many of the proposals currently on the table. After all, it is difficult to argue with the basic premises of industrial policy—that people need and want jobs, the kind that pay well and are secure; that government should establish a policy framework for industrial development; and that government policies should not be unintended obstructions to the expansion of the employment base. It is also difficult to forget that previous efforts at government tinkering with the economy may be responsible for some of the problems we face today.

Above all, in its search for a national industrial policy, Congress must be mindful that its policies to reindustrialize America may help some workers and investors, but at the expense of others. To ensure that government's powers are used to promote the general interest (not special interests), Congress should resolve (1) that it is in favor of government doing what it can to save and create jobs, but (2) that it is against any program that saves or creates jobs in some industries while limiting growth or destroying jobs in other industries.

Acceptance of this point is especially crucial in cases where the wages of workers whose jobs are saved are higher than the wages of workers whose jobs are destroyed. Automobile workers in Michigan, for example, who earn substantially more than the average manufacturing wage, should not be beneficiaries of an industrial policy that destroys or jeopardizes the jobs of textile workers in North and South Carolina, who earn significantly less than the average manufacturing wage. Textile workers, meanwhile, should not benefit from an industrial policy that causes other workers, who may earn even less, to lose their jobs.

Congress should resolve further that government programs to channel investment funds—grants, subsidized loans, and loan guarantees—to selected industries ("winners") be undertaken only after identifying those industries ("losers") that would be denied private investment funds as a result. We have noted that the Chrysler bailout had a laudable objective, saving Chrysler workers' jobs. At the same time, government loan guarantees diverted investment funds from other uses to Chrysler and, to that extent, reduced employment opportunities in other firms, even other automobile firms.

In other words, Congress should declare, as a matter of political integrity in policy formulation, that any industrial policy proposal is a two-edged sword, with both positive and negative effects, and that the intent of Congress is to increase employment and investment opportunities, not to reduce them. It should also declare, as a guiding principle, that no action will be taken under the guise of an industrial policy unless *compelling* reasons are given for government efforts to save or create jobs in the selected "winning" industries while destroying or jeopardizing jobs in "losing" industries.

To judge industrial policies fairly and accurately, the Congress and the public need to know who the winners and losers from government policies are likely to be and why the selections were made. Therefore, all industrial policy proposals should be accompanied by an "economic impact statement" that explains in clear and emphatic language:

- a list of the industries selected for aid ("winners");

- a list of the industries that will be harmed by the policy ("losers");

- estimates of the jobs saved and/or created in the selected industries and destroyed and/or jeopardized in other identified industries;

- a statement of purpose and an affirmation of the national and public interests that are sought both by the saving and creating of jobs in the "winning" industries *and* by the destroying or jeopardizing of jobs in the "losing" industries.

If such a resolution, or one similar to it, were adopted, Congress would retain considerable policy flexibility. However, it would also be acknowledging that greater federal expenditures, which create employment opportunities, give rise to greater taxes and/or deficits, which reduce employment opportunities; that restrictions on imports, which create or save jobs, reduce exports and the employment base in exporting industries; and that government grant loans and loan guarantees that direct investment funds *into* selected industries, maintaining or expanding employment opportunities there, also divert funds *away* from other industries, in which employment opportunities will be lost. Congress will also be forced to explain the reasons why it is willing to hurt some workers in order to help others. To this extent the Congress can be held more accountable for its actions.

Such a resolution does not mean that there is nothing in the way of industrial policy that the Congress can do to pursue the public purpose. It would mean, however, that pursuit of the public purpose through industrial policy would be undertaken more openly and more carefully.

The Necessary Macroeconomic Framework

More than anything else, the federal government must get its macroeconomic policy house in order if any industrial policy agenda is to have any hope of being effective. Markets can operate tolerably effectively in a stable economic environment. A prime reason for our economic and industrial difficulties over the past two decades has been instability in government policies, principally macroeconomic policies. Fiscal policy has been characterized by a long-term trend toward higher tax rates on capital and labor, growth in government expenditures in real terms and as a percentage of gross national product, and accelerating dependence on deficit spending (which is a hidden form of taxation on the nation's resources). There have also been major shifts in the composition of government expenditures, first toward greater transfer and welfare programs in the 1960s and 1970s and then toward defense expenditures in the early 1980s. The budget process itself has become unwieldy, resulting in final budgets not being approved until months after they are supposed to take effect. Uncertainties over budget totals and allocation adds unnecessarily to the risk of doing business in the private sector.

Monetary policy has been characterized by a long-run expansion in the rate of growth in the money stock, which is a major explanation for the inflationary spiral of the 1960s and 1970s. Rapid annual increases in the money stock in the late 1970s were followed by equally rapid decreases in the money growth rate in the early

1980s. The abrupt month-to-month changes in the money stock in recent years have, without question, contributed marginally to the relatively high real interest rates in the country via increasing the riskiness of holding monetary assets. Given projected budget deficits that range upwards of $200 billion for the next several years and the tendency of the Federal Reserve to accommodate the loanable fund demands of the Treasury, money market analysts understandably forecast a continuation of past policy cycles: spurts of inflation followed by recession, due to expansion and contractions of the money growth rates.

Realistically, policies designed to revitalize the American industrial economy must be predicated upon government getting its own fiscal and monetary houses in order. A first priority in any economic revitalization program is for the federal government to bring its deficits under control. Economic growth is dependent upon greater investment, and projected federal deficits are expected to continue to take more than half of the personal and business saving pool. The projected deficits can be expected to severely retard development, most importantly by crowding out private investors.

Government deficits should be brought under control through two mechanisms, one long-run and one short-run. The long-run approach would require adoption of the proposed balanced budget–tax limitation amendment to the Constitution, which would require a balanced federal budget and which would tie growth in federal expenditures to growth in national income. Between now and the time that amendment is adopted, a realistic means of moving the federal government toward a balanced budget would be to have the Congress commit itself to freezing per-capita federal expenditures at the current 1984 level (if a freeze on total real expenditures appears unacceptable), while undertaking a thorough review to identify those government programs that could more appropriately be provided by non-government organizations—that is, those that could be privatized.[3] This would mean that while government services could expand with population, Congress would have to face difficult decisions on how its dollars should be allocated among competing department interests, and the federal government would slowly become a relatively smaller component of the national economy. Also, in the near term government must reform

[3]See Stuart Butler, "Privatization: A Strategy for Cutting Federal Spending," Heritage Foundation Backgrounder (Washington, 1983).

its budget process, eliminating current delays in approving the budget on schedule and hence eliminating the growing threat of government shutdowns when the budget has not been approved by the start of the fiscal year.[4]

Monetary policy must be brought under control. The most preferred policy would be to require the Federal Reserve to follow a monetary growth rate rule (which would likely be defined as a "monetary band" within which the growth rate must stay) and/or to encourage competing monies. Barring the acceptance of a money growth rule or competing monies, the political independence of the Federal Reserve must reconsidered. Evidence continues to mount that the Federal Reserve tends to follow the monetary policies of the administration in office. The present institutional arrangements permit administrations to shirk responsibility for the fate of adverse monetary policies, while allowing them to take credit for favorable monetary policies.

Concluding Comments

In the final analysis, in rethinking America's industrial future, we as a country must come to grips with the fact that many of our current economic difficulties stem from the breakdown of constitutional constraints on government. There is now virtually nothing government cannot do in the way of intervening in private markets, including industrial markets. Hence there are virtually no constitutional constraints on how interest groups, industrial or otherwise, can use government in the pursuit of their own narrow ends, which often include the transfer of income from the larger society to themselves. It is therefore understandable why many industrialists fervently support various industrial policies: they see in them a means of easing competitive pressures, increasing their firms' and industries' profits, and improving their own welfare. Many of these industrialists also understand that if they do not seek industrial policies for themselves, others will, and then their competitive positions may be eroded under the pressure of taxes collected to pay for benefits going to other industries and by subsidies that

---

[4]For a review of the avenues for reform in the budget process, see John Palffy, "Giving the Budget Process Teeth," Heritage Foundation Backgrounder (Washington, November 1983); and Stuart M. Butler, ed., *A Heritage Foundation Report on Taming the Federal Budget: Fiscal Year 1986* (Washington: Heritage Foundation, 1985).

enable other firms in other industries to compete more aggressively for the nation's scarce resources.

The case against managed capitalism, or for "unmanaged" markets, is actually a set of arguments for constraints on the economic powers of government. Namely, government must be relegated to the very important and difficult task of developing the economic climate in which all firms operate, and it must be denied the capacity to manage market outcomes, which inevitably translates into a power to pick "winners" and "losers." The case against managed capitalism is a set of arguments directed toward the goal of restricting established economic power groups from using their political clout to their own narrow advantage. It is an argument for encouraging industrialists and workers alike to direct their energies toward producing the goods and services that we all want, not toward manipulating government policies. That is the kind of economic future we must seek in order to remain prosperous and free.

Index

Democratic Caucus Committee on Party
  Effectiveness, 14
DiLorenzo, Thomas, 38, 41
Displaced workers (*see also* Retraining
  programs)
  number of, 71–73
  skilled employment, decline in, 68–69,
    68 tbl
  work force structure and, 69–71, 70 tbl
Dualism in the labor force, 66, 70–71

Economic Bill of Rights, 13, 34
Economic Cooperation Council. *See*
  Planning councils
Economic decline of the U.S., 17–18, 35
Economic democracy, 12–13, 19–20, 35–36
Economic growth, 197–98
Economic impact statements, 75, 205
Economic problem
  definition of, 104–5
  information problems, 110
  price-quantity combination, 108
  production, 105–6, 106 fig
  resources, 105
  scarcity, 105, 107
  supply and demand, 107–8, 107 fig
  wants, 105
Economic revitalization plan
  antitrust policies, 201–2
  budget concerns, 199
  education policies, 203
  international trade, 201
  investment policies, 203–4
  labor policies, 202–3
  markets, reliance on, 199–200
  regulation criteria, 201
  resource allocation, 199
  services, provision of, 200–201
  tax policies, 202
Economics education, 108–9
Education expenditures, 13–14, 203
Emerging industries, 120
Employment
  full employment, 9
  in manufacturing, 21, 38, 43, 44–45, 69
  nonmanufacturing, 44–45
  protectionism and, 168–70
  Reconstruction Finance Corporation,
    effects of, 90–93
Employment relationships, 130–31
Entrepreneurship, 15–16
Environmental regulation, 200
Equilibrium tax rate, 150

Europe. *See* Western Europe
Exchange rates, 165
Externalities, 29, 76–80

Fair Trade in Steel Act of 1982, 160
The Fatal Conceit (Hayek), 103–4
Federal Deposit Insurance Corporation,
  203
Federal Trade Commission (FTC), 180, 181
Ford, William, 10–11, 19, 81n, 136
FTC. *See* Federal Trade Commission
Full employment, 9

General Motors, 183–84
Gephardt, Richard, 84, 91
Gevirtz, Don, 15–16
Gordon, David, 13, 126n
Guarini, Frank, 81n, 82, 85

Haberler, Gottfried, 179, 180, 181
Hager, Wolfgang, 18, 161–62, 164, 165
Harrigan, Anthony, 160
Harrison, Bennett
  capital mobility, 143
  economic decline of the U.S., 17, 18, 35
  national industrial policy proposals,
    11–13
  plant closings, 19
Hart, Gary, 1, 3–5, 18, 126n
Hatsopoulos, George, 16
Hayek, F. A., 29, 103–4, 109, 111, 118
Heilbroner, Robert, 105
Henderson, David, 23
Hickel, James, 23, 95, 97
High-tech sector, 70–71, 71 tbl, 72 fig
Hollings, Ernest (Fritz), 2, 13–14, 18,
  81, 82
Hoover, Herbert, 85

Iacocca, Lee, 97, 190
Income-demand curve, 146 fig
Income transfers, 167–68, 185, 187–88
Industrial democracy, 6–7
Industrial policy. *See* National industrial
  policy
Interest, real rate of, 16
Interest groups, 28
International Monetary Fund, 9
Investment fund allocation, 100–101

Japan
    industrial development projects, 62–63
    industrial growth in, 54, 58
    national industrial policy, 19, 22, 23, 63
    real rate of interest in, 16
    trade policies, 164–65, 169, 176, 177 fig
Jefferson, Edward, 16–17
Job losses, 37, 64, 74–75
Job openings, 68 tbl
Job rights
    contract concerns re, 131–32
    employment relationship and, 130–31
    equity and efficiency goals, 125–27
    government role in, 124–25
    intrinsic right to jobs, 124–25
    job ownership, 127–30
    job resale rights, 129–30
    legal rights of workers, 137–38, 139
    legislated, 132–33, 134, 137
    market uncertainty and, 140–41
    negotiated, 133–34, 138
    plant closing rights, 134–36
    as public good, 134–35
    risk elimination goal, 138–39
    tradeoffs in, 132–33
Job security
    contract guarantees re, 133–34
    legislation re, 123
    plant closings and, 123
Johnson, Chalmers, 164
Johnson, Manuel, 83
Jones, Jesse, 86, 87

Kendrick, John W., 60, 61
Kipling, Rudyard, 185, 195–96
Kline, Eugene, 160
Kotkin, Joel, 15–16
Kuttner, Bob, 65, 68, 69, 160, 165, 173

Labor contracts, 132–34, 138
LaFalce, John, 41, 81n, 83
Laffer curve, 147–48, 147 fig
Laissez-faire theory, 160
Lavoie, Don, 115
Lawrence, Robert Z., 45
Lee, Dwight, 22, 31, 144, 145, 148, 150
Lodge, George, 36
Logue, Dennis E., 62

Managed capitalism
    coordination of policies and agencies,
    117, 118

information problems, 117
    objectives of, 116–17, 122
Manufacturing sector (see also Automobile
    industry; Steel industry)
    employment in, 21, 38, 43, 44–45, 69
    management problems, 45–46, 54
    output value, 41, 42 tbl
    plant and equipment spending, 60,
    62 tbl
    production in, 38, 39–40 tbl, 41
    recessions, effects of, 45
    research and development spending,
    59, 60 tbl, 61 tbl
    trading by, 48, 50, 51 tbl, 52, 52 tbl, 53–
    54 tbl, 55–57 fig, 58
Market ownership, 182–83
Market system, 25–26, 199
Marx, Karl, 151
Maybank Amendment, 91–93
Mercantilism, 2
Middle class, decline in, 65–66
Miller, G. William, 95
Modernization of industry, 172–73
Mondale, Walter F., 65
    Chrysler bailout, 94–95
    national industrial policy proposals, 7–8
    plant closings, 10, 136
    protectionism, 159, 175
Monetary policy, 206–7, 208
Money markets, international, 74
Monopoly power, 186–88
Multinational corporations, 155
Munger, Michael, 58, 59, 178
Murtha, John, 81n

Nader, Ralph, 136
Nardinelli, Clark, 85n, 86
National Commission on Employment
    Policy, 77, 78
National Employment Priorities Act of
    1979, 12n
National Employment Priorities Act of
    1983, 11, 12
National industrial policy (NIP) (see also
    Capital taxation; Centralized planning;
    Job rights; Managed capitalism;
    Protectionism; Reconstruction Finance
    Corporation; Retraining programs)
    adaptation goal, 2, 5, 30–31, 46
    Askew proposals, 16
    Bluestone-Harrison proposals, 11–13
    conceptual problems, 24–30

214

employment consequences of, 90–93
incentives, effect on, 98
intervention philosophy, 84
investment fund allocation, 100–101
legislation re, 81–82
loans and investments by, 86–88, 87 tbl, 89 tbl
politicization of, 93–94, 100
proposals re, 7, 8, 10, 34
purpose of, 81–82
targeting of expenditures, 91–93
Regional development banks. *See* Reconstruction Finance Corporation
Reich, Robert
adaptation concerns, 30–31, 46
economic decline of the U.S., 17, 18, 35
economic democracy, 20
job security, 123
managed capitalism, 122
national industrial policy proposals, 2, 5–7
Reconstruction Finance Corporation, 84, 99
Relocation of industries, 43–44
Rent seeking
beneficiaries of, 190
creation of, 185–86
definition of, 188
investment, effect on, 188, 189–90
by monopolists, 186–88
problems of, 191
tax/compensation policies, 192–95, 196
wastefulness of, 188–89, 190–91
Research and development spending, 59, 60 tbl, 61 tbl
Resources, definition of, 113
Retraining programs (*see also* Displaced workers)
double training through, 75–76
externalities of, 76–80
federal funding for, 66–67, 73–75
locally funded, 80
worker incentives, effect on, 76
Reynolds, Morgan O., 128n
RFC. *See* Reconstruction Finance Corporation
Road to Serfdom (Hayek), 29, 118
Robbins, Lionel, 104
Rohatyn, Felix, 8–9, 84
Roosevelt, Franklin D., 85–86, 126n
Rumberger, Russell, 35, 126n

Sakoh, Katsuro, 23, 63
Samuelson, Robert, 22

Schmenner, Roger, 37
Schultze, Charles, 60, 62, 191
Service sector, 21–22, 41, 42 tbl
Severance pay, 131n
Shearer, Derek, 35, 126n
Smith, Adam, 26–27, 101, 159, 183
Social welfare, 26, 67
Static analysis, 186
Steel industry, 160, 171, 172–73, 191
Stein, Herbert, 22, 90
Subsidies, foreign, 173–74
Supply and demand, 27, 107–8, 107 fig, 114–15
Supply-side economics, 148

Targeting of expenditures, 91–93
Tariffs, 169, 179–82
Taxation (*see also* Capital taxation)
centralization of authority, 154–57
long-run revenues, 148–50, 149 fig
revitalization plan policies re, 202
short-run revenues, 149–50
tax rates, 145, 146–48, 150, 146 fig, 147 fig
unitary, 157
Tax/compensation policies (buyouts), 192–95, 196
The Theory of Moral Sentiments (Smith), 26–27, 101
Thurow, Lester
economic decline of the U.S., 17, 18, 35
job security, 123
middle class, decline of, 65
national industrial policy proposals, 9–10
plant closings, 19
Tollison, Robert, 188–89
Trade, international (*see also* Protectionism)
bilateral nature of, 164–65
comparative (cost) advantage, principle of, 163–64, 165–66, 169, 170–71, 175
comparative costs of production, 162–64
foreign competition, benefits of, 167
industrial survival and, 166–67
reasons for, 164
Trade, U.S. (*see also* Protectionism)
balance of trade, 49 tbl, 174–79, 177 fig, 178 fig
deficits in, 46
growth in, 48
manufactured goods, 48, 50, 51 tbl, 52, 52 tbl, 53–54 tbl, 55–57 fig, 58

215

216

About the Author

Richard B. McKenzie is the John M. Olin Visiting Professor of American Business at the Center for the Study of American Business at Washington University of St. Louis. He is on leave from his position as professor of economics at Clemson University. He is the author of several books, including *Fugitive Industry: The Economics and Politics of Deindustrialization* (Pacific Institute, 1984) and *Bound to Be Free* (Hoover Institution, 1982), and the editor of *Constitutional Economics: Containing the Economic Powers of Government* (Lexington Books, 1984). *The New World of Economics*, fourth ed. (Richard D. Irwin, Inc., 1984), which he coauthored with Gordon Tullock, is widely used in colleges and universities. McKenzie is an adjunct scholar of the Cato Institute.

Cato Institute

Founded in 1977, the Cato Institute is a public policy research foundation dedicated to broadening the parameters of policy debate to allow consideration of more options that are consistent with the traditional American principles of limited government, individual liberty, and peace. Toward that goal, the Institute strives to achieve a greater involvement of the intelligent, concerned lay public in questions of policy and the proper role of government.

The Institute is named for *Cato's Letters,* pamphlets that were widely read in the American Colonies in the early eighteenth century and played a major role in laying the philosophical foundation for the revolution that followed. Since that revolution, civil and economic liberties have been eroded as the number and complexity of social problems have grown. Today virtually no aspect of human life is free from the domination of a governing class of politico-economic interests. A pervasive intolerance for individual rights is shown by government's arbitrary intrusions into private economic transactions and its disregard for civil liberties.

To counter this trend the Cato Institute undertakes an extensive publications program dealing with the complete spectrum of policy issues. Books, monographs, and shorter studies are commissioned to examine the federal budget, social security, regulation, NATO, international trade, and a myriad of other issues. Major policy conferences are held throughout the year from which papers are published thrice yearly in the *Cato Journal.* The Institute maintains an informal joint publishing arrangement with the Johns Hopkins University Press.

In order to maintain an independent posture, the Cato Institute accepts no government funding. Contributions are received from foundations, corporations, and individuals, and other revenue is generated from the sale of publications. The Institute is a non-profit, tax-exempt, educational foundation under Section 501(c)3 of the Internal Revenue Code.

CATO INSTITUTE
224 Second St., S.E.
Washington, D.C. 20003